'A funny and compulsively readable picaresque adventure through a paranoid shadow world'   **Louis Theroux**

'A funny, superbly controlled account of Ronson's wanderings through the wonderland of fanaticism and delusion . . . The result is high comedy'   *New Statesman*

'Often entertaining, more often disturbing . . . Ronson has gotten closer to these people than any journalist I can think of'   *New York Times*

'Ronson has a deft, ironic touch and a brilliant way with scene-setting and direct speech'   *Guardian*

'Made me laugh out loud, as well as shudder . . . As we all reel from the consequences of September 11, his book seems even more relevant'   **Justine Picardie**

'Ronson manages to get the best out of people by trying to understand them'   *Evening Standard*

'The strength of Ronson's book is that it reminds us not only that extremists are weird but also that their fantasies take sustenance from the real world'   *Sunday Telegraph*

'This is an investigation where comedy is married to a stomach-churning potential for violence . . . Ronson weaves his tale like a master [and] has proved, with an often hilarious account that does to world domination what Bill Bryson has done so exhaustively to travel, that Picador is no part of the shadowy New World Order'

Irish Independent

'Ronson's wide-eyed, guileless tone collapses the gap between "them" and "us" and brilliantly conveys the larger picture'   *Metro*

'It is how [Ronson] reveals the all-too-real machinations of Western society's radical fringe and its various minions that makes this enjoyable work rather remarkable'

Publisher's Weekly

THEM:

Adventures with Extremists

Jon Ronson is an award-winning writer
and documentary maker. He is the author of
many bestselling books, including *Lost at Sea*,
The Psychopath Test, *The Men Who Stare at Goats*
and *Them: Adventures with Extremists*. His first
fictional screenplay, *Frank*, co-written with
Peter Straughan, starred Michael Fassbender.
He lives in London and New York City.

Also by Jon Ronson

The Men Who Stare at Goats

Out of the Ordinary: True Tales of Everyday Craziness

What I Do: More True Tales of Everyday Craziness

*The Psychopath Test: A Journey Through
the Madness Industry*

Lost at Sea: The Jon Ronson Mysteries

Frank: The True Story that Inspired the Movie

THEM:

Adventures with Extremists

JON RONSON

With an introduction by Russell Brand

PICADOR CLASSIC

First published 2001 by Picador

First published in paperback 2002 by Picador

This Picador Classic edition first published 2015 by Picador
an imprint of Pan Macmillan, a division of Macmillan Publishers Limited
Pan Macmillan, 20 New Wharf Road, London N1 9RR
Basingstoke and Oxford
Associated companies throughout the world
www.panmacmillan.com

ISBN 978-1-4472-7546-6

1 3 5 7 9 8 6 4 2

A CIP catalogue record for this book is available from the British Library.

Printed and bound by CPI Group (UK) Ltd, Croydon, CR0 4YY

Visit www.picador.com/classic to read more about all our books
and to buy them. You will also find features, author interviews and
news of any author events, and you can sign up for e-newsletters
so that you're always first to hear about our new releases.

Introduction

When I first read *Them* ten years ago I was a bit of a conspiracy boffin and a David Icke aficionado. I was not long free from drugs and not yet pacified by dollars and comfort. I was a lot more open to the possibility that there was a shady cabal meeting in the smoky room that Jon set out to find. Back then, like Alex Jones, the gung-ho, hang-'em-high, gum-chewing Texan libertine who Jon portrays with such winning warmth, I saw the contemporary news narrative as a duplicitous zoetrope to distract the 'masses'.

Since that early reading I have stayed clean, earned money and chatted to Julian Assange, a man who could be forgiven for thinking there were coordinated and malevolent bodies who govern the world. Instead though he believes there is no plan, just a greedy Mongol horde of capitalists charging towards profit, decimating anything that stands in their way and improvising structures that suit them as they go. That sounds reassuringly simple and comes from a man with bloody good access to the CIA mainframe who is now shacked up in a pretend bit of Ecuador for not keeping his gob shut. Surely he would know about the smoky room that Jon set off to find and its by now wheezy occupants.

I was hustled, shanghaied into writing this introduction by a literary agent. Jon Ronson's series of interwoven essays on conspiracy, his now legendary trip through paranoia and legitimate fear from the perspective of a man who suffers from both, is preceded by a professionally leveraged foreword. So even here, in these very pages, there is evidence of an invisible network, behind the scenes imposing power.

Natasha, I think her name was, Jon's agent, a nice lady.

The fact is, though, I admire Jon Ronson and love this book. I think he is brave and funny. He respects us as readers and never overwrites. Instead he leads us, like a nervous Sherpa, through awkward questions and deft jokes to the doorstep of his preferred conclusion and leaves us there, having rung the doorbell for us, waiting for the truth to swing open in our startled faces. That is a good example of the kind of metaphor that Jon would never use, it is too laboured and instructive. Plus it started on a mountain and ended at a pebble-dashed semi in suburbia. Likely with a posturing Ayatollah in residence.

As well as this restraint and devotion to consistent and pithy metaphors, Jon also manages to somehow become charmingly entangled with his subjects whilst maintaining a degree of detachment and objectivity. How does he do that? How can anyone roll along with Dr Ian Paisley, a man who Jon makes clear would gnash any overt or garish opponent into nothingness in an effortless blur of spittle and fang if they strayed from Debrett's to Tourette's for a millisecond? Can it just be because Jon has that nerdishly disarming humility while he is being casually caustic? It cannot be as simple as that. I think, as the Paisley episode in this lovely book demonstrates, Jon observes deep nuances in his subjects and renders their complex humanity and vulnerability in a way that is surprising and deceptively plain.

I have met David Icke a few times and I like him and have got time for the sport-casual soothsayer, but I have never found him more genuinely heroic than in the moment that Jon describes at a Canadian book signing, in which some earnest twerp, in an attempt to undermine Icke, flings a flan at him. Icke's fleeting acknowledgement of the bungled character assassination as recorded by Jon makes the Nostradamus of newt-ma-geddon sound like James Bond.

Neither had I previously particularly noticed the incredible devotion and kindness of Ian Paisley prior to re-reading *Them*. Even when Dr Paisley died and his long-time nemesis Martin McGuinness said, 'I've lost a friend,' I did not open up to the possibility that there was a greatness to the man that I had missed. Jon Ronson, though, by journaling Paisley's missionary work in Africa, his volatility and integrity, in tandem with his own doubts and queries, has awakened in me a surprising warmth towards the hollering Ulsterman. Often in this book you will read unappealing details and damning conjecture and yet primarily be charmed by the protagonists. Jon Ronson is the alchemic ingredient that makes these base characters glisten.

I notice in many cases the apparatchiks of the main players are vehicles for the more negative prejudices I had harboured. An anti-Semitic hiccup from one of Icke's staffers, Presbyterian inflexibility from Paisley's wingman. Surprisingly though in most cases the subjects themselves for all their hysteria, Sturm and Drang come across as well intentioned and now, in some cases, fourteen years after the original release of the book, perspicacious.

In Jon's own preface to a previous edition he recounts the tale of inadvertently overhearing Icke and a compadre washing their hands in a lavvy while he himself was concealed in a cubicle. The two men discussed the futility of Jon's venture, documenting Icke's journey when everything in the world was about to change so radically. 'Doesn't he know how redundant all this will be when his book comes out?' giggles David. Jon laughs along in the loo, knowing this too is perfect gonzo content. I mentioned this to Jon when chatting to him in preparation for writing this introduction and he told me that in the short time between the eavesdropping and the original release of this book 9/11 happened, so my assumption that Icke was the intended target of that gag was wrong, Jon was laughing at himself, inferring that Icke's bathroom smugness was actually prescience.

Elsewhere (in *Lost at Sea* and *The Psychopath Test*) Jon has written about his own neurosis and hysteria, his paranoia that his wife and son could befall some terrible mishap if he did not compulsively and ritualistically phone home. He would trouble his missus with nocturnal mithering and was unable to stop until the intervention of Neurolinguistic hypnotists Paul McKenna and Richard Bandler. The bizarre techniques pioneered by Bandler, a controversial and confusing character, stopped Jon's paranoid obsession on the spot. Is Jon drawn to these quirky peripheral figures because at his core he too is driven by a relentless inner suspicion that all is not well? Is it only Jon's wit and humour and system of outer checks and regulations that prevent him becoming a survivalist or tender Klansman?

I like this book because I do not trust the establishment. There is no doubt that the powerful keep a lot of things quiet for dubious reasons. Where there is a margin for doubt and query our fictive capacity can spiral. Our consciousness, the seat of all enquiry, is itself an unexplained mystery that rests upon an anatomy that conducts a million complex functions without our bidding or consent. Each of us lives aboard a conspiracy of organs and nerves that we cannot control and do not understand. So I suppose it is natural that we are suspicious that something sneaky is going on, it is, it is us.

Yet here we are a decade later; Icke was right about the network of establishment paedophiles, more and more it appears there are alliances between neocon extremists and religious fundamentalists, the power and veracity of the Bilderbergers is water-cooler chitter-chatter and One Direction fans know all about the Illuminati.

Perhaps by the time this Picador Classic edition is published this introduction will also be obsolete, the lizard overlords will have been exposed and confronted, humankind will have formed into a one-world revolutionary army to confront our scaly foe, with an apology to David Icke embroidered on every flag. If that is true, we will need Jon Ronson more than ever to report from the front line, wryly, to remind us that no matter how trivial or grand the stories we tell ourselves to make sense of ourselves and our world are, we the heroes of this collective tale are both trivial and grand, warm and cynical, neurotic and brave and with Jon, the perfect chronicler for this contradictory world, we will never be allowed to forget how funny that is. Thank God.

RUSSELL BRAND
22nd November, 2014

THEM:

Adventures with Extremists

For Joel

'I think it bodes well for world peace that *Friends*
is a success everywhere in the world.'

Lisa Kudrow

'When I was coming up, it was a dangerous world, and
you knew exactly who they were. It was us vs. them,
and it was clear who them was. Today, we are not so sure
who they are, but we know they're there.'

George W. Bush, 21 January 2000

'I want to hug strangers. I want to hurt other strangers.'

Jay McInerney, New York City, 15 September 2001

Contents

Preface and Acknowledgements

One evening, in 1999, I was in a toilet at a lecture theatre in Frome in Somerset when David Icke, the subject of chapter six of *Them*, walked in. He didn't know I was in the cubicle, and he began talking about me to the man standing next to him at the urinal. I sat there and eavesdropped.

I'd been travelling with David Icke for a few weeks, on and off, while he spread his message that the shadowy elitists who secretly rule the world are actually extraterrestrial, shape-shifting giant lizards. The reason why I wanted to chronicle this chapter in David's extraordinary career was because a coalition of prominent anti-racists were convinced that when he said 'extraterrestrial, shape-shifting giant lizards' he was using code, and what he really meant was 'Jews'.

I thought the David Icke story would be a funny, burlesque way of examining the burgeoning anxiety on both sides. It was like an escalating cold war of paranoia. The extremists were getting crazier, and so were our responses towards them.

Some of the radicals and conspiracy theorists and fundamentalists compared this intensifying paranoia with a pressure cooker, ready to explode, but I thought they were just being overly dramatic, and nothing bad was going to happen. Perhaps, in retrospect, this book can be read as a snapshot of life in the Western world on 10 September 2001.

In the toilet in Frome, the man standing next to David Icke asked him why I was following him around.

'He's wasting his time,' replied David. 'His book isn't coming out until 2001. Doesn't he know how radically different the world will be then? Anything he writes now will be utterly redundant!'

'You're right,' chuckled the other man at the urinal, wryly. 'He's completely wasting his time.'

I chuckled wryly too, inside the cubicle.

David Icke's website – as I write this, in mid-October 2001 – has become something of a monument to the words, I Told You So. He quotes his own writings from 1998:

> With fear as the reptilians' greatest weapon, the plan is to engineer events, real and staged, that will create enormous fear. This includes a plan to start a third world war either by stimulating the Muslim world into a 'holy war' against the West or by using the Chinese to cause global conflict. Maybe both.

Those people featured in *Them* – Islamic fundamentalists, American militias and separatists and neo-Nazis – have more in common now than ever. Most are convinced that the power elites of the Western world, in one guise or another, secretly orchestrated the events of 11 September. This is what they *do*, they say. They create chaos, and from the ashes of this chaos will rise their terrible World Government.

Here is another belief most of them share: that the financial traders who worked inside the twin towers were the foot soldiers, conscious or otherwise, of the New World Order, an internationalist Western conspiracy conducted by a tiny, secretive elite, whose ultimate aim is to destroy all opposition, implement a planetary takeover, and establish themselves as a World Government. This is a book about this conspiracy theory – about the secret rulers of the world, and those people who believe in them.

The subject of chapter one of *Them*, Omar Bakri, has often referred to himself as Osama Bin Laden's man in London. He has claimed to have sent as many as 700 of his British followers abroad to Jihad training camps, including Bin Laden's in Afghanistan. On 13 September 2001, Omar began to initiate his own endgame. He posted a message on his website, which read: 'The final hour will not come until the Muslims conquer the White House. As America declares war on 1.5 billion Muslims worldwide, what is your duty?'

He then gave an interview to the *Daily Mail* in which he said, 'When I first heard about it, there was some initial delight about such an attack. I received a phone call and said, "Oh, wow, the United States has come under attack." It was exciting.'

Then he called for a fatwa against President Musharraf of Pakistan for supporting American action against the Taliban. The Conservative leader, Iain Duncan Smith, during an emergency session of Parliament, called for a change in the law so Omar could be deported. Scotland Yard arrested Omar, and then released him. He had committed no crime.

I telephoned Omar on the evening of his arrest. I expected to find him in defiant mood. But he seemed a little scared.

'This is so terrible,' he said. 'The police say they may deport me. Why are people linking me with Bin Laden? I do not know the man. I have never met him. Why do people say I am Bin Laden's man in Great Britain?'

'Because you have been calling yourself Bin Laden's man in Great Britain for years,' I said.

'Oh Jon,' said Omar. 'I need you more than ever now. You know I am harmless, don't you? You always said I was laughable, didn't you? Oh Jon. Why don't people believe you when you tell them that I am just a harmless clown?'

'I have never thought you were a harmless clown,' I said.

I telephoned Omar again a few weeks later. I asked him if I could follow him around some more, now that a conclusion to his story seemed imminent. His response was startling to me.

'You portray me as a fool,' he said. 'I will not let you anywhere near me ever again. You hate the Muslims.'

'I don't hate the Muslims,' I said.

'You are a Muslim-hating Zionist Jew,' said Omar.

He hung up on me then. I don't know why Omar's tone of voice and attitude had taken such a turn. Perhaps there were other people in the room.

*

This book began its life in 1995 as a series of profiles of extremist leaders, but it quickly became something stranger. My plan had been to spend time with those people who had been described as the extremist monsters of the Western world – Islamic fundamentalists, neo-Nazis, etc. I wanted to join them as they went about their everyday lives. I thought that perhaps an interesting way to look at our world would be to move into theirs and stand alongside them while they glared back at us.

And that's what I did with them for a while. But then I learnt of their shared belief in the New World Order: that a tiny elite rules the world from inside a secret room. It is they who start the wars, I was variously told, elect and cast out the heads of state, control Hollywood and the markets and the flow of capital, operate a harem of under-age kidnapped sex slaves, transform themselves into twelve-foot lizards when nobody is looking, and destroy the credibility of any investigator who gets too close to the truth.

I asked them specifics. Did they know the actual whereabouts of the secret room? But their details were sketchy. Sometimes, they said, these elitists meet in hotels and rule the world from there. Every summer, they added, they team up with presidents and prime ministers to attend a Satanic summer camp where they dress in robes and burn effigies at the foot of a giant stone owl.

I took it upon myself to try to settle the matter. If there really *was* a secret room, it would have to be somewhere. And if it was somewhere, it could be found. And so I set about trying to find it.

This turned out to be a hazardous journey. I was chased by men in dark glasses, surveilled from behind trees, and – unlikely as it might sound right now – I managed to witness robed international CEOs participate in a bizarre owl-burning ritual in the forests of northern California.

One night, in the midst of my quest to find the secret room, I was back in London playing poker with another Jewish journalist, John Diamond. He asked me what I was up to. I ranted about how it was all true, how the extremists were onto something, how they were leading me to a kind of truth, and so on.

John, who suffered from throat cancer and consequently needed to write everything down, immediately found a blank page in his notepad and furiously scribbled: 'You are sounding like one of THEM.'

The word THEM was written with such force that it left a mark on the page below. Was John right? Had I become one of them? Whatever, I would have liked to have expressed my gratitude to John for giving me the idea for the book's title, but he died shortly before its publication.

Many thanks to David Barker, John Sergeant, Peter Grimsdale, Saul Dibb and Fenton Bailey. I could not have written this book without them. Well, I probably could have written it without them. I couldn't, however, have written it without Ursula Doyle at Picador who commissioned and edited it, Derek Johns who brokered the deal with aplomb and Camilla Elworthy, who is the best publicist I have ever worked with. Peter Straus, Stephanie Sweeney, Richard Evans, Chantal Noel and Neil Cross at Picador couldn't have been more supportive.

Geoff Kloske, at Simon and Schuster in New York, was trusting and appreciative, and I am enormously grateful to him.

I would also like to thank Janey Walker, Tim Gardam, Janet Lee, Janis Hadlow, Steve McCarthy, David Malone, Emily Fielden, Natasha Fownes, Mike Whine, Vivienne Clore, Sam Bickley and Emma Forrest.

I would say that my wife, Elaine, possessed all the patience and understanding of a loving wife, etc., but in fact she just said to me: 'Oh, will you just shut up about it and finish it.' The loving wife in this situation was Adam Curtis.

All the words within are my own, except for the paragraphs I have appropriated from Neal Gabler's *An Empire Of Their Own (How The Jews Invented Hollywood)*.

Shorter versions of *A Semi-Detached Ayatollah* and *Dr Paisley, I Presume* were published in the *Guardian Weekend* magazine (in 1997 and 1998). I'd like to thank Deborah Orr, my editor at that time, Kath Viner, my current editor, and whoever it was at the *Guardian* who came up with the title *A Semi-Detached Ayatollah*. Before that it was called *Tottenham Ayatollah*.

A question I've been asked is by what criteria I have defined the people within this book as extremists. The answer is, I haven't. My only criterion is that they have been called extremists by others.

One thing you quickly learn about them is that they really don't like being called extremists. In fact they often tell me that *we* are the real extremists. They say that the Western liberal cosmopolitan establishment is itself a fanatical, depraved belief system. I like it when they say this because it makes me feel as if I have a belief system.

JON RONSON
October 2001

1. *A Semi-Detached Ayatollah*

It was a balmy Saturday afternoon in Trafalgar Square in the summertime, and Omar Bakri Mohammed was declaring Holy War on Britain. He stood on a podium at the front of Nelson's Column and announced that he would not rest until he saw the Black Flag of Islam flying over Downing Street. There was much cheering. The space had been rented out to him by Westminster Council.

The *Newsroom South-East* TV reporter talked the afternoon's events up with a hard, fast, urgent but cool-headed voice. She was a Muslim. In his speech, Omar Bakri referred to people like her as Chocolate Muslims. A Chocolate Muslim is an Uncle Tom.

(The next day, the *Daily Mail* would run a photograph of a cold-eyed Omar Bakri on their inside front page under the headline, *Is This The Most Dangerous Man In Britain?* From his cold eyes, he looked as if he could be.)

There were maybe 5,000 of Omar Bakri's followers there in Trafalgar Square. After his speech, their plan was to release thousands of black balloons, carrying the call to war on little attached postcards. The balloons would fly high into the London sky, painting it black and then falling across London and the Home Counties. The balloons were being stored in a net, underneath the podium from which Omar Bakri was outlining his post-Jihad vision for the UK.

He who practised homosexuality, adultery, fornication or bestiality would be stoned to death (or thrown from the highest mountain). Christmas decorations and shop-window dummies would be outlawed. There would be no free mixing between the sexes. Pubs would be closed down. The landlords would be offered alternative employ-ment in something more befitting an Islamic society, like a library, and if they refused to comply they would be arrested. Pictures of ladies' legs on packets of tights would be banned. We would still be able to purchase tights, but they would be advertised simply with the word 'tights'.

I very much wanted to meet Omar Bakri and spend time with him while he attempted to overthrow democracy and transform Britain into an Islamic nation.

I visited Yacob Zaki, a Muslim fundamentalist who often shared a platform with him.

Yacob Zaki is white and Scottish, a former Presbyterian who converted to Islam when he was a teenager. He lives in Greenock, a port near Glasgow. He is Greenock's only militant Muslim convert. He said he had suffered much bullying at school as a result of his conversion, but it was well worth it.

'Do you think that Omar Bakri might succeed in over-throwing the western way of life?' I asked him.

'Well,' said Yacob, 'Omar is our best hope at this time.'

'Why him?'

'Charisma,' said Yacob. 'He's the most popular leader of the disaffected youth. People queue around the block to see him talk. Although we disagree on some matters.'

'Like what?'

'Well,' said Yacob, 'one time I wanted to release a swarm of mice into the United Nations headquarters. Women hate mice, you know. I thought it was a brilliantly simple idea. One swarm of mice would have crushed the whole UN process, don't you think?'

'Women standing on chairs,' I agreed.

'But Omar said no,' said Yacob. 'He said it was a stupid idea.'

'What other disagreements have you had with Omar Bakri?' I asked Yacob.

'Well,' he said, 'Omar got very angry with me when I announced that Hillary Clinton was a lesbian. But I have the proof.'

Yacob and I spent the day together. It was that afternoon I first heard about the Bilderberg Group, the secret rulers of the world, a tiny group of pernicious men and one or two pernicious women who meet in a secret room and determine the course of world events. It is they who start the wars, Yacob said, own the media and destroy – by covert violence or propaganda – anyone who gets too close to the truth.

'One mysterious case,' said Yacob, 'is that of the peanut farmer who attended a Bilderberg meeting and overnight became the most powerful man in the world. Yes. I'm speaking of Jimmy Carter. So you can see that they are extremely secretive and powerful.'

I didn't really take it in. I stared blankly at Yacob. I didn't realize that the people Yacob spoke of would come to occupy – in the most unpleasant ways – a tremendous part of the next five years of my life.

Yacob looked at his watch. He wanted our meeting to end. He had a tip on where he could purchase Hitler's binoculars, and he didn't want another collector to beat him to it. He gave me Omar Bakri's address. I got his telephone number from the phone book.

It turned out that Omar Bakri lived a couple of miles away from me, in Edmonton, north London, in a small semi-detached house at the end of a modern, fawn-coloured council-built cul-de-sac. His offices were at the Finsbury Park Mosque, at the bottom of my road, not far from Highbury football ground.

I wrote to ask him if I could follow him around for a year or so while he attempted to transform Britain into an Islamic nation. He called back straight away. There were so many anti-Muslim lies, he said, generated by the Jewish-controlled media. So much misinformation, in the newspapers and the movies. Perhaps this would be an opportunity for the record to be set straight. So, yes. I was welcome to join him in his struggle against the infidels. And then he added, 'I am actually very nice, you know.'

'Are you?' I asked.

'Oh yes,' said Omar Bakri, 'I am delightful.'

At 9 o'clock the next morning I sat in Omar's living room while Omar played with his baby daughter.

'What's your daughter's name?' I asked him.

'It is a difficult name for you to understand,' said Omar.

'Does it have an English translation?' I asked.

'Yes,' said Omar, 'it translates into English as "The Black Flag of Islam".'

'Really?' I said. 'Your daughter's name is the Black Flag of Islam?'

'Yes,' said Omar.

'Really?' I said.

There was a small pause.

'You see,' said Omar, 'why our cultures can never integrate?'

The Lion King was playing on the video. We watched the scene where the warthog sings 'Hakuna Matata', the song about how wonderful it is to have problem-free philosophies and no worries. Omar sang along, bouncing the baby on his knee.

'We always watch *The Lion King*,' he said. 'It's the only way I can relax. You know, they call me the Lion. That's right. They call me the Lion. They call me the great warrior. The great fighter.'

Omar showed me his photo album. His teenage photographs make him look like a matinee idol. He came from a family of twenty-eight brothers and sisters. His father had made a fortune selling sheep and pigs and cows. They had chauffeurs and servants and palaces in Syria, Turkey and Beirut. Omar escaped Saudi Arabia in 1985. He had heard that he was to be arrested for preaching the Jihad on university campuses. So he ran away. He escaped to Britain. Now he is a big man with a big beard.

'I was thin because I always worried,' he said. 'I was always on the run. Now I live in Britain, I never worry.

What's going to happen to me here? Ha ha! So I got fat. A leader must be big in stature. The bigger the body, the bigger the leader. Who wants a little scrawny leader?'

Omar's plan for the morning was to distribute leaflets outside Holborn tube station entitled: 'Homosexuality, Lesbianism, Adultery, Fornication and Bestiality: THE DEADLY DISEASES'. He said he'd planned to travel by public transport, but he couldn't help but notice my car in his driveway, so perhaps I would give him a lift instead?

'OK,' I said.

I dropped him off near the tube station. I went to park the car. Ten minutes later, I found him standing in the middle of the pavement with a stack of leaflets in his hand.

'How's it going, Omar?' I asked.

'Oh, very good,' he smiled. 'The message is getting across that there are some deadly diseases here and there.'

He turned to the passers-by.

'Homosexuality!' he yelled. 'Beware the deadly disease! Beware the hour!'

Some time passed.

'Homosexuality!' yelled Omar. 'Beware! There are homosexuals everywhere!'

I expected to see some hostility to Omar's leaflets from the passers-by. But the shoppers and tourists and office workers seemed to regard him with a kindly bemusement. Nonetheless, after ten minutes nobody had actually taken a leaflet.

'Beware the hour! There are homosexuals everywhere! Beware the hour!' continued Omar, cheerfully. 'Be careful from homosexuality! It is not good for your tummy!'

Omar Bakri was unlike my image of a Muslim extremist.

Then he told me that he had a good idea.

'Just watch this,' he said.

He turned the leaflets upside down.

'Help the orphans!' he yelled. 'Help the orphans!'

'Omar!' I exclaimed, scandalized.

The passers-by started to accept his leaflets.

'This is good,' chuckled Omar. 'This is good. You see, if I wasn't a Muslim I'd be working for . . . how you say . . . Saatchi and Saatchi.'

At lunchtime Omar said he needed to buy some collection boxes for his regular fundraising endeavours for Hamas and Hizbullah. Hamas had orchestrated a bus bombing in Jerusalem three weeks earlier which had killed eleven people.

'There is a Cash and Carry just off the ring-road near Tottenham,' said Omar, 'that sells very good collection boxes. Could you give me a lift?'

'OK,' I said.

So we drove to the Cash and Carry. Omar sat in the back seat, which made me feel a little like a taxi driver.

'Left,' said Omar. 'Left at the junction. No. Left!'

At some traffic lights, I asked Omar where his wife was when I was at his house.

'She was upstairs,' he said.

'Really?' I said. 'The whole time I was in your living room, watching *The Lion King*?'

'Yes,' said Omar. 'She wouldn't come down until after you left.'

'What would happen if I tried to interview her?' I asked.

'I would declare fatwa on you,' said Omar.

'Please don't say that,' I said.

'Ha ha!' said Omar.

'Even as a joke,' I said.

We arrived at the Cash and Carry to discover that the only collection boxes they had in stock were large plastic novelty Coca-Cola bottles. Omar paused for a moment. He scrutinized the collection boxes. He furrowed his brow. Then he placed half a dozen of them in his trolley.

'These are good collection boxes,' he said. 'Very big and lightweight.'

'It seems strange to me,' I said, 'that you plan to collect for Hamas and Hizbullah in novelty Coca-Cola bottles.'

'Ah,' said Omar Bakri. 'Very good. I am not against the imperialist baggage. Just the corruption of the Western civilization.'

'But nevertheless,' I said, 'Coca-Cola is such a powerful symbol of Western capitalism.'

'Yes, indeed,' mumbled Omar.

'So you are utilizing our symbols in your attempt to destroy them?' I said.

'Oh yes,' he murmured, distantly.

Omar didn't seem too keen on this line of questioning. He seemed uncomfortable talking about his allegiance to Hamas and Hizbullah. He was in the process of applying for a British passport, and the Conservative government was attempting to pass a law criminalizing those who raised money at home for terrorists overseas – a law that was widely believed to be targeted primarily at Omar.

'I do not collect only for Hamas,' said Omar. 'I collect for all the Muslims worldwide.'

He wandered away, pushing his six large novelty Coca-Cola bottles in a trolley through the Cash and Carry. He stopped at a shelf full of picture frames. The manufacturers had filled the frames with a sample photograph, portraying a sunny beach. A young woman in a one-piece bathing costume lay on the sand underneath an umbrella. She was licking a vanilla ice-cream cone in a borderline-suggestive manner. Omar shook his head sadly.

'This,' he said, 'is the corruption of the Western ideology. You want to buy frames. What do you do with the woman in the frames?'

Nonetheless, he lifted a dozen or so picture frames from the shelf and put them in his trolley, next to the Coca-Cola collection bottles.

'So I will take these frames,' he said, 'and replace the picture of the woman with a decent message taken from the Koran.' He paused. 'OK, Jon,' he said. 'I am ready to go.'

'OK,' I said. 'I'll bring the car round.'

We packed the Coca-Cola bottles and the picture frames into the boot of my car, and I drove Omar to the Finsbury Park Mosque, where he was to deliver a speech at a conference entitled 'Democracy or Dictatorship?' Omar was speaking on behalf of dictatorship.

This was my first opportunity to meet some of Omar's followers. There were maybe five hundred of them in the audience. Things did not start well.

'Are you a Jew?' asked a young man.

'Uh, no,' I said.

He apologized.

'Don't worry about it,' I said.

Omar Bakri was fast-talking on the podium, as if he couldn't contain the words that needed to be said. He filled the room. He quoted from a letter he'd just received from an old friend of his, Sheikh Omar Abdel-Rahman, the Blind Sheikh.

The Blind Sheikh was in jail for life in Missouri for 'inspiring' the 1993 World Trade Center bombing. This law of 'Inspiration' had not been utilized since the American Civil War. Omar used to eat with the Blind Sheikh back in Saudi Arabia. Now he was a martyr throughout the Islamic world, who believed he was framed by the New World Order, a secret clique of international bankers and globalist CEOs and politicians determined to crush Islamic freedom.

Omar reiterated the theory I had heard from Yacob Zaki – that this elite was secretly scheming to implement a sinister planetary takeover. I began to wonder whether I should attempt to locate the whereabouts of this secret room. If it existed it would, after all, have to be somewhere. Could one get in?

The Blind Sheikh's letter – entitled 'Sheikh Omar's Lonely Cry From The Dungeon of "Free" America' – had been smuggled out to Omar from the jail in Missouri, where the Sheikh was held in solitary confinement. It read:

Have you heard of the strip searches? They order me to remove all my clothes, open my thighs and bend forward. Then, like beasts, they search my private parts intimately while the others stand around watching and laughing. They humiliate me because I am a Muslim and because what they do is expressly forbidden by God.

Omar and the audience were enraged by this letter. As Omar read it out, one or two members of the audience gasped and shouted, 'No!'

Omar said, 'The world must hear of this. The world must know what they are doing to Sheikh Abdel-Rahman who is, I must remind you, an old blind man who has committed no crime. We will shake up the world. Together, we will shake up the entire world.'

Afterwards, Omar said he needed to do some errands in town, and could I give him a lift?

'OK,' I said. 'I'm meeting someone in Soho, so can I drop you off there?'

'No,' he said, anxiously. 'It is forbidden for me to go into Soho. Please don't take me there.'

Soho would be razed to the ground, explained Omar, once the Holy War had been won.

'It is important for people to understand these things,' he explained, 'so they will be ready to adapt to the new ways.'

'Which people?' I asked.

'The people of Britain,' said Omar.

'Have you ever been to Soho?' I asked.

'Oh, no,' said Omar. 'It is forbidden.'

'What do you imagine Soho to be like?' I asked.

'There are naked women everywhere,' he replied. 'Naked women standing on street corners.'

So I drove Omar into town by a route that avoided Soho. We passed a poster advertising the Spice Girls' debut album.

'Such a very stupid thing,' mumbled Omar. 'Spicy Girls.'

'What will become of the Spice Girls when Britain is transformed into an Islamic nation?' I asked.

'They will be arrested immediately,' he replied. 'They will not even be existing in an Islamic state. OK. We can go on. Turn right at the lights.'

Geri Spice was wearing a Union Jack dress in the poster, which made me wonder about the future of our flag.

'There will be no Union Jack,' said Omar. 'The Union Jack represents the old order. And it must, therefore, be eliminated.'

We got talking about the word 'fundamentalist'. Omar said it had been redefined by the infidels of the West as a pejorative term.

'You use it as an insult,' he said. 'Turn left, please.'

'But surely you *are* a fundamentalist,' I said, 'in the sense that you live your life by the rules set down in the Koran.'

'That is true,' said Omar. 'The Koran rules every aspect of my life. It tells me how I eat, how I sleep, how I fight, and even how I will die.' Omar paused. 'You know,' he said, 'the Koran even tells me which direction I must break wind in.'

There was a short silence.

'And which direction *do* you break wind in?' I asked.

'In the direction of the non-believer!' Omar said. 'Ha ha ha! *The direction of the non-believer!*' Omar laughed heartily for some time and slapped me on the back.

'OK,' said Omar, as I pulled up near Piccadilly Circus. 'Thank you very much. Goodbye, Jon.'

As I drove away, I gave my horn a little beep and I mouthed the words, 'I'll call!'

Omar Bakri nodded and smiled, and he disappeared into the crowd.

A month or so later, I was sitting in the passenger seat of a Porsche listening to 'Benny And The Jets' by Elton John turned up very loud. We were tearing up the balmy streets of Torquay, the jewel of the English Riviera. The ocean glistened past us, as the driver drummed his fingers on the steering wheel in time to the music. He wore a blue blazer and an open-necked shirt. His hair was bouffant, and his glasses were tinted. All in all, he cut a dashing figure. He went by two names. He was Nigel West, the internationally acclaimed spy writer, and rarely had a novelist so resembled his characters. He was the image of a debonair gentleman spy. And he was also Rupert Allason, the Conservative Member of Parliament for Torbay, which included the town of Torquay. Rupert and I were on our way to a garden party.

Rupert was leading a campaign in the House of Commons to see Omar Bakri deported. Rupert was determined to ensure that Omar's passport application was rejected. He wanted to see Omar sent back to Saudi Arabia, or Syria, or anywhere but here.

'He can preach his message of hate anywhere he likes,' said Rupert, drumming his fingers on the steering wheel. 'But not in Great Britain.'

As we drove to the garden party, it crossed my mind that

perhaps Rupert and Omar were not as unalike as they imagined. For instance, both were opposed to gay and lesbian rights and both were vigorously in favour of the death penalty. But Rupert considered my thesis to be fanciful and inaccurate.

'I believe,' he said, 'that every man is entitled to a fair trial. If he is convicted, he would be taken to a lawful place of execution where he'd be put down in the most humane method known to science, either by hanging or by lethal injection. Whereas Omar Bakri believes in dragging someone to the nearest square and stoning him to death in a manner I consider to be not only barbaric, but also wholly uncivilized.'

We pulled up at the garden party, a Conservative party fundraising event, and Rupert made his way into the crowd. There were maybe a hundred of his supporters there, and they gathered around him, shaking his hand and offering him words of condolence. This was the week that the *Daily Mirror* had exposed Rupert, in a four-page spread, as an adulterer. Adultery was a crime which, under Islamic law, is punishable by stoning to death.

An elderly lady approached Rupert with a reproachful wag of her finger.

'I saw you in the newspaper,' she said, 'and I thought to myself, Rupert! You made me a promise!'

Rupert smiled urbanely.

'Did I?' he said. 'Oh, dear.'

'Never mind,' she chuckled.

I imagined that Rupert's constituents would forgive him anything.

'You know,' I said to Rupert, 'under Islamic law a quintessentially English occasion like this one would probably be outlawed.'

Rupert nodded. He played the garden some more, a glass of white wine in his hand. Then it was time for him to make a speech about Omar Bakri. He took his place next to the raffle stall, and the garden fell silent.

'I've long been campaigning against an Islamic extremist,' he began, 'a terrorist who believes in planting bombs and blowing up women and children in Israel.' Rupert paused. 'This man is applying for a British passport. Well, my message to him is that he can apply for a passport anywhere he likes, but not in Great Britain.'

There was a smattering of applause.

Rupert scrutinized the garden. The sunlight made the swimming pool glitter. By a meteorological quirk involving the positioning of nearby hills in relation to the Atlantic drift emanating from the Gulf of Mexico, Torquay is one of Britain's very warmest places. This geographical fluke, says the Torbay Meteorological Department, makes Torquay's climate uncannily similar to the climate of Istanbul.

'This man,' announced Rupert, 'would like to see quintessentially English occasions like this lovely afternoon outlawed. In his totalitarian vision for Britain, the ladies would not be allowed to bare their arms nor wear the clothes of their choice, and doubtless there would be other disagreeable constraints on the men present. And I for one am not having it.'

There was thunderous applause. And then Rupert announced the raffle winners.

After the prizes were handed out, Rupert became solemn.

'So, ladies and gentlemen, thank you very much indeed for attending what is, we all agree, a quintessentially English occasion. We have much to be proud of. But we're not going to win the next election without the grassroots support only you can provide. Go out onto the streets. Campaign and campaign and campaign. Let's not hear gripes and groans. Let's remember all the wonderful things that the Conservative party has done for this country. Thank you.'

There was more applause, and we took our place at a table of elderly ladies. The conversation quickly turned to the issue of Omar Bakri.

'I believe in hanging,' said a local magistrate called Margaret. 'I believe in flogging. I believe in bringing the young people up to respect someone in higher authority. But this man . . .'

'This man,' agreed Rupert, 'is living among us, and he's trying to overthrow *our* way of life.'

'Well,' muttered Margaret's husband, Frank, 'I don't think he'll get very far. Particularly not in Torquay.'

'Torquay in particular wouldn't stand for this sort of extremism,' agreed Margaret.

'I suppose,' said Frank, 'everyone is entitled to their freedom of speech . . .'

'But it *is* extremism,' said Margaret. 'It really is. And not only would the people of Torquay not stand for it, I think that the whole West Country would feel the same way.'

'I'll be seeing Omar soon,' I said to Rupert. 'Would you like me to deliver a message to him?'

'Yes I would,' said Rupert. 'My message to him is this: Peddle your extremism elsewhere.'

Rupert folded his arms. He sat back in his chair. I was impressed at the way in which he'd stolen my line about the Islamic assault on quintessentially English afternoons and turned it into the centrepiece of his address. It takes a skill to be able to plunder a fragment of fleeting small-talk in this manner. I imagined that Rupert could turn pretty much anything to his advantage, even the *Daily Mirror*'s elaborate chronicle of his adultery, a scandal the likes of which had destroyed many a backbench politician in these times of political sleaze. But today Rupert responded with a glint and a wily smile, and I heard one young woman turn to her friend and describe Rupert as foxy.

I considered Rupert's warnings about the two encroaching foes, Omar Bakri and New Labour, to be overly cautious. It was a beautiful, hot Istanbul-esque afternoon. The garden party seemed indestructible, and so did Rupert.

But I was wrong. Rupert's political career was shattered by a bizarre chain of events that began one evening soon after the garden party at the Thatched Tavern in nearby Maidencombe. It was a Saturday night, a fortnight before the 1997 General Election. Rupert had taken a break from his campaigning schedule to have a quiet meal with a friend. Perhaps he felt he'd earned a respite from the intense affability a politician must display during the weeks leading up to polling day, for that night, at the Thatched Tavern, Rupert was demanding.

'We went out of our way,' said Suzanne Austin, Rupert's waitress that night, 'and got him the very best table in the restaurant. I noticed that the flowers on his table were red, so I even rushed out into the garden to find him some blue ones.'

'Do you think Rupert appreciated the attention you paid to him?' I asked.

'I don't think he even noticed,' said Suzanne. 'Anyway, he wasn't *rude*, he was just very demanding.'

'So what happened?' I asked.

'Well,' said Suzanne, 'at the end of the night, the waitresses always sit down, have a chat, and share out the tips. So another waitress said to me, "I bet Rupert gave you a very big tip." And I said, "No. As a matter of fact, he didn't give me a tip at all." And she said, "I can't believe it. You were running around after him all night. I bet you're not going to vote for him now." And I said, "Certainly not. I'm going to vote for the Lib Dems." '

There was, said Suzanne, a murmur of agreement. Some of the other waitresses announced that, in sympathy, they would change their allegiance from the Conservatives to the Liberal Democrats also. They went home and told their husbands, some of whom agreed that a man who behaved like that in a restaurant couldn't be trusted to represent his constituents' needs in Westminster.

In total, it was estimated, Rupert lost fourteen votes as a result of his inappropriately demanding behaviour at the Thatched Tavern and his refusal to leave a tip. Two weeks later, Rupert lost his seat in Parliament to the Liberal Democrats. He lost by the smallest margin of the election: twelve votes.

On my return to London there was a message from Omar on my answerphone. The Israeli Army had bombed a UN safe haven in Qana, southern Lebanon, killing a hundred Muslim civilians, women and children. Bill Clinton referred to the massacre as 'a tragedy', as if it was a natural disaster. This choice of words angered Omar almost as much as the attack itself.

'It was not a tragedy,' he said. 'It was an act of terrorism.'

Omar decided to organize a demonstration outside the Israeli Embassy in Kensington High Street. He needed to get some leaflets photocopied. If I had a minute, could I drive him to Office World?

I agreed, although I feared I was beginning to cross the line between journalist and chauffeur.

Also, I didn't think Omar had realized I am Jewish. He hadn't mentioned it, and neither had I. He had once called Jews the lowliest disbelievers on Earth. I felt I was letting down my people somewhat in helping him co-ordinate his Jihad.

Office World is a hub of revolutionary political and religious activity in north London, primarily because of their special Price Promise.

'If you find a photocopying service that's cheaper,' explained Omar on the way, 'then Office World will give you a discount.'

'Capitalism,' I said.

'Capitalism,' said Omar. 'Oh, yes. I benefit from your capitalism to convey the message. I benefit from your freedom of speech.'

A Hasidic Jew stood next to us at the Office World counter. He wanted sheet-music copied for a barmitzvah.

Omar sized up the Hasidic Jew, and the Hasidic Jew sized up Omar. Then the Office World employee said, 'Finished!', and handed Omar two hundred leaflets.

The Hasidic Jew glanced at them with some curiosity. They read: 'Crush the Pirate State of Israel'. He glared at us. Omar smiled awkwardly.

'This,' he whispered to me, 'is a very sensitive moment.'

We paid and left. As we walked towards the sliding doors, I looked over my shoulder and grinned apologetically at the Hasidic Jew, but he pointedly turned away, back to the man doing his photocopying.

'Come on!' said Omar. 'Very busy. Very busy.'

And so I brought the car around.

When I arrived at Kensington High Street for Omar's Israeli Embassy demonstration, I was surprised to see only ten or so of his followers sporadically yelling, 'Down, Down Israel!' and 'Israel You Will Pay!' at the passing traffic. I asked Omar why the turnout was so disappointing. He explained that when he telephoned Directory Enquiries to get the address of the Israeli Embassy, they deliberately gave him a false address in Knightsbridge. By the time Omar discovered the correct address it was too late. Many of his followers were already on their way and they didn't have mobile phones. They were now presumably lost, wandering the streets of Knightsbridge. This, Omar said, was proof that Scotland Yard's Muslim monitoring unit was in league with British Telecom's directory enquiries service.

'It cannot be a coincidence,' he said.

'So,' I said, 'let me get this clear. You dialled 192, and asked for the address of the Israeli Embassy—'

'Yes,' said Omar.

'And they gave you a false address in Knightsbridge?'

'Yes,' said Omar.

'But how did they know that you were an Islamic militant?'

'Oh, Jon,' said Omar, sadly. 'You are naive. Anyway. I have higher plans. Just you wait and see.'

'Mmm?' I said.

'I will stage an event that will shake up the entire world,' said Omar. 'Just you watch. I will put London at the centre of the Islamic map.'

'Really?' I said.

'Oh, yes,' said Omar. 'This is just the beginning. I can promise you this. By autumn, I will have shaken up the entire world.'

'Really?' I said.

'You don't believe me?' said Omar. 'Just you wait and see.'

As the months progressed, I found my life becoming increasingly determined by Omar's whims.

'If you turn up late,' he often said, 'I'll give you sixty lashes. Ha ha!'

On many occasions Omar would telephone and call me over urgently. I would cancel nights out with my wife and drive over to discover that he'd forgotten all about me and had taken the train to Plymouth, or Nuneaton, or to his secret Jihad training camp near Crawley. I sometimes felt I was getting a unique insight into what it would be like living under Islamic rule, with Omar as Ayatollah.

Omar's plans for Britain's biggest ever Islamic rally, the rally that would shake up the world, began to gain momentum around late summer. He put a deposit down on hiring the mammoth 14,000-capacity London Arena, in a scheduling gap between a Tom Jones concert and a show called The Wonderful World of Horses. Omar had never heard of Tom Jones and he was shocked to discover that women throw their underwear at him on stage.

'My God,' he said, as we stood in the London Arena foyer, waiting for the management to show us around, 'that is the sign of the hour, when women take off their own knickers and their own underwear. That is the sign of the hour.'

'Do I look smart enough?' asked Anjem, Omar's second in command, adjusting his tie. Anjem was a bookish, res-olute young man, the plodding administrator realizing the wild plans of the idealist.

'You look very smart,' said Omar. 'I hope they don't recognize me. Will they recognize me?'

'No,' said Anjem. 'They won't recognize you.'

They didn't recognize him. Omar told the management that he was a teacher of Islamic affairs, and this would be an educational conference. Inside, we wandered around the huge, cavernous hall.

'Yes,' said Omar, quietly to himself. 'Yes. This will do.'

Although I was unaware as to what Omar had in store for the rally, I was a little doubtful about whether this venture would be a success. His recent track record in these matters was shaky. Perhaps I *was* being naive about the Israeli Embassy debacle, as Omar had suggested, but I couldn't help speculating that Directory Enquiries had given him the correct address and Omar had written it down wrong.

Also, there was an unfortunate incident that had occurred at the end of Omar's famous Trafalgar Square speech the previous summer. When the thousands of black balloons carrying the call to war on little attached postcards were unleashed from their netting, it became evident that the postcards were too heavy. The cardboard/helium weight ratio had not been accurately calculated, and the messages anchored the balloons to the Trafalgar Square pavement. The afternoon culminated in many of Omar Bakri's followers kneeling amid five thousand grounded balloons, waving their arms about in an ultimately fruitless attempt to generate enough of a breeze to get them airborne. One or two of the followers eventually untied the messages and allowed the balloons to float away. But without the messages, the balloons lost their raison d'être, and they soon stopped doing this. The last thing I saw was one young man, his face covered by a scarf, defeatedly kicking a listless black balloon and stomping off.

So now, as we stood in the midst of the vast, empty London Arena, I couldn't imagine how Omar intended to fill the 14,000 seats. And then he explained to me his masterplan. The rally would include videotaped messages and personal appearances from an extraordinary cast of Islamic extremists. There was the Blind Sheikh, Omar's old friend, jailed for life for 'inspiring' the 1993 World Trade Center bombing. There was Hizbullah's spiritual leader

Mohammed Hussein Fadlallah. There was Osama Bin Laden, who had not yet been labelled 'a man as dangerous as any state we face' by Bill Clinton for his alleged role in the American Embassy bombings in Kenya and Tanzania, but had already been linked to a number of truck bombs in Saudi Arabia, killing US servicemen and Australian tourists, and had financed the Taliban in Afghanistan with some of his vast inherited personal fortune. There was Dr Mohammed Al Masari, the Saudi dissident who had called for the annihilation of the Jews. And so on.

'So?' said Omar, when he'd finished reading me his list. 'What do you think?'

There was a long silence.

'But what about your application for a British passport?' I asked him.

'Mmm?' said Omar.

'Don't you think that when the Home Office hears about your list of speakers they'll be reluctant to grant you British citizenship?'

'It is freedom of speech,' chuckled Omar. 'What can they do? We are breaking none of your laws.' He chuckled. 'If I lived in Saudi Arabia, I could never get away with what I do here!' He paused. 'Anyway. It is ironic. You want to get rid of me? Give me a passport! I will be on the first plane out of here. I will go to India for a holiday. I will visit my mother in Syria.'

Within days of the announcement of the London Arena rally, Omar and his roster of Islamic extremists were being debated across the world. Omar's tiny offices at Arsenal were thrust into the limelight of international politics.

The Egyptian government summoned the British chargé d'affaires in Cairo to demand an explanation. There was talk of Egyptian sanctions against Britain.

A communiqué from the Algerian Foreign Office read, 'Algeria expresses its firm reprobation at this London rally. This permissive attitude clearly goes against the declarations of the G7 conference at Lyon where a new co-ordinated international effort was mounted to fight this menace to international peace and security.'

Gay rights groups and the Board of Deputies of British Jews appealed to the Home Office for the rally to be banned.

The Foreign Secretary announced to Parliament that the rally couldn't be stopped unless laws were broken, and laws were so far not being broken.

But the Home Office issued an open letter to Omar: 'The British Government condemns any statement made at the rally in support of terrorism. We will monitor the rally and gather evidence to prosecute anyone breaking the law.'

In the space of one week, Omar had received 634 interview requests. Now, whenever I turned up to see him, I had to vie with dozens of other journalists for Omar's attention. Omar was headline news worldwide. Day after day, newspaper and television editorials debated whether Omar, Osama Bin Laden and the Blind Sheikh should be allowed their freedom of speech. Most sided with the no camp. The *Mail on Sunday* wrote:

'This Man Is Dedicated To The Overthrow Of Western Society. He Takes £200 A Week In Benefits And Is Applying For British Citizenship'.

*

This report was illustrated with a large and somewhat sinister portrait of Omar scowling.

'They took many, many photographs of me,' said Omar when he showed me this photograph, 'and they were just looking for one to make me look angry. They said to me, "Say Teese, Cheese." They wanted me to show my teeth. I said, "What? You want me to do *this* for you?"'

Omar held his hands out in front of his face and gnarled his fingers like a Nosferato vampire.

'And they tried to take a picture of me when I was joking with them!'

Only an editorial in the *Independent* newspaper took Omar's side.

> Britain has a glorious history of hospitality to political radicals. Banning the rally would diminish the principles that uphold our society and be a victory for those who seek its destruction.

In late August, Omar took a break from the rally preparations to attend a secret weekend social get-together with all of Britain's Islamic fundamentalist leaders at a large Edwardian manor house in the countryside near Birmingham. There had been some in-fighting within radical Islamic circles, and this weekend's fishing and table tennis was intended to help rebuild bridges.

The house was down a long lane, past some 'No Unauthorized Entry' signs. It was once the country pile of a mining baron, but now it was a college for Muslims. I arrived at 10 p.m., and parked the car. It was dark outside, and I could hear cheerful noises coming from the front parlour. I peered in through the window, and I saw a lot of men in robes shaking hands and hugging each other. Omar was there, laughing and joking.

It had been said that Omar was not popular within many of Britain's Muslim communities. Certainly many moderate Muslims – Chocolate Muslims, as Omar called them – considered him dangerous PR in a society that could be furiously Islamophobic. But even within his own militant world, there had been conflict. Many of Omar's rival leaders thought that he'd made a mistake in calling for the assassinations of John Major and Tony Blair, for example. The London Arena rally too had generated some hostile debate. I imagined that this weekend social get-together had much to do with the rifts caused by his recent actions.

I was caught peering through the window by a tall young man in a white robe.

'Can I help you?' he said.

'Ah,' I said, 'I am personal friends with Omar Bakri.'

There was a long silence. He looked me up and down.

'Are you?' he said.

'I really am,' I said.

Doubtfully, he went inside. He returned, a few moments later, with Omar.

We were then left alone in the car park.

'Oh my God,' laughed Omar. 'They told me not to communicate with the media. They expressly said no journalists.' He laughed. 'What can I do?'

Some more Islamic militants arrived, and they embraced Omar warmly. Then they stopped and looked at me.

'This is my friend,' said Omar. 'He is writing about my

life. Nothing to do with the meeting. He is following me around for maybe ten or fifteen years.'

And then I heard a voice behind me. A small group of Omar's fellow militants had formed, and one of them said, softly, 'I have brought a spare suitcase. Dr Al Masari has brought a spare pair of shoes. You, Omar Bakri, have brought a spare journalist.'

'Maybe I can come inside?' I said, quietly, to Omar.

'Wait here in the car park,' said Omar. 'I'll do my best.'

Omar vanished inside the country house. I waited. Some time later, he returned.

'I'm sorry,' he said. 'They said no way. There's nothing I can do. You have to go away now. Goodbye.'

'What's going on inside?' I asked.

Omar grinned. 'Everyone's here!' he said. 'Really! Everyone!'

'And what are you all talking about?'

'Oh, it's very informal,' he said. 'We are splitting into groups. Tomorrow we will go fishing.'

'There seemed to be some tension before,' I said. 'I was wondering if some of the other leaders consider you to be too extreme.'

'What is this word "extreme"?' said Omar. 'Words like fundamentalist or terrorist or extremist mean nothing here. Those are your words. For you, a terrorist is somebody who blows up a bus here and there. But for the people here, I am on the front line. I am a great warrior, a great fighter.'

At this point, I think that Omar registered my disappointment. He brightened.

'Would you like an ice cream?' he said. 'I can get you an ice cream.'

'Yes, please,' I said.

'OK,' said Omar. 'I will get you an ice cream.'

Omar wandered inside again. He came out a few minutes later with a vanilla choc ice.

'OK,' said Omar. 'So I am cooling down the temperature and also the tension with an ice cream for you.'

'Thank you very much,' I said.

'You must go now,' said Omar. 'So, goodbye.'

I drove into Birmingham and checked into a Holiday Inn. I decided to return the next morning. I was keen to see Omar at play, which was something he rarely does.

'I get dizzy when I am not furthering the cause of Islam,' he had once said to me. 'I cannot take a day off, an hour off, even a minute off. I will take time off when I am with Allah, when I die in the battlefield and become a martyr.'

But he was due to make a rare exception this weekend, fishing in the pond in the grounds of this country house.

At six the next morning, I drove once again into the long lane. I spotted Omar immediately. He was taking an early-morning stroll with a small group of robed men. I beeped and waved merrily.

To my surprise, however, Omar seemed furious to see me.

I pulled up, and jumped out of the car.

'Hi!' I said, cheerfully. 'Omar!'

Omar pointedly ignored me.

'Omar?' I said, quizzically. 'What's wrong?'

'How did you know I was going to be here this weekend?' barked Omar. 'Who told you? Why have you tracked me down here?'

'Omar?' I said, confused. 'What's going on?'

'What do you want from me?' said Omar, sharply.

'I just wanted to see you fish,' I said, hopelessly.

'Who told you I was going to be here?' snapped Omar. 'Tell me their name!'

There was a long silence.

'I have no idea,' I said, finally.

There was another awkward pause.

'Well, now you're here,' said Omar, 'you may as well stay.'

'Thank you,' I said.

We carried on walking. When Omar was looking away, one of his fellow walkers smiled softly at me.

'That was quite a show Omar put on just then,' he said.

'Yes it was,' I replied.

'So,' said Omar, merrily, turning around to us, 'where is everybody and where is the fishing?'

And then, ahead of us, was a small, shady pond. It was a lovely rustic sight. A cluster of Islamic militants were gathered around fishing rods. For bait, they were using sweetcorn. We wandered over. The first thing Omar said was, 'How many fish did Hizb-ut-Tahrir catch?'

The other leaders glanced at each other and raised their eyebrows. Omar's split from Hizb-ut-Tahrir – the group he had previously led before branching off to form Al Muhajiroun – had been painful and acrimonious, and now there seemed to be some competition between them.

'He didn't catch any fish,' came the reply.

'Ha ha!' says Omar. 'No fish! Really? Ha ha! Somebody give me a fishing rod.'

Soon after casting off, Omar's rod began to twitch. He had caught a fish.

'Praise be!' he exclaimed. 'I've got a fish! I've got one! Ha ha!'

He lifted his rod out of the water, and the bedraggled fish struggled mid-air on the line, while all the Islamic fundamentalists gazed at it.

'Ha ha!' said Omar. 'It looks like one of the Jewish Board of Deputies.'

There was a smattering of polite laughter.

'What do I do now?' said Omar.

'Pass me the green knife,' said a man to Omar's right. 'Quick! The green knife!'

In a panic, Omar reached for a tin opener.

'Not the tin opener! The knife! Hold the fish, Omar Bakri. Just hold the fish.'

'No,' said Omar, quietly, 'I cannot hold the fish.'

There was a silence.

'Hold the fish!'

'No. I cannot hold the fish. What do I do with a fish?'

'Oh, give it to me!'

'OK,' said Omar. 'You hold the fish.'

The other leaders glanced despairingly at Omar. And then one of them sighed, reached for the fish, and said, 'How do you expect to fight the Jihad, Omar Bakri, if you cannot hold a fish?'

Omar didn't return my calls for a few days after the fishing trip.

*

31

It was midnight, back in London, a few days later. Omar and his people were flyposting for the rally. Omar asked me to join in, so I could provide a lift for some of his supporters. They covered Piccadilly Circus and Trafalgar Square. They flyposted telephone boxes, stop signs, no-right-turn signs, buses, tube trains, pelican crossings, and age-old statues of generals on horseback.

'Who the hell is that?' said Anjem, referring to a statue of Field Marshal John Fox Burgoyne in a street behind the Mall.

'Who gives a tinker's toss who that is,' replied a young man called Naz, pasting glue over the statue's base.

They stuck a JIHAD! sticker on a gold knob at the end of an iron railing outside Buckingham Palace. But there were too many air-bubbles. Gold knobs are not suitable for rectangular stickers. They spent five minutes or so attempting to iron out the bubbles. They stood around the gold knob in silence. Finally, one of them said, 'It's not working, is it?'

Within the next few days, the London Arena received complaints from twenty-eight local councils about the flyposting. There had been bomb threats too, and the Arena announced that they intended to charge Omar £18,000 for extra security. When I paid the Arena an impromptu visit to ask them how they were coping with being in the midst of a burgeoning international incident, they threw me out. They wouldn't even let me stand in the foyer.

That afternoon, they called Omar and told him that, on top of the cost of removing the flyposters and the £18,000 extra security charge, they wanted to renegotiate the car-parking facilities. This was a strange new twist. Omar sent Anjem to the Arena to explain that, firstly, the flyposting could only have been the work of an unknown band of supporters. Omar was just a simple man. He couldn't control the enthusiasm of all the Muslim people.

'But, Omar,' I said, 'your phone number was printed on the bottom of the leaflets.'

'Do *you* know my phone number?' said Omar.

'Yes,' I said.

'And how did you first find it,' he asked, 'all those months ago?'

'The phone book,' I said.

'Exactly,' said Omar.

'Ah,' I said. 'Clever.'

And in response to the Arena's second demand: what possible need could there be for security guards at an educational conference on Islamic affairs? All this talk of bombs and terrorism and extremists was just lies generated by media infidels.

And finally, everyone, Islamic fundamentalists included, had an inalienable right – by *law* – to park their cars.

Omar was confident that these arguments were watertight.

Every morning, Anjem would buy all the papers, and Omar would read about himself and the rally, and listen to debates about himself on BBC Radio 4. His offices in the basement of the Finsbury Park Mosque were besieged by reporters and TV crews. When Omar prayed, television crews filmed him praying. Later, shots of Omar praying were broadcast on the news with the following commentary:

> There are more Muslims in south-east London than anywhere else in Europe. The vast majority of them are horrified by Al Muhajiroun. They believe the group only generates prejudice against all Muslims in the West.
>
> Sheikh Omar Bakri Mohammed is the leader of Al Muhajiroun. He's a Syrian living in Britain on state benefits. What he wants is a Holy War that is unashamedly violent.

Omar hadn't eaten properly in days – just crisps and chocolates and fig rolls. His health was suffering. And he was getting woken up in the middle of the night by anonymous phone calls. 'Enough is enough. You fundamentalists are going to pay the price. You are dead meat.'

'Very silly messages,' said Omar. 'But the one that came last night had an Arabic accent. "If the rally goes ahead, we will blow it up, you traitors." '

But in spite of this, I'd not seen Omar quite so happy.

He was asked to appear on a Carlton television discussion programme called *Thursday Night Live*. The producers told Omar that it would be an intellectual and even-handed debate about the issues surrounding the rally. Omar was excited.

The night of the broadcast, I turned on Carlton TV to see a television studio full of young white males. They wore Fred Perry shirts and smart-casual sports tops, the uniform of the modern-day south-east London racist. There was a great deal of shouting.

The presenter, whose name is Nicky Campbell, was wandering amongst the audience holding a microphone. He pointed it at random shouting men, and their amplified cries drifted briefly above the general noise. Omar sat, very quiet and still, on a stage.

'The gentleman in the striped shirt,' said Nicky Campbell, passing the microphone across.

'I don't wanna get into depth about Islamic or Islam and all that,' he said, 'but I believe if anyone comes into this country, like this geezer 'ee's on benefit – I think if you're gonna be in this country, you should be *British*.' There was thunderous applause. 'Not Islamic or Islam or nothing, but *British*.'

Nicky Campbell said, 'How much money in benefit are you getting every week?'

'One hundred and fifty pounds,' replied Omar softly. You could barely hear him over the shouting.

'If you wanna change something,' interrupted the man in the striped shirt, 'you wanna get a *job*!' There were howls of support from the audience. 'Not ponce down the bleedin' DSS.'

'I used to have a job,' replied Omar, 'and many people like you worked for *me*.'

'Well, go down the corner shop and get one then,' said the man in the striped shirt.

Nicky Campbell intervened. 'OK,' he said. 'The man in the front row with the glasses.'

'We have our laws, and all that,' he said, 'so shouldn't it

be a simple thing? As in Rome, do as the Romans do. You're a bloody terrorist and you should swim home to—'

His final words were drowned out by howls of approval.

I arrived at Omar's offices early the next morning. This was the day before the rally. Omar was laughing.

'Did you see me on TV last night?' he said, shaking his head. 'My God!'

'Were you upset?' I asked.

'Oh, no,' said Omar. 'It was very silly. Did you *see* them?'

The offices were packed as always with supporters and news crews from around the world waiting to interview him.

'You know, Jon,' he said, 'there have always been plans. And the first two plans have already been put into operation. Plan A was to announce the rally, and we announced the rally. Plan B was to shake up the entire world, and we have shaken up the entire world.'

'How many plans are there in total?' I asked.

'Four plans,' said Omar.

'So you're now on to Plan C?' I asked.

'That's right,' said Omar.

'What's Plan C?' I asked.

'I will tell you now,' said Omar, 'because we are ready to implement it. OK. Do you know how many journalists have asked to interview me and have requested a press pass for the event of the rally?'

'Six hundred and thirty-four,' I said.

'Exactly,' said Omar. 'I don't think that any member of

Parliament, or even Lady Diana herself, had this many journalists requesting a press pass.'

'What has this got to do with Plan C?' I asked him.

'OK,' said Omar. 'Today, I will announce that all journalists are banned from entering the London Arena.'

Omar grinned. He looked at me to gauge my response to Plan C. I was confused.

'Why?' I said. 'What's wrong with letting them in?'

'It will be a Muslim-only conference,' says Omar. 'Ha ha! What do you think of that?'

'I think it's a little bit of a shame,' I said, 'and I don't quite understand the rationale behind it.'

'It is a Muslim-only conference,' said Omar, a little sharply.

Then Omar was called away for a private meeting with Anjem, his deputy. I considered Plan C. I knew that ticket sales had been disappointing. Only two or three thousand had been sold, which left eleven thousand empty seats in the London Arena. Also, few of the pledged video messages from incarcerated terrorists and fugitives from justice had arrived – not even the one from Omar's old friend, the Blind Sheikh. As I watched Omar wandering away, I realized what his final plan, Plan D, must be.

At lunchtime, Omar and Anjem disappeared again into a room together. Then they reappeared, looking grave. Omar cleared his throat. He had something he wanted to say. The room fell silent. Omar didn't announce it as such, but this was Plan D.

'The rally,' said Omar, 'has been cancelled. It is over.

There will be no rally. They have blackmailed us. The London Arena have blackmailed the Muslims. They wanted to charge the maximum cost of security. Eighteen thousand pounds. They know we can't afford this sort of money. So do not blame us for the cancellation. We were blackmailed. Any questions?'

'Are you disappointed?' I asked Omar.

'Oh, no,' said Omar. 'It is a great victory for Muslims worldwide. It is a victory because we said we would shake up the world, and we shook up the world. We promised it would become a historical rally and it has become a historical rally. It blew up the whole world.'

'And financially?' I asked. 'Has it been an expensive endeavour?'

'Oh, no,' said Omar. 'I am entitled to a full refund from the London Arena.'

As word of the cancellation spread, rumours began to circulate that Omar would have his rally after all, but at a different location.

'Is there going to be a march in the streets?' asked the journalists. 'Somebody mentioned Hyde Park.'

'We will have our rally,' said Omar. 'Speaker's Corner. Hyde Park. Ten-thirty on Sunday morning. Come along. The world's press will be there.'

'And what about your supporters?' I asked. 'What about the audience?'

There was a moment's pause.

'They are very welcome to come along too,' said Omar, 'of course.'

*

I arrived early at Speaker's Corner on Sunday morning. It was an unusual choice of location for Omar's alternative rally. This corner of Hyde Park was a notorious asylum for the theologically and politically overwrought to exercise their democratic right, on Sunday mornings, to be heard on top of soap-boxes and stepladders. The flaw was that the audience turned up only to be amused by the speakers' eccentricities. It was a tourist attraction. I could not understand why anybody who felt he had something crucial to impart would choose to make himself heard at Speaker's Corner. If I was far-fetched in this manner, I wouldn't pigeon-hole myself. I'd try to slip into the mainstream.

I spotted Omar. He was surrounded by film crews. Although he had often said he would relish the opportunity to die in the battlefield, security was tight today. Omar's people were holding walkie-talkies and eyeing passers-by as if they were potential assassins. I waved a hello, but Omar didn't respond. Now he was at the centre of world events, our relationship had cooled a little. He didn't need me any more.

I noticed Mohammed, one of Omar's teenage sons, in the crowd. He was standing alone. He looked a little anxious and he seemed not to be sharing in the excitement of the day. He told me that he had seen the movie *Malcolm X* on the video a few nights before, and he recognized some worrying parallels between this story and his father's.

'You see what happened to Malcolm X?' said Mohammed. 'Too much publicity, and you see what happened? Bang.'

'Is that what your dad's becoming?' I asked.

'I didn't exactly like that video,' he said. 'Even Mum says she's worried. But it's all in the hands of God. I guess.' Mohammed paused, sadly. 'I guess,' he said, 'it's all in the hands of Allah.'

Then there was a shrill noise to our left, screeching and cat-calls. Everyone looked over. We saw a mass of pink flags surrounded by a police escort. It was Outrage, the gay rights group, who'd arrived for a counter demonstration, a Queer Fatwa. They held placards sentencing Omar to '1,000 Years Of Relentless Sodomitical Torment'.

'Al Muhajiroun!' they chanted. 'Anti-gay! Anti-women! Anti-you!'

The TV crews abandoned Omar en masse to film the Queer Fatwa.

'That's the decline of this nation,' Omar announced to the few journalists still listening to him.

One of Omar's young followers, a teenager with a wispy beard and a Jihad baseball cap, spotted me watching the Queer Fatwa.

'You *cannot* put the homosexuals in Omar's life story,' he said, furiously. 'No way. If you do that, you will get *so many* death threats. You will get more death threats than the entire State of Israel gets. Which is two or three billion, actually.'

'Just if I put Outrage in Omar's life story?' I said.

'No way,' he said, 'can you do that.'

This worried me. Whenever I told people I was spending a year with Omar Bakri, they invariably looked concerned and said, 'But what about the fatwas?' I had shrugged these concerns off. But now a Muslim extremist had actually said the words *death threat* to me. Admittedly, it wasn't a tangible death threat, per se, more a death threat precursor. But that was still one step closer to a death threat than I'd ever hoped to come. I felt the need for some comforting words from Omar, but I couldn't get anywhere near him for all his bodyguards.

I did not see Omar for two months. We spoke on the phone from time to time, but he didn't seem to want to have me about. Things had taken a turn for the worse. He had been evicted from his offices at the bottom of my road. His landlords, the Finsbury Park Mosque, were sick of all the film crews. Also, the DSS had stopped his unemployment and disability benefits. Rupert Allason claimed victory for this.

'I would love nothing more than to get a job,' Omar told me over the phone. 'But how can I, with all the terrible publicity your media gives me?'

'So you've lost your offices and you've lost your unemployment benefit,' I said. 'You've lost everything.'

'I have lost every material thing in this life,' said Omar, 'but I have not lost my belief or my struggle or the cause I believe in. I may not have money but I have dignity.'

'Omar,' I said, 'there's something I'm a little worried about which I wanted to talk through with you.'

'Oh, yes?'

'One of your followers said that if I put Outrage in your story, I would get two or three billion death threats.'

'Ah,' said Omar. 'They are terrible people. They are always putting death threats on people, those homosexuals.'

'No, no,' I explained. 'It wasn't the homosexuals who put a death threat on me. It was one of *your* people. I was wondering if you could put in a word for me. Smooth things over.'

'I don't talk to homosexuals,' Omar replied.

'It wasn't the homosexuals,' I said, exasperated. 'It was a young man, with a wispy beard. And he was wearing a Jihad baseball cap.'

There was a long silence.

'There are a lot of people with beards,' said Omar, finally. 'And a lot of people wearing Jihad baseball caps.'

There was another silence.

'Omar,' I said, 'I can point him out to you. I don't know his name, but I've often seen him standing next to you.'

'Jon,' said Omar, quietly, 'this cannot have happened. No Muslim would ever put a death threat on to anybody. Anyway. I've got to go now. Goodbye, Jon.'

'Goodbye, Omar,' I muttered.

A month passed, and then it was January, the first day of Ramadan. For months now, I'd been asking Omar to take me to his secret Jihad training camp in Crawley – which seemed a rather incongruous location for a Jihad training camp. Finally he agreed. We were picked up at Crawley station by some young local followers. These were people I had never seen before. Omar said that in every town and city in the country, and many towns abroad, there was a cluster of Al Muhajiroun supporters.

'When you put all those people together,' said Omar, 'you have an army. Oh yes, there is a time when a military struggle must take place in the UK. Jihad. It's called "Conquering". One day, without question, the UK is going to be governed by Islam. The Muslims in Britain must not be naive. They must be ready to defend themselves militarily. The struggle, as I always say, is a struggle between two civilizations, the civilization of man against the civilization of God.'

We were driven to the Jihad training camp, a well-stocked gym in a scout hut in a forestry centre. Snow lay on the ground. Inside, a young man wearing boxing gloves was beating a punchbag, and Omar immediately instructed him to focus his assault.

'On the head,' he said. 'That's it. The head! Easy. Easy. OK, stop now. Rest, rest! You kill him! You kill him!'

The group laughed, and I laughed too.

I was standing in one corner, with my back against the wall. I found this situation slightly uncomfortable. And then, apropos of nothing, Omar made an announcement to the group.

'Look at me!' he said. 'Here I am with an infidel. Jon' – Omar paused for effect – 'is a Jew.'

There was an audible gasp, followed by a long silence.

Of all the locations in which Omar could have chosen to disclose this sensational revelation, a packed Jihad training camp in the middle of a forest was not the place I would have hoped for. I found myself searching for the fastest path to the door.

'Are you really a Jew?' said someone, eventually.

'Well,' I said, 'surely it is better to be a Jew than an atheist?'

There was a silence.

'No, it isn't,' said a voice from the crowd.

'When did you know that I was Jewish?' I asked Omar.

'From the beginning,' he said. 'I could see it in your eyes. Why didn't you tell me?'

'Well,' I said. 'You know—'

'You are ashamed to be a Jew?' said Omar. 'You deny it?'

'No,' I said.

'I am not offended that you are a Jew,' said Omar. 'We are all Semites. If you were Israeli, if you were Zionist, that is a different matter. But what offends me is that you hide it. You assimilate. That you have no pride.'

'I am proud,' I said, unconvincingly.

Of course, Omar was right. I should have told him.

'Assimilation,' tutted Omar. 'Integration. That is the worst thing of all. Be a Jew!'

I left the Jihad training camp soon after. I was to see Omar on only one more occasion. It had been a year since he bought his novelty Coca-Cola Hamas collection boxes from the Cash and Carry. They were full now of loose change and £50 notes. There was a cheque for £5,000 in one. Anjem and Omar were taking the collection boxes to the bank. The money would be converted into foreign currency and shipped off to the Middle East, where it would be used in the fight against Israel.

Omar had some business to finish. Anjem packed the bottles in the back of his car. Then he remembered that he'd left his coat inside. He said, 'Could you guard the money for a moment? I won't be long.'

'OK,' I replied.

Anjem disappeared and I was left standing guard over

thousands of pounds, money that would go to Hamas, to kill the Jews in Israel.

For a while I stood there.

And what the hell was I doing, guarding money that would be used to kill the Jews? And then I understood that I had to take the money. I had to reach into the car, grab the Coca-Cola bottles, and make a run for it. This was my responsibility, my duty. I had an obligation to do this. I had the strength to carry two bottles. How many lives might that save? Omar and Anjem were still inside. The car was unlocked.

But I didn't do it, of course. I just stood there. And then Anjem and Omar returned, thanked me for my help, and took the money to the bank.

2. *Running Through Cornfields*

Rachel Weaver is eighteen. She lived with her boyfriend, Josh, in a large, plain ranch house in northwest Montana. I sat at her kitchen table, drinking her apple juice and eating from a jar of Certs mints, while Josh lifted weights in the spare bedroom.

Rachel said, 'The gun I really fell in love with is the .45 70. I'm not even sure who makes it. It's a lever action. It's not like it's a big machine gun. It's not a hard kick. It's a . . . *whoa* . . . it lugs you back.'

When she said 'whoa', she slid her shoulder back as if she was dancing.

'Do you want to try it out?' she said.

'OK,' I said.

Rachel disappeared into the back room and she returned holding two semi-automatic rifles.

'This is the .45 70,' she said. 'And this one is an AR15. Honey . . .?'

'Yeah?' called Josh.

'Will you get the mini .14?'

'OK,' he yelled.

Josh appeared holding a silver revolver. They laid the guns out on the kitchen table – a mini cache, almost like a photograph of a police seizure – and loaded them one by one.

'How did you two meet?' I asked them.

'High school,' said Rachel.

'She didn't like me in high school,' said Josh.

'What a dork,' said Rachel.

'Ha,' said Josh.

'He was a jock,' said Rachel. 'Mr "I'm A Stud".' She rolled her eyes. 'I was always, "OK, whatever . . ." '

But now they were engaged to be married.

'Josh is one of the boys that your mom says not to go around with,' said Rachel.

We put on our coats and our baseball caps and we headed out into the fields behind Rachel's house. Before we started, Rachel wanted to give me a talk about the basics of sensible shooting, but Josh just shoved a loaded rifle into my hands.

And then, once Rachel's four horses had been shooed to a safe distance, and I had propped the gun onto my shoulder: Bam!

'Look at him!' laughed Josh. 'He's grinning all over his face!' Josh was delighted. 'You see that?' he said. 'Big smile.'

This was true.

Bam! I went. Bam! And then: Bam bam bam bam!

'*Now* I understand why you people don't want to give up your guns!' I yelled.

'Once you've fired your first shot,' said Josh, 'there's no going back.'

Bam bam! I tried out a fancy manoeuvre. Bam bam! . . . Bam!

'Careful, Jon,' said Rachel. 'You're starting to look a little radical!'

'Ha!' I said.

'You've crossed over now,' said Josh.

It was Josh's turn to shoot, so Rachel and I sheltered from the snow in the woodshed.

'You know,' she said, 'I don't see guns as a big political thing.'

'Why not?' I asked her.

'Well,' she replied. 'The reason—'

Bam! went Josh. Bam bam bam! Bam!

'The reason—' said Rachel again.

Bam! Bam! Josh continued shooting into nothing.

'Come on,' said Rachel, impatiently. We waited for Josh to stop, which he finally did in order to reload.

'OK,' said Rachel. 'The reason why I don't see it as a big political thing is because even if I had my rifles it's not going to do me any good if the government wants to wipe me out. They can just fly over in a helicopter and drop a fire bomb.'

We both involuntarily looked up to the sky.

'Trying to go up against the government?' said Rachel. 'That's just . . .'

She trailed off. Then she added, wistfully, 'Unless the whole country did it.' She laughed. 'Now that would be different, I guess.'

She turned to Josh.

'Honey?'

'Yeah?'

'I've got about five minutes. Then I've really got to get into town.'

'OK,' said Josh.

We shot some more. Rachel found some tin cans. She said that shooting into nothing was pointless. She shot three times and hit the tin cans twice. Then she looked at her watch.

'I've got to go,' she said. 'Honey . . .?'

'I'm going to shoot these last five,' said Josh.

'OK,' sighed Rachel.

'I'm going to shoot these five,' repeated Josh, thinly.

'Why?'

'*Because I want to*,' snapped Josh.

'Watch the horses, honey,' said Rachel. 'They're—'

BAM BAM BAM BAM BAM!

But Josh had finished it. He finished it in a manner I would have called testy had guns not been involved – but guns were involved so I will call it frenzied – by pumping his pistol senselessly and abruptly into the ground.

Rachel stared daggers at Josh.

'Easy as that,' he said, icily.

'You *enjoy* just wasting bullets?'

'Yes,' said Josh.

We wandered back to the house. Sensible, safety-conscious Rachel led the way, dumb gung-ho me and even dumber gung-ho Josh followed. I had never seen a domestic quarrel punctuated by gunfire before, and it had startled me into an awkward silence. Rachel was silently furious with Josh for behaving like a gun-toting idiot in front of a journalist. Josh was silently seething for his own unfathomable reasons. Nobody said anything.

When Rachel was two years old, in the early 1980s, her parents, Randy and Vicki Weaver, took her from the city to live on top of a mountain in Idaho. Her father, an ex-Green Beret in the US Special Forces, built them a plywood cabin, 25 foot by 32 foot, 4,000 feet up in the Selkirk Mountains, at the top of Farnsworth Road overlooking Ruby Creek, among the bears and the mountain lions.

There was Rachel, her parents, her nine-year-old sister Sara, their seven-year-old brother Sammy, and some dogs and chickens. Later on Vicki would give birth to baby Elisheba up there.

If you can't opt out on top of a mountain in Idaho, her parents figured, you can't opt out anywhere. If the government won't leave you alone there, where can you be left alone?

'They just wanted to get away,' said Rachel, 'away from the bad things they show on TV.'

The children were home schooled. Rachel's parents believed that the world was being secretly ruled by a clique of primarily Zionist international bankers, global elitists who wanted to establish a genocidal New World Order and implant microchips bearing the mark of Satan into everyone's forehead. But they had no intention of doing anything about it. The international bankers were a long way off.

They were pioneers back in 1982. Nowadays many people, including Omar Bakri and his friends, believe that the New World Order, the international bankers, are secretly ruling the world from a room somewhere. But Randy and Vicki were among the first. They hammered a sign outside their cabin that read: 'STOP THE NEW WORLD ORDER'.

Some of the things they believed up there might seem crazy, but they were a long way off.

Rachel poured me some more apple juice and gave me some more Certs mints to eat while she told me about her early memories of life in that cabin.

'There are just so many things that people don't understand,' she said. 'When I was little I would go out and watch a wasp dig a hole in the ground for hours. Then I'd follow him and he'd go and paralyse a worm or a cricket and he'd drag it into his hole and he'd lay an egg and the egg would feed on it and it would hatch and crawl out of the ground. Little things that nobody would ever notice. But I noticed.'

She passed me some strawberry twisties.

'The media said we were crazy up there and had landmines everywhere and all we cared about was guns. I do like guns. I still do. I did then. But it's not weird or crazy.'

Rachel showed me photographs of her family. Sammy looked about ten, a little skinny blond-haired boy, but he actually was fourteen when the photograph was taken.

'What are your early memories of Sammy?' I asked her.

'That would have to be me being called a tag along.' Rachel smiled. 'Sara and Sammy were closer in age. They went hiking. They had horses. They'd go and hang out in a tree fort. I was just tripping and falling. So I'd have to pacify myself by playing with lizards and bugs. I remember the day before everything happened, Sammy went down to collect the seeds from his radish plants, and I followed him down to watch him and talk to him, and he was all, "Leave me alone. Quit following me." And I went behind this blown-over tree and I was sitting there crying and he came over and apologized to me and told me he loved me, and I remember that because he'd never said anything like that to me before.'

She showed me more photographs. Her father Randy was dressed in a biker jacket, the big sky behind him.

Her mother Vicki looked like a Bible scholar.

Rachel and Sara looked like typical American children, pretty, long black hair.

Elisheba was just a baby.

Rachel picked up the photograph of her mother.

'She was dainty,' she said. 'Petite, very feminine, never burped in front of anybody. Just wonderful. Dad was always the final yes or no, but Mom was always very persuasive. She was the brains, and she just let him think he was running the show. Dad probably still doesn't know it.' She laughed. 'When you see him you'd better not tell him that I told you that.'

It was Vicki's idea to move to the cabin. As much as Randy shared his wife's beliefs about how the separatist Weavers needed to isolate themselves from the tyranny of the impending world government and so on, Randy liked to cut loose once in a while and go drinking in populated areas.

Unfortunately, one of the populated areas he chose was

the nearby Aryan Nations, a militant neo-Nazi community and gathering place for skinheads and racists. They wore their hearts on their sleeves, in the form of swastika armbands.

Aryan Nations holds a big summer camp every year, and Randy visited four years running, sometimes taking the children along. He says now that he would invariably get into fights with the neo-Nazis about their beliefs. (He says their disagreement centred on who, exactly, constituted the secret clique of global elitists who were implementing a planetary takeover. The neo-Nazis blamed the Jews exclusively, whereas Randy felt that focusing antipathy onto a single race was a mistake. He didn't consider himself to be a white supremacist. He was a *separatist*. This may sound pedantic, but it wasn't pedantic to him. But, still, he liked the neo-Nazis as people, and he thought their countryside and picnic areas were nice.)

Randy was finally kicked out of the place for smuggling in a six-pack of beer. Aryan Nations is terribly intolerant, about beer drinking too.

But he did make friends there. One of his friends was Gus Magisano. Gus asked Randy to rob banks with him, and hoard machine guns. Gus told Randy that the New World Order, the secret clique of international bankers, could be overthrown only with ordered violence. Randy told Gus that he wasn't interested.

One day Gus asked Randy to sell him two sawn-off shotguns. Randy said OK. He asked Gus where he wanted them sawn. Gus pointed to a spot on the barrel which was a quarter of an inch outside the legal limit. Randy sawed away.

Gus wasn't his real name, of course. He was an under-cover informant for the Bureau of Alcohol, Tobacco and Firearms. The plan was to entice Randy into sawing off the shotguns below the legal limit, and then offer him a deal. He could either become a government informant and spy on Aryan Nations, or he could go to jail for illegal gun running.

'I don't understand it,' said Rachel. 'We were just good people who didn't even have any *intention* of doing any-thing wrong. I totally don't understand why they even came to my dad to ask him to saw off shotguns. It makes no sense to me. It just blows my mind that they'd even *care.*'

For the government, though, Randy had the makings of a perfect informant – a slightly crazy person who was friends with far crazier people, a family man with bad finances. How could he turn them down?

He didn't just turn them down, he made a great big burlesque show of turning them down.

'Hey, Vicki!' he yelled. 'Come out here. Take a look at these guys! Guess what they just asked me to do! Write down their names.' And so on.

Six months later, Randy was indicted on the shotgun charge. In a preliminary hearing, the magistrate told Randy that he'd lose the cabin if he lost the case. Randy and Vicki considered themselves to be in a no-win situ-ation. They would lose the cabin if they failed to appear, but they were bound to lose the case so they would lose the cabin even if they *did* appear. They decided not to show up in court any more. They buried their heads in the sand. A young family friend, Kevin Harris, moved in with them.

The family took to carrying guns at all times. They became increasingly convinced that the New World Order was watching them from the bushes.

They discovered that they *were*, in fact, being watched from the bushes. They found a surveillance camera and tore it down. Randy let it be known that he would not be taken off the mountain alive, although most of the people who knew him considered these words to be just bravado. Vicki gave birth to Elisheba.

And then, one day in August, it all began.

'I remember the first part,' said Rachel. 'I was out on the back porch with Mom and my little sister Elisheba who was at that time ten months old. Sara came through the house and said the dogs were going crazy, and Kevin and Sammy were going out to see what it was.'

Sammy grabbed his gun. Rachel grabbed Elisheba and a mini .14. She tagged along as far as the front of the cabin.

'I had only ever had a glimpse of a mountain lion. I loved mountain lions. The dogs didn't usually go crazy wild when people came up. So I was hoping I'd see a bear or something. Then I remember hearing gunshots.'

This was 21 August 1992. What had happened was this: three US marshals had been staking out the cabin for weeks, hoping to arrest Randy for failure to appear on the shotgun charge. That morning they got too close to the cabin door. Striker the Labrador began barking and running after them. Sammy and Kevin followed the dog down the hill. Suddenly, an agent jumped out from the bushes in jungle camouflage and shot Striker in the back.

Sammy yelled, 'You killed my dog you son of a bitch.'

He fired two random shots, which hit nobody. He was 4 foot 11 inches tall, and his voice hadn't broken. The US marshals then opened fire, nearly blowing off Sammy's arm.

Sammy yelled, 'Dad! I'm coming home, Dad!'

He turned around to run back to his father, but the US marshals shot him dead in the back.

Kevin Harris opened fire. The marshals shot back and one of them was killed, either by Kevin or by friendly fire, as they call it.

'We were all standing on that rock that overlooks our driveway,' said Rachel. 'Mom and Sara and Dad and I. Kevin came running up the hill and said that Sammy had been shot and he was dead. And it was just . . . we just let out a cry and broke down. Dad fired Mom's .223 into the air. Full clip. And Mom asked Kevin if he was sure, and he said, yeah.'

For Randy and Vicki, the responsibility for Sammy's death lay not with the US marshals, not with the government, but with the New World Order, the Secret Rulers of the World, the clique of world bankers and globalist CEOs and media moguls who meet in secret rooms to plot the carve-up of the planet.

Vicki Weaver wrote in her diary that night that Striker and Sammy had been killed while chasing the 'servants of the New World Order' down Farnsworth Road.

The US marshals called for back-up, and an army of four hundred troops was dispatched within the next twenty-four hours to surround the cabin and the nearby roads and the meadow below. There were US marshals and FBI snipers in gas masks and face paint and camouflage, local police, state police, the BATF, the Internal Revenue Service, the US Border Patrol, Highway Patrol from four states, City Police and the Forestry Service. They had tanks and armoured personnel carriers.

The FBI's elite Hostage Rescue Team took control. They sealed off an area of twenty square miles at a cost of a million dollars a day. More federal troops were flown in by helicopter. They built a new road up the mountain for the tanks. Martial law was declared by the state governor, who called the Weaver cabin an 'extreme emergency and disaster area'.

Two local journalists reported seeing the FBI load fuel into cylinders and load the cylinders into a helicopter which they flew above the cabin. Perhaps they intended to firebomb the family to eliminate the witnesses (Randy, Rachel, Sara, Vicki, Kevin and Elisheba). It is a matter of debate. Whatever, the FBI saw that the journalists had witnessed the manoeuvre and the helicopter landed again.

This military operation was undertaken with such stealth, such silence, that – besides from hearing a few sirens down in the valley – the Weaver family had no idea that they were now surrounded.

The neighbours came out of their houses and saw the army roll past them up the hill. They scribbled messages onto placards and held them up at the troops. The placards read:

> 'Death To The New World Order!'
> 'New World Order Burn In Hell!'

The morning after Sammy's death, Randy wanted to see his son's body one last time (they had carried him from the road and wrapped him in blankets and placed him in the tool shed) so he opened the cabin door and looked around the hillside and saw nothing (the snipers being heavily camouflaged).

He walked the few yards to the shed. As he put his hand on the latch, an FBI sniper called Lon Horiuchi yelled, 'Freeze, Weaver!' and then he shot Randy in the arm.

Rachel saw this as she stood at the cabin door with her mother, Vicki, who held the baby Elisheba in her arms.

'You bastards!' yelled Vicki.

Then the sniper shot Vicki through the face.

The bullet went right through Vicki's head, taking with it fragments of her skull, which embedded themselves in Kevin's arm and ribcage and lungs. Vicki dropped dead to the floor at Rachel's feet, with Elisheba underneath her. Randy ran back to the cabin.

'Dad picked Elisheba up off from underneath Mom and handed her to me,' said Rachel. 'She had blood and stuff all over her head and we were afraid she'd been shot too, but she was OK. It was just Mom's blood. Dad brought Mom in and put her on the kitchen floor. That's when we drew the curtains around all the windows and shut the door, obviously, and we didn't come out after that.

'I remember feeding Elisheba a whole box of sweets so she wouldn't cry, poor girl.

'I remember having to crawl through Mom's blood every time I needed to go into the kitchen to get food.

'I don't think of it as this day or that day after that. I just remember it as one long terrible day.'

*

The military set up base camp a few hundred yards down the mountain. The rumour went that some army person hammered a sign into the ground outside the tents calling their temporary barracks 'Camp Vicki'.

'I remember hearing people underneath the house rustling through our stuff,' said Rachel. 'I remember the floodlights coming in through the cracks in the curtains and hearing their stupid half-tracks rolling over our stuff in the yard.'

Rachel told me this as we sat at her kitchen table. There are very few ornaments in her house. Where you might have a painting, binoculars hang from a nail in the wall next to the front window. (Rachel told me they were there for birdwatching, but during our time together a car happened to stop on the road near the front of her long driveway and she grabbed the binoculars and peered through them and only sat down again once it had driven away.)

'The tanks crunched our generator,' said Rachel, 'rolled over our outhouse. Not to mention, after they shot our dog and my brother, they ran over the dog.'

Rachel said, 'Just sick.'

She said, 'Every day they would shout at us through some bullhorn. They'd yell, "Vicki! Vicki! Tell Randy to pick up the phone. Vicki! We're having blueberry pancakes for breakfast. What are you having for breakfast?" And Dad would scream out, "You sons of bitches, you shot her. You know she's dead." And they'd never answer us. I *know* they could hear us through the walls. These were just plywood walls. I remember being really mad at them for acting like nothing was wrong.'

The spinning had begun straight away. The FBI said that

Randy himself might have shot Sammy in the back. They said the marshals had been ambushed, that they were pinned down and had not returned fire. They said that Randy was wanted for bank robberies, that he was a white supremacist, that the Weavers lived in a 'mountain fortress', and then 'a bunker', and 'a stronghold protected by a cache of fifteen weapons and ammunition capable of piercing armoured personnel carriers'.

They said that the two shotguns Randy sold the undercover informant were 'the chosen weapons of drug dealers and terrorists'.

Most of this was unnecessary, of course. The two crucial words were 'white supremacist'. That did it. Randy was henceforth referred to in all media as, 'White supremacist Randy Weaver'.

I dug out a tape of a chat show aired at the time, *Politically Incorrect* from New York, in which Randy's case was discussed by the comedian Bill Maher, Nadine Strossen of the American Civil Liberties Union and Garry Marshall, the creator of *Mork and Mindy* and *Pretty Woman*.

BILL MAHER: He was in Aryan Nations. Come on. Oh, boo hoo!

NADINE STROSSEN: Belonging to Aryan Nations is not a crime. That's his right.

GARRY MARSHALL: In my neighbourhood if a guy puts swastikas on his kids, I would be a little suspicious. I wouldn't say: 'Come on over! We'll have some fruit!'

AUDIENCE: (*Big laugh*.)

BILL MAHER: They shot the dog in the back. Can you

believe that, Garry? Oh, man, that's a Canine
American! He has his rights!

AUDIENCE: (*Laugh*.)

GARRY MARSHALL: That was the worst thing that
happened!

AUDIENCE: (*Laugh*.)

NADINE STROSSEN: He wasn't causing any danger to
anyone.

BILL MAHER: If you're bringing up your kids in Aryan
Nations you are causing danger because you're
spawning hate in America.

AUDIENCE: (*Applause*.)

The white supremacist angle was clearly working.

I left Rachel that evening. Before I got into my car, she told
me I should be careful not to over-romanticize her family.
She said that the people who did not call them white
supremacists tended to go on about fields of cotton and
running through cornfields.

'Running through cornfields?' I asked.

'A friend of my dad,' she said, 'started writing a book
about what happened, and Dad was reading the first
chapter, which was all about him as a boy running through
cornfields. And Dad said, "What a bunch of bullshit." He
never ran through cornfields. But Dad's friend likes to
write and he wanted to make it great.'

Rachel laughed.

'Running through cornfields,' she said.

*

I left Rachel's house and drove two hundred miles – through Missoula, near where the movie stars live (Meg Ryan, Peter Fonda, Whoopi Goldberg, etc.), and into Idaho, through the Bitterroot Mountains, past a sign that reads 'Winding Road Next 77 Miles' – and I stopped twelve miles past Kamiah, where Jack McLamb lives.

Jack McLamb lives in a trailer home in a small Christian community called Doves of the Valley. He looks like a friendly church minister, with a bouffant of white hair. In fact he is an ex-policeman, drummed out of the force after he created an organization called Police Against The New World Order.

I asked Jack how he first heard of Randy Weaver.

'They were calling him a neo-Nazi on the radio,' he said, 'an anti-Semitic hatemonger, a violent radical, any nasty name you can think about. You're the scum of the earth and they have a right to kill you, see?'

'I guess that the worst thing you can be called is an anti-Semite,' I said.

'Boy,' said Jack, 'the *worst* thing. Not racist. Not homophobe. Anti-Semite. There's such a power there. Boy. You get labelled an anti-Semite you're in *big* trouble. The media picked it up, of course, and used those words. They needed to demonize these people in case it ever got to court. They knew they were in big trouble. I mean, oh my goodness, talk about jury appeal. When you machine gun a little boy in the back and shoot a mother holding a baby in the head, you've got yourself some jury appeal.'

Jack said, 'Anti-Semite. That's the first thing they hit you with when you start to investigate the New World Order. I'm learning this myself. I've been labelled an anti-Semite just because I'm speaking out against this damnable world system.'

'Who is calling you an anti-Semite?' I asked.

'The Anti-Defamation League out of New York,' said Jack. He quickly added, 'It isn't true, of course. I am an honorary member of Jews for the Preservation of Firearms.' Jack paused. 'Some people think this is a Jewish conspiracy, some think it's a Catholic conspiracy, some people think it's a Masonic conspiracy. But I know what it really is.'

'What is it?' I asked.

'It is a satanic globalist conspiracy,' said Jack.

I was surprised to hear from Jack that the first thing Randy Weaver yelled through the cabin walls at him, the very first thing he yelled to the outside world, having been under siege for a week, was not, 'They killed Vicki. They killed my bride.' (That was the second thing he yelled.) It was not, 'I've been shot too.' (That was the third thing he yelled.) The first thing he yelled was, 'Why is the radio calling me a white supremacist when those are not my views?'

Jack said to me, 'The saddest days of my life were spent on the top of that mountain. It just broke my heart.'

It was a warm evening, and so we sat outside.

'You know why they shot Vicki Weaver?' said Jack. 'They knew Vicki was the strongest member of the family. This is what you learn in military training. Take out the head. This was a family. But they were treating them just as a military target. I get tears in my eyes thinking about it.'

'How did you end up being there?' I asked Jack.

'OK,' he said. 'I was living in Arizona at the time, and Colonel Bo Gritz came into town campaigning for the presidency of the United States. Colonel Bo Gritz is the most decorated Green Beret in the US army. Movies have been made about his exploits. So Bo said, "Jack, can I have breakfast with you?" I said, "Sure." He said, "There are some things going on in Idaho. A guy by the name of Randy Weaver is barricaded into his home with his family, and his son has been killed and it looks like there could be more death if something doesn't happen. I've been asked by the FBI to become involved because Randy Weaver served under me in the Special Forces, and they believe he will talk to me. So I'm going up there and will you come along as my back-up?" '

'Why did he feel he needed backing up?' I asked.

'Colonel Bo and I are hated by the government,' said Jack. 'He was worried that he'd go up there and all the guns would be pointed at him. They'd blow him to pieces and blame it on Randy Weaver. So I was his insurance.'

'What happened when you arrived?' I asked.

'It was surreal,' said Jack. 'It was incredible. I've never seen so many FBI agents, US marshals, local police, state police, in one place in my life. There were bullet-proof vehicles that were used to transport troops in, armoured personnel vehicles, military uniforms, face paint on their faces, bullet-proof vests. They had completely taken over this very small town.'

Jack paused.

'And by now there were around two thousand people on the other side of the barricade, there to support the Weaver family. You had a mixed bag from preachers, to neighbours, to people like me, to neo-Nazis from Aryan Nations up the road, to even some liberals.'

'Aryan Nations were there?'

'You know what,' said Jack. 'There are probably no more than fifteen of those radical crazies up at Aryan Nations at any one time, but the media likes to portray that there's thousands up there. But the neo-Nazis were down at the roadblock for the wrong reasons. You've got the radio saying that an anti-Semite has killed a US marshal, and Aryan Nations thought, "Good. Let's go down there and support him." So there are citizens on one side of the barricade and military and police on the other side of the barricade.'

'And when you got up onto the mountain,' I said, 'what conversations did you have with the Weaver family?'

'Randy was crying and the children were crying,' he said. 'So I would speak for a while and then Bo would speak for a while. We're trying to calm the girls down, get them to stop crying and to focus on something other than their mother lying underneath the kitchen table in a pool of blood. This was unbelievable trauma. Every time they had to get food, there was her body.'

'And this was a week after she'd been killed?' I said.

'A week after,' said Jack, 'in a cabin that was very stuffy. And Kevin had gangrene, having been shot by the sniper. They had blocked the windows and the doors with rags so the government couldn't see them and shoot them. So it was real stuffy.'

'What were the conversations about?' I asked.

'Bo found a stick about this long,' said Jack. 'He got

onto a stump and he was holding this big staff. He looked like Moses.'

'So you were still outside at this time?'

'The girls didn't want to let us in,' said Jack. 'They didn't know us and they didn't trust us. Anyway, it was really something. Bo had found out that Randy and the girls knew all about this world conspiracy. Randy and Vicki were very good parents. They'd explained it all to the kids, about how this group of very powerful people are setting up a New World Order. So Bo went over all these stories about how the money is controlled, about these secret organizations like the Bilderberg Group. But Randy and the girls already *know* this. So what Bo's doing, see, is he's talking to the five hundred militarized police lying in the bushes. He's talking to *them*. So he had a captive audience all day Saturday.' Jack laughed. 'The government *hated* us for that. These guys are not supposed to know about all this, and Bo's giving dates and names and times. Randy and the girls knew what he was doing. It was really neat.'

This is what Jack said that Bo talked about that day: he said that the secret rulers of the world call themselves the Bilderberg Group and they rule the world from a secret room somewhere. He said that every year this global elite go to a secret summer camp north of San Francisco called Bohemian Grove, where they get together and 'do all types of debauchery, sexual perversion, you name it. It's a really weird club and the same people who belong to the Bilderberg Group belong to it. They're witches and warlocks, and they are into anything that is evil.'

Jack said that what happened at Randy Weaver's cabin was a great awakening, not just for him and for Colonel

Bo Gritz and for the five hundred troops lying in the bushes in full jungle camouflage, but for the world in general and the United States in particular.

It is true to say that during the months that followed the end of the siege, the United States militia movement – which had not previously existed, to speak of – reported a massive upsurge in their membership. Jack was inundated with enquiries about how to fight the New World Order.

It was the Monday lunchtime, ten days into the siege, that Bo and Jack finally convinced the Weaver family to come out of the cabin and take their case to court.

'It was so wonderful to see the door opening and those little girls come out and take off their weapons,' said Jack. 'And they were the saddest days of my life that were spent on the top of that mountain. When I realized that my fellow police officers and soldiers were capable of that. These militarized men in their woolly bully outfits had executed the boy. When Sammy Weaver saw his little dog being shot, when little Sammy saw that and he opened fire, they almost cut his left arm off. Little Samuel who looked like he was ten, they shot his left arm to where it was hanging by the flesh, and he yelled, "Dad, I'm coming home, Dad", and at that time my fellow officers took this MP5 machine gun and just sprayed him up the back . . .

'Well, I carried the little girls down to the military force, these *big* guys, face paint, they all looked like trees and bushes, and their tears were coming down and streaking their face paint. They were all crying.'

Jack cried as he recounted this story. Then he said, 'And

that's why there are so many people today that are speaking out against this damnable New World Order.'

In the end, Randy Weaver and Kevin Harris were charged with murder, conspiracy and assault. The trial was a disaster for the government. The jury acquitted Kevin Harris of all charges, and convicted Randy only of failing to appear on the original firearms charge. He served sixteen months in jail.

The government paid Rachel and Sara and Elisheba $1 million each in an out of court settlement, hence Rachel's house and horses and mini-gym in the spare bedroom.

The American media, while continuing to refer to Randy Weaver as a white supremacist – which they still do – became highly critical of the handling of the case by the FBI and the BATF. It was just about the worst publicity these two law-enforcement agencies had ever received. The judge declared that the government had shown a 'callous disregard for the rights of the defendants'.

Jack McLamb said it was no coincidence that at the height of this bad press, the BATF announced with some pride that they were taking military action against a violent, child-abusing gun-hoarding religious cult holed up in a compound down in Texas.

I don't know if it was a coincidence or, as Jack said, an exercise in public relations. Whatever, six days into Randy Weaver's trial, fifty-three adults, including David Koresh, and twenty-three children were burnt to death at Mount Carmel in Waco.

The remains of the Weaver cabin became a place of pilgrimage for this new army of believers in the secret rulers of the world. One of the pilgrims was Timothy McVeigh who visited Randy Weaver's cabin, alone, some months before blowing up the Alfred P. Murrah Building in Oklahoma City, and killing 168 people. McVeigh considered the Murrah Building to be local New World Order headquarters.

ONE OUT OF EIGHT AMERICANS HAS HARD-CORE ANTI-SEMITIC FEELINGS

This quarter-page advertisement occupied the front page of the *New York Times* a few weeks after I visited Jack McLamb. The ad had been paid for by the Jewish defence organization, the Anti-Defamation League of B'nai Brith.

When journalists report stories about American anti-Semites, they often end up paying a visit to the ADL in their New York headquarters. The ADL provide you with fact sheets. They have fact sheets on pretty much everyone – from obscure, uncelebrated militia leaders through to famous Ku Klux Klansmen and neo-Nazi organizers.

They have offices in every state in America, a budget big enough to take out front-page adverts in the *New York Times*, and a direct line to the President and the State Department and the FBI, who act on the information they provide.

It is no exaggeration to say that the ADL has the last word on who is an anti-Semite and who is not. They are the ones who decide. Then they inform the rest of the world, and the rest of the world, including me, goes along with it.

So I visited Gail Gans, their chief researcher into anti-Semitism in the American heartland.

Gail told me that one out of eight Americans has hard-core anti-Semitic feelings. She said that much of that has to do with those people who like to mythologize the Weaver siege as evidence that the 'New World Order' – which is a code word for 'International Jewish Conspiracy' – really exists.

Gail said that the job of the ADL has become akin to that of a code breaker.

'We lay out the program to the people of the world,' she said. 'This is who the anti-Semites are. These are the words they use. This is a code word and this is what it means.'

Gail rifled through her drawer and she handed me pamphlets with titles such as 'Armed And Dangerous'. They referred to Colonel Bo Gritz as 'an extremist', Randy Weaver as 'an extremist', and Jack McLamb as 'an anti-Semitic extremist conspiracy theorist'.

'I'm surprised,' I said. 'And also shocked. I've been with Jack McLamb, and he really didn't strike me as an anti-Semite.'

'That's because he's clever,' said Gail. 'He doesn't come right out and say anti-Semitic things. He uses code words.'

I asked Gail to list for me the code words – the words that mean Jew without actually saying Jew. Here are some of them:

'International Bankers'. 'Internationalists'. 'Cosmopolitans'. 'Secret Government'.

'New World Order'. 'International Financiers'. 'That Strange Group Behind the Media'. 'Culture Manipulators'. 'The Middle Men in New York'. 'The New Yorkers'.

And, yes, Jack McLamb had said some of those things to me. Could they be code words? They seemed so abstruse. If people couldn't figure out that they meant 'Jew' – and I am usually sensitive to these matters – what was the point of having them? Where would it end? Was Jack McLamb being clever?

'Randy Weaver,' said Gail, 'is now going round the country giving speeches about what happened to him. And, on a human level, I'm sorry for what happened. But I also know that a' – Gail paused, grappling for the right words – 'a *sane* person upon being asked to surrender wouldn't have taken their children and their dog and gone into a mountain cabin. This wasn't a game.'

'But that makes it sound as if Randy Weaver was fleeing justice and holing up in some cabin, when in fact all he did was stay home with his family,' I said.

'Randy Weaver could have surrendered,' said Gail. 'He didn't have to take his family up to that cabin *at all . . .*' (What, I wondered, did Randy Weaver's choice of accommodation have to do with protecting the Jewish people from anti-Semitism?)

'He says it was trumped-up charges. *Trumped-up charges*? He tried to sell weaponry to an undercover BATF agent.'

'But Sammy Weaver was ambushed and he didn't have a chance,' I said.

'So Weaver says,' smiled Gail. She shrugged. Then she said, 'Do I feel critical of law enforcement in this case? Yes. I'm sad it played out that way. But I'm also sad that the people in charge didn't make it stop before it started.'

'The people in charge?' I asked.

'I mean Randy Weaver,' said Gail.

'In charge?' I said.

'Randy Weaver has become a martyr to a government gone crazy.' She sighed. 'A martyr to an unfeeling, masterly, all-powerful government that's trying to take the population of the United States and rub it under its heel. That's the way the extremists see the government . . .'

But the word extremist was suddenly indistinct to me. *Unfeeling*, *masterly* and *all-powerful* seemed smack-on when it came to outlining what befell the Weaver family. Or was I imagining my own family in that cabin? After all, Randy Weaver *could* have surrendered (I would have). He *did* attend Aryan Nations (I wouldn't have).

'Randy Weaver and his friends see themselves as the only stand-up guys against the New World Order,' said Gail. 'And when you stand up against the New World Order bad things happen to you, and now you have Randy Weaver as a martyr and now you have David Koresh as a martyr.'

'Ooh! White supremacist!'

Randy Weaver grinned and he gnarled his face up like he was a movie villain.

'That's *big* news. Who wants to report on the ice-cream social? That won't sell a damn thing. This is exciting stuff. People go to car races to see wrecks. They love blood and guts. People are cruel. On the whole,' said Randy Weaver, 'I don't trust people.'

It was Saturday. I had picked Randy up from Dallas airport and we drove down towards Mount Carmel in

Waco, the site of the Branch Davidian church that had been besieged by the same team, right down to the individuals, that had organized and executed the Weaver siege.

(Randy's siege became widely known as 'The Siege at Ruby Ridge' even though there was no such place as Ruby Ridge. The Weaver family lived in a nameless place somewhere between Caribou Ridge and Ruby Creek. Rachel had told me that 'Ruby Ridge' probably sounded kitschy to the reporters at the time, which was why it stuck.)

Randy drove down Interstate 35. He smoked just about an entire packet of cigarettes during our two-hour drive. His enormous biker sunglasses hid half of his face.

'I can joke about Ruby Ridge now,' he said, 'and keep going. I couldn't for a while. I can watch a Western again now. Post-Traumatic Stress Disorder. I know we all had it. Even Elisheba. Elisheba remembered that shit until she was two and a half: "Blood! Mama fall down! Mama needs help!" She made everyone in the room start crying. She still says, "I wish Mama hadn't died." Well. Hell, yeah.'

Randy turned the air conditioning on full.

We stopped off for breakfast in a mall en route to Mount Carmel.

'Did Rachel talk to you about what happened after we locked ourselves into the cabin?' asked Randy.

'A little,' I said.

At this, Randy leant forward. He took off his sunglasses.

'What does Rachel remember?' he said.

'She remembers the tanks smashing the generator,' I said.

'I didn't talk to Rachel about these things for years,'

73

said Randy. 'I didn't even know that Rachel had seen them shoot me and shoot her mother. I just didn't know that.'

'What else happened after you locked yourself in the cabin?' I asked him.

'Vicki used to make up little songs to sing to the kids, and so we sang those songs. Oh, I can't remember. Did Rachel talk to you about it?'

'A little,' I said.

'I remember the radio,' he said. 'The radio said, "Crazy bastard, white supremacist, has murdered a US marshal." So this was a big deal now. You've got a dead cop. They didn't mention that Sam had been killed. This cop is worth more than my son? I don't think so. Duh. He isn't worth more than my dog. But a US marshal had got murdered. That was the big thing. Well. It wasn't the big thing to us.'

Randy had never visited the ruins of the Branch Davidian church at Waco. But for hundreds of thousands of Americans, perhaps even millions, the Weaver siege and the burning of David Koresh's church are forever linked, proof of a government gone crazy, a New World Order coming to kill whoever does not bow down to them.

We paid the bill and drove the last few miles. We asked directions. Everyone knew the way. And then the place appeared, among flat green fields, a landscape that looked almost English, off a country road, behind a lake.

We pulled into the car park, near burnt-out school buses and razor wire and wreckage from the old church, lying in the grass. Amongst this wreckage was a shining new building. For six months local volunteers had been spending their weekends rebuilding the church. It was nearly finished.

We jumped out of the car. The volunteers stopped working and looked up at us and I heard some of them whisper, 'Is that Randy Weaver?'

Randy was hugged by strangers. When people asked him how he was doing, he said, 'I ain't been shot at lately. Yep. Things are looking up.'

There was a little laughter.

The volunteers hammered and sawed and painted the doors. Some wore T-shirts that read 'Death to the New World Order'. I saw one man wearing an official Ruby Ridge T-shirt: 'Ruby Ridge – Freedom At Any Cost'. Randy sold these T-shirts most weekends at gun shows around the United States, along with the opportunity to 'Have Your Photograph Taken With Randy Weaver. $5'. This was how he earned a living. The photographs were taken by his new wife, Linda, on a Polaroid Instamatic, and Randy would sign them, 'Freedom At Any Cost'. But contrary to what Gail Gans at the ADL had said, Randy did not give speeches about what happened to his family. He was not a public speaker, he told me. Even the thought of it made him nervous.

Inside the new church – it looked just like a normal country chapel – they hung chandeliers. Outside they mowed the lawn between the memorial trees (one for each person who died at Waco – it was now a small forest). Randy glanced at the volunteers. He said, quietly, 'I wonder which of them are undercover snitches.'

'Might some be here?' I whispered.

'I wouldn't doubt it for a minute,' he said.

'Right here now?'

'They blend right in,' said Randy.

More volunteers approached Randy, shook his hand, and asked him to pose for photographs.

I got talking with an elderly man called Ron Dodge. Ron started telling me about the Bilderberg Group.

'I keep hearing about the Bilderberg Group,' I said. 'Who are they?'

'They're the men that run the world,' said Ron. 'They start the wars. They cause the famines. They control the governments. They choose the presidents. Both candidates. They're setting up the one world order.'

'Do you believe that there's a connection between the Bilderberg Group and what happened to Randy Weaver?' I asked him.

'Sure,' said Ron. 'Their plan is pretty basic. They go into a nation. They create chaos. This is their philosophy. Stir up the people. Take over the power. And why have we never heard of them? They own the media.'

'They say that the people who control this world can sit around one large table and have lunch,' chipped in a passing militiaman from Michigan called John. '*That's* the Bilderberg Group.'

'What's the Michigan Militia doing here?' I asked John.

'We are here to ask these people's forgiveness for sitting around on our butts and watching it on TV,' he replied. 'What happened at Ruby Ridge and Waco will *never* happen again, under any circumstances. If it does there will be immediate retaliation, armed resistance, from the Michigan Militia.'

The volunteers sawed and drilled in nails, and I could no longer hear what Ron and John were saying, so we took a walk through the memorial garden towards the lake.

'Television's an interesting thing,' said Ron. 'When this siege started here at Waco, I could not imagine that they would burn these people up. But they did. Then I thought there'd be such an outcry it would bring down the government. But the silence was deafening. When I asked people about it they said, "David Koresh was a bad guy. He deserved it." I started thinking, what's *wrong* here? There's something wrong. I kept thinking about it. Then I found out one day that television is not a steady light, it's a rapidly flashing light. As soon as I got that little bit of information, I realized what had happened. One of the ways you hypnotize people is with a rapidly flashing light. Everybody is hypnotized. What happened here, and what happened at Ruby Ridge, was that they programmed the world to accept that murder is OK.'

'Tell me more about the Bilderberg Group,' I said. 'Where do they meet?'

There was a silence.

Dusk fell, and Colonel Bo Gritz arrived in a glistening trailer home. He helped with the hammering for a while, and then the volunteers lit camp fires and ate from a barbecue and Bo and Randy hugged each other and reminisced about the siege at Ruby Ridge.

I joined them after a while. We sat on plastic chairs next to Bo's trailer home. Bo Gritz looks just as a retired Green Beret colonel should look. He is heavy set, with a shock of white hair.

As Randy and Bo and I talked, we began to attract a small audience. Alex Jones came and sat down with us. Alex is a popular radio talk-show host from nearby Austin. His anti-New World Order radio show – *Info Wars* – is syndicated to forty cities across America.

Randy said to Alex, 'Let me shake your hand. I'm a big admirer of yours. I love your show. You've got some guts.'

More volunteers came and sat down, and our chat became something like the after-dinner entertainment.

Randy has changed since the siege, since the death of his wife. I imagine that Vicki was the one with the passionate hatred for the New World Order, and Randy was happy to go along with it because he loved her, just as long as she didn't object to him cutting loose once in a while to go drinking with his friends from Aryan Nations. Back then they read the Bible most nights. Now Randy is an agnostic. He no longer believes that the New World Order, the Bilderberg Group, the secret clique of international bankers, were responsible for the murders of his wife and son. Now he puts it down to a battle of egos – that moment when he made a big burlesque show of refusing to become a government informant.

'I laughed at them,' he said. 'I don't laugh any more.'

But in this interpretation, Randy was pretty much alone. Just about everyone else sitting around the camp fires considered the international bankers to be responsible for what happened at Ruby Ridge.

'I want to tell you something remarkable,' said Bo, 'about what happened when we got Vicki's body out of that cabin. I expected in August for there to be an extreme smell of death inside that cabin. Remember there were blankets all over the windows. It was very stuffy. Yet I didn't have that powerful smell. This has got to be tough on Randy.'

Randy lit a cigarette.

'Besides from the terrible evidence of Vicki being shot in the face with a .308,' said Bo, 'you would not have known that she wasn't just asleep. Her skin was still supple.'

'And for how long had she been dead?' I asked.

'Eight days,' said Randy.

'Eight days,' said Bo.

'Eight days,' said Randy.

'I was in awe of her condition,' said Bo. 'The Catholics believe that if the body is not corrupted, they consider that person to have died under grace. They look upon it as one of the criteria for sainthood.' Bo shrugged. 'All I know,' he said, 'is that her body was unlike any other of the hundreds I have personally handled. Eight days dead.'

'Eight days,' said Randy.

'It wasn't anything like it was supposed to be,' said Bo Gritz.

'How could the Aztecs sacrifice *ten thousand* people on some public holiday, eat their children's *hearts*? I've been to their temples, I've seen the skulls buried in their *walls*, some nightmare horror. How could the Romans rip people *apart*, burn their city, just to *do it,* just to blame it on people? And we see decadent empires in their final stages of corruption, as they become *insane*. Engaging in mass murder. Just to do it. This is what is happening *today*. The New World Order are a bunch of *sick control freaks*!'

This was the voice of Alex Jones, every word in capital letters, no light or shade, all bellow, broadcasting live from Austin, Texas, right now, to five million people across America, and live on AOL, broadcasting to the world, if the world wants to hear it.

'When *you* allow the government to murder folks at Ruby Ridge, at Waco, at Oklahoma City, at the World Trade Center bombing – *all government actions* – when you allow this to *happen*, when you sit back and *laugh*, and you think you're on the *big* team, the A-Team. Boy! You're rooting for the government's side! Because you're a coward! And you sense that you'll keep your little ostrich neck safe. And then *your* day is coming.'

Endearingly, Alex was hollering his powerful apocalyptic vision down an ISDN line from a child's bedroom in his house, with choo-choo train wallpaper and an *Empire Strikes Back* poster pinned on the wall.

'Are *you* going to be that Aztec villager who hands his child over to be *lunchmeat* for the *priesthood*? That's what's going to happen to *you*! In a hi-tech form! We'll be right back.'

'*From his central Texas command centre, deep behind enemy lines, the information war continues with Alex Jones and his GCM radio network, after this break . . .*'

After I had met Alex at Mount Carmel, I discovered that it was his own idea to rebuild David Koresh's church. He raised the $93,000 needed through donations from his listeners.

Randy had told me that Alex Jones was a true and tireless warrior. Now, Randy had flown home to his new wife in Iowa – 'She'll shoot me if I miss my plane,' he said – and so I asked Alex if I could watch him broadcast his show.

'I am a war reporter,' yelled Alex to me, off the air. 'That is what I do. There's a whole buffet of corruption out there.'

'Are you sure that the people behind Ruby Ridge and Waco were also behind Oklahoma City and the World Trade Center bombings?' I asked him.

'That's not even *debatable*!' he roared. 'Well. I guess you could debate Oklahoma City. But the World Trade Center is not even *debatable*. Clinton's Reichstag. Horror.'

Alex lit a cigarette. He flicked the ash into a styrofoam cup.

'We've gotta cut the Hydra's head off,' he yelled, 'and *drive it back to its black abyss*.'

'I still don't quite understand,' I said, 'the relationship between the Bilderberg Group and what happened to Randy Weaver.'

'The Bilderbergers,' said Alex, 'are the Roman Senate. It's a pyramid. They're way up there. Below them you've got the IMF, the World Bank, the United Nations, then you've got us down here, the cattle, the human resources. And Randy Weaver is way out over *there*. See? He left. They *hate* that! So they *scare* the cattle back into the pen. See? Burn 'em out! I'm living in a place where black helicopters, one hundred and fifty miles south of me, are burning buildings, terrorizing people, and *I'm* the extremist?'

'Who says you're an extremist?' I asked.

'The Anti-Defamation League!' he yelled. 'The ADL are

a bucket of *black paint* and a *brush*. They're worse than the Klan. They get *massive* funding from the globalists. It doesn't matter if your girlfriend's Jewish, your little sister's Korean' – Alex's little sister is Korean – 'anybody who wants to live free is a *racist*. The ADL is the scum of the earth. You aren't going to use that last line out of context are you?'

'No, no,' I said.

He turned back to his microphone.

'OK! We're back!'

But we weren't back. Alex was off the air. The ISDN line had mysteriously died.

'Damn!' he yelled. 'Not again! *This* is the New World Order!'

Alex thumped the table and looked out of the window and saw a telephone engineer out on the pavement, fiddling with the box that held his ISDN line.

'*There* he is. You little *turd*. I've caught you this time.'

Alex ran outside to the pavement, leaving me in the studio with Violet, his girlfriend.

'This does not scare me,' said Violet. She looked out of the window. 'The point is,' she said, 'it does not scare me.'

'What does scare you?' I asked her.

'Nothing,' said Violet. 'Not even the death threats. We've had phone calls, describing our house, describing our animals, voices like out of *The Exorcist*. Alex definitely has stalkers.'

'Sir!' bellowed Alex at the engineer. I could hear him through the window pane. 'It's starting to get ridiculous. My nationally syndicated radio show has gone down.

Again! You people have been cutting my lines, giggling and smiling. And your bosses deny you even *exist . . .*'

'Sorry,' said the engineer.

Defeated by technology, or by covert censorship, we headed off to the local TV studio where Alex was scheduled to present a live TV talk show. We sat in the foyer while he prepared himself for his broadcast. There was a bank of monitor screens behind the reception desk, broadcasting all of Austin's TV output.

For a while I watched all the channels at once. Then I noticed a figure on one of the screens. He had a face I recognized from somewhere, long ago, a middle-aged man with long, greying hair and sharp blue eyes. I walked over to the screen and turned up the volume. He had an English accent. He seemed to be talking about lizards – specifically about how the leaders of the New World Order, the clique of international bankers, are genetically descended from giant lizards.

And then, suddenly, I realized who it was. It was David Icke.

'Alex!' I called. 'What's David Icke doing on television?'

'Oh,' sighed Alex. 'He's big news.'

'Really?'

'You know him?'

'Well,' I said, 'he once announced on the Terry Wogan chat show on the BBC that he was the son of God.'

'That figures,' said Alex, wearily.

'He seems to be saying that the Bilderberg Group are twelve-foot lizards,' I said.

'DAVID ICKE,' yelled Alex, suddenly, 'IS A TURD IN A PUNCHBOWL!'

'What do you mean?'

'He talks about the global elite, the Bilderberg Group, these power structures which are *all* real, *all* true. Meat and potatoes! Something you can bite into! And then at the end of this he says, "By the way, they're all *blood-drinking lizards.*" '

'Really?'

'Al Gore needs blood to drink. So does Prince Philip. He's discrediting the whole thing. You've got a nice fruit punch. Icke takes a great big dump right in the middle of it, and now *nobody's* going to drink out of that punchbowl. That's his job, and he's doing his job well.'

'Are you suggesting that David Icke is in league with the global elite,' I said, 'employed to make the whole thing seem ridiculous?'

'He's either a smart opportunist con man,' said Alex, 'or he's totally insane, or he's working for them directly.'

'Let's take some calls.'

'Hi. This is Marsha.'

'Hi, Marsha. What's your point?'

'I just wanted to ask you a little about your background,' said Marsha. 'Have you travelled a lot?'

'Yes,' said Alex.

'Where have you been?' asked Marsha.

'Where have *you* been?' said Alex.

'You haven't answered my question,' said Marsha.

'*You're an aggressive twit, ma'am!*' yelled Alex.

'Well, there's no need to be rude.'

'I don't like *snivelling passive–aggressive people like you*!'

'I just wanted to know your background.'

'I'm taking *action*!' roared Alex. 'I've rebuilt the church at Waco. I've exposed black helicopters. Lady, you don't want to face the truth of what's happening! I KNOW ALL YOUR LITTLE PSYCHOLOGICAL SICKNESSES, LADY! YOU DON'T COUNT! YOU ARE FURNITURE! WE'RE FACING THE ENEMY AT THE TOP OF THE PYRAMID! CAN'T YOU FEEL IT? IT'S EPIC! *NOW* IS THE TIME. *NOW!* WE'RE ENGAGING IN AN INFO WAR, SIX HOURS A DAY! GIANT SHORT-WAVE TRANS-MITTER TOWERS WORLDWIDE BEAM MY VOICE! SO THANK YOU FOR CALLING, *LADY*.'

I was getting a bit of a headache, so I slipped out of Alex's TV studio for what I assumed to be the relative calm of the production booth. By now, Mike Hanson, Alex's producer, was himself addressing Marsha on the phone.

'WE'RE TRYING TO RUN A SHOW HERE!' screamed Mike. 'WHAT YOU ARE YOU? SOME KIND OF HIGH AND MIGHTY . . . YOU KNOW WHAT? YOU DON'T KNOW YOUR ASS FROM A HOLE IN THE GROUND! FUCK YOU, TOO.'

Mike slammed down the phone.

'That was a B minus,' said Alex, once the TV show was off the air. 'I do A-plus shows all the time.'

'You have a very powerful voice,' I said.

'Yep,' said Alex.

'So has Mike, your producer,' I said.

Alex looked confused.

'What do you mean?' he said.

'Well,' I said, 'when I left the studio I went into the

production room and Mike was yelling at Marsha down the phone.'

'Was he now?' said Alex. 'Is that so?'

'WHAT ARE YOU TRYING TO DO?' screamed Alex at Mike. 'UPSTAGE ME? OH, I KNOW WHAT YOU'RE UP TO! MAKE A BIG SHOW OF SHOUTING DOWN THE PHONE! STEAL THE LIMELIGHT! AND THEN JON WILL WRITE ALL ABOUT *YOU*!'

'FUCK YOU!' yelled Mike. 'YOU'RE PARANOID!'

'FUCK YOU!' yelled Alex.

'STOP IT! BOTH OF YOU!' screamed Max, the young and until now serene bespectacled vision mixer in the corner.

Both men abruptly stopped yelling and turned to Max.

'What's wrong?' said Alex.

'I'm just sick of you two shouting at each other all the time,' sobbed Max. 'I've had enough.'

Max grabbed his coat and ran out of the studio. Alex and Mike glanced quizzically at each other. They shrugged.

'What was *that* all about?' said Alex.

In the summer I flew back to Montana to visit Rachel Weaver. The last time I had seen her – when we had gone shooting in her back garden with her now ex-boyfriend Josh – she had offered me an open invitation to visit what was left of the cabin.

Ruby Creek was a two-hour drive from Rachel's home in Montana. She did the driving. The bumper sticker on her 4 by 4 read: 'HEY DUMB ASS! IT'S NOT GUNS! IT'S BAD PARENTING!' She put CDs into her car stereo. She played Fatboy Slim and the Jungle Brothers, and a song she said was one of her mother's favourites, the Statler Brothers' 'Flowers On The Wall'.

We stopped off for lunch. We sat at the counter. I asked her more about her family's religious and political beliefs up in the cabin. She said it was hard to remember now. After her mother was killed they pretty much gave it all up.

'Let me think,' she said. 'We didn't have pictures or stuffed animals because we believed that was a recreation of what the Creator had already made. We didn't eat meat unless it had a split hoof and chewed its cud, like a cow or a deer. Marine life had to have fins and scales. No shark or eel. Um. Marrying your own race. Keep your race pure. Oh, I can't really think. It was way deeper than that. I just can't remember it.'

Rachel paused.

'Oh, yes. We held our Sabbath on Fridays.'

'Like the Jews,' I said.

'The Hebrews are *not* Jews,' said Rachel. 'It's all been twisted and rewritten.'

I looked quizzically at her.

'You should have seen some of the literature Mom showed us as kids,' she said. 'It *totally* proves that the Hebrews were not Jews. I'm sorry if I'm offending you.'

'And you definitely weren't white supremacists?' I asked.

She looked at me aghast.

'No way! We had *nothing* against Jews. Mom wouldn't have turned anyone out. Never! She had the biggest heart. We *never* felt the white race was supreme to all others. Plus, we were the *safest* people when it came to guns. That's why I've got such a problem with Josh. Yeah, we carried our guns a lot. I can see why that would be intimidating if you didn't know us, but we'd *never* aim a gun at anyone.'

I believed Rachel. Once the siege had begun – once they'd locked themselves into the cabin – the only shots that were fired came from the outside, from the FBI snipers.

We paid up and got back into her jeep and Rachel played me some more songs: The Bloodhound Gang and Hot Chocolate – 'You Sexy Thing'– and Dusty Springfield's 'Son of a Preacher Man'.

'Do you remember visiting Aryan Nations?' I asked her.

'Yeah,' she said. 'I remember the treasure hunts. We'd get together and find little pieces of paper that would lead us to clues. It was fun.'

'You don't remember any weirdness?' I asked.

She narrowed her eyes. 'I remember a cross lighting. Oh. And they tried to do a swastika one year.'

'What do you mean?'

'They put a big old swastika on top of a couple of 2 by 4s. They were going to burn it. But it was top heavy. So it fell over.'

We drove through Bonners Ferry, a lovely little town on the banks of the Kootenai River, and then out into the country, past the Deep Creek Inn, the bar and restaurant where the Weavers used to go for special occasions, birthday meals and so on.

The cabin wasn't as far from civilization as I'd imagined. There was a golf course within three miles. We drove up a little mountain lane, the jeep bouncing precariously along the potholed roads. Rachel's gonk, her little red and black stuffed toy, fell off the dashboard. The tree branches scraped the windscreen and the paintwork.

'Oh, I should have bought pruners,' she winced, her hands clutched tightly on her zebra-print steering-wheel cover. The road narrowed even further.

'We used to build tree forts around here,' she said. 'We used to play war games.'

I remembered the surveillance video the FBI had released to the media during the siege. The surveillance tapes were shot in the weeks before Sammy and Vicki were killed, grainy footage filmed from across the mountain, showing Rachel and Sammy and Sara running around with guns.

We reached a small clearing.

'OK!' she said. 'This is it!'

She parked up next to a giant rock that overlooked their driveway, the rock upon which Randy had fired Vicki's .223 into the air, full clip, on hearing of his son's death. She jumped out of the jeep and ran around the corner. I followed her. Then I stopped.

Rachel was standing on a square of linoleum where her kitchen used to be. The walls and the roof had gone now. They collapsed in the snow in 1998. All that was left of the cabin was the floor, jutting out over the ridge to a panoramic view of the Kootenai river valley, thousands of feet below. Rachel stepped into where her living room once was.

'Mom and Dad's bedroom was above the kitchen,' she said. 'Sam's bedroom was right here.' Rachel indicated a space in the air.

'The sink was over here on this side,' said Rachel. 'We

used to have a back porch right there. About right here was where the front door was.'

An overturned cooker lay in the doorway. There was a book on the floor. Rachel picked it up.

'*Restoring Junk*,' she read. She rested the book back on the floor. 'Mom was good at that.'

There were more books and magazines scattered around – *The Borrowers*, and an old copy of the *Spotlight* newspaper: 'Everything you ever wanted to know about the men who control our world . . .'

There were bottles of a 'delicious whey-based drink' called Yenka Nutri-Whey, a hanging basket, an old pair of Sam's shoes.

'Can you hear that?' said Rachel. I couldn't hear anything. 'Someone's on their way up. Now we can run out onto the rock and see who it is!'

Rachel bounded over to the giant rock that overlooked the driveway. She climbed on top of it and listened.

'Nah,' she said. 'It's someone going up even higher. Yep. That's what we used to do every time we heard a car. We'd all yell "Ooh! Somebody's come to see us!" Jeez. Something so simple can bring back all that excitement.'

I rummaged through the debris scattered around the cabin floor and the surrounding land, finding remnants of life in the cabin before the siege. I picked things up – cardboard boxes containing some empty spice bottles her mother used to keep, Elisheba's baby chair.

'What are you doing?' said Rachel. 'It's just a bunch of junk.' She laughed. 'All the things that used to be important to us were junk to other people,' she said. 'The books and stuff. Now it's junk to me and important to you.'

We wandered back to the jeep.

'Funny to think that they called this place a mountain fortress,' I said.

'Yeah,' said Rachel. 'Our plywood house. They said it was a compound. That's why they could sneak up within fifteen feet of us.'

We drove back to the Deep Creek Inn and ate dinner on the porch overlooking Ruby Creek. Just as we were finishing, a man wandered out of the inn. He was holding a guitar.

'My name is Dallas Pike,' he said to Rachel. 'I'm a musician. I moved up here about a year ago. What happened to your family is the reason why I moved to Idaho. I've been coming up here to that bridge every August, and I've been praying that I would finally get a chance to meet you or your sister or your dad. I have a feeling you might appreciate this song.'

And, without warning, Dallas began to play.

Blood stains in the snow, bloody ridge, Idaho
Blood stains in the snow, bloody ridge, Idaho
Some buffalo hunters and the FBI
Killed this land before our eyes
Blood stains in the snow, Vicki Weaver and Waco.

I looked over at Rachel. She was in floods of tears. Dallas finished his song. He began crying too. He touched her hand.

'What happened up there happened to a lot of people,'

he said. 'I can't tell you what an honour it is to meet you and to be able to sing my song for you.'

'Thank you,' said Rachel. 'It really is a great song.'

Dallas stood up and walked back into the inn. Rachel was quiet for a while. Then she said, 'I don't know what to say to people when they do that.'

I got the sense that Rachel had enough on her plate without becoming a legend of the Wild West.

Rachel went to bed and I found Dallas sitting at the bar. We took a walk out to the river.

'Vicki Weaver was butchered like a buffalo,' he said, 'standing in the doorway of her own home, holding her baby and crying out to God to protect the rest of her family from the mad dogs that had already shot her son in the back from an ambush.'

Dallas looked out at the river.

'But it's beautiful out here in Idaho,' he said. 'Sometimes you have to sit back and smell the pine trees. I come as often as I can. I stay as long as I can. I listen to the water. I'm very content here. I play my song and I travel hither and yon. I didn't sing that song to make her cry. I sang it so she'd know she wasn't alone. Just last week I played it down at the Rainbow Festival in south-east Montana, and this great big biker guy, tears were running down his face, he got up and came over and threw his arms around me and hugged me and kept crying. I played it at Nashville. You could have heard a pin drop.'

Dallas told me that he thought Vicki Weaver was one of God's prophets.

'She spoke about how close we are to a totalitarian

government,' he said. 'She spoke about the one world order, the single world currency. The military-industrial complex. She spoke about the Bilderberg Group. I did my own research and I found out just how right she was.'

We sat and listened to the river for a while.

'The truth is out there,' said Dallas. 'Just like in the *X Files*. You just have to look between the bullshit and the murders.'

3. *The Secret Rulers Of The World*

At the National Press Club on Pennsylvania Avenue, Washington, DC, Big Jim Tucker left a coded message on the answering machine of a friend.

'Mother. Your dutiful son is playing kick the can on Pennsylvania Avenue, Tuesday morning, 10.30 a.m., thank you.'

Big Jim placed the telephone back on its receiver. He lit a cigarette and glanced around the lobby with a routine vigilance. Even here at his club, his gentleman's *club*, he considered himself not entirely safe. Anyone could discover that this was where he had breakfast every day, three strong black coffees and some pastries on the side.

'If they ever got me,' he said, 'they'd make it look like a typical Washington mugging. A mugging on the sidewalk. Killed for a couple of dollars. Another three paragraphs in the newspaper. Or maybe they'd dump my body outside some bar somewhere. Oh yes, they're smooth operators.'

Jim paused. He pulled on his cigarette. His heart is not strong due to his habit of smoking unfiltered Camels at all times, pack after pack. He is quite huge, an elderly southern gentleman in a crumpled suit and a newshound trilby. He has a voice like gravel (a result of cigarette-induced emphysema which, by a happy accident, gives his speech an enigmatic rhythm, like a charismatic Sam Spade down on his luck) and an office downtown with venetian blinds.

He said, 'The thing is, we don't know how much time we've got left. And suppose I just so happen to "drop dead" in my office on Tuesday afternoon. It could be the following Monday before someone says, "Where *is* that boy?" I don't want to be burnt bacon when they find me. I guess I'm just too vain to be found that way.'

Big Jim laughed in a hollow manner.

'So I phone my friend every day just to announce I'm still kicking the can and still hunting the macaroon. Still breathing, see? The day she doesn't get that call is the day she makes enquiries.'

Here at his private members' club, Big Jim could pass for a venerable old star commentator for a heavyweight daily newspaper, but he isn't. He works for an underground paper called the *Spotlight*. Mainstream journalists keep away from him. This is, Jim says, because certain high-ranking members of the overground media, even some members of his own *club*, are in league with the secret rulers of the world.

And it is they who would make his death look like a typical Washington mugging.

When I began hearing about the Bilderberg Group – about the notion that a tiny band of insidious and clandestine powermongers meet in a secret room from which they rule the world – I was sceptical. But I kept hearing about them, and I finally decided to try to settle the matter once and for all.

Which is why I visited Big Jim Tucker. Within anti-Bilderberg circles Big Jim is considered a pioneer, a trail-blazer, risking his life to attempt to locate the geographical whereabouts of the secret room.

'They exist all right,' said Big Jim, 'and they're not play-ing pinochle in there.'

Big Jim Tucker has spent thirty years documenting the facts. He's been after them since the 1970s when he first got the hunch that they existed. He abandoned a good career in sports journalism on a big city paper. It has been cat and mouse ever since, he said. Good against evil.

'Those sick luminaries are always on the move,' said Jim. 'They never come together in the same place twice, so as to evade detection. They only meet once a year, for a long weekend in May or June.'

They have been ruling the world in secret since 1954, Jim said, when a man called Joseph Retinger, whose name rarely appears in the history books, decided to create them. One of many mysteries is how Retinger – a Polish immi-grant employed as secretary to the novelist Joseph Conrad – had the wherewithal and the contacts to organize such a mighty endeavour.

Their first meeting took place in the Bilderberg Hotel in Holland, which is why the secret rulers of the world go by the name of the Bilderberg Group.

*

Big Jim said that I happened to have caught him at a very good time. He was ready to take things further, to turn up the heat and cause some trouble.

'So you've actually managed to obtain the address of the next Bilderberg meeting?' I asked Jim.

'Yes, sir,' he said.

'You know *exactly* where it is?' I asked.

'Yes I do,' he said.

Big Jim said he fully intended to thwart their security and barge in unannounced to catch them red-handed going about their covert wickedness. I was welcome to tag along, he said, 'Just so long as you don't step on twigs or fall off walls while we're on the prowl.'

'The plan is this,' said Jim. 'We'll leave Washington on the last day of May, and we'll arrive at the target destination on the Sunday morning. We'll start patrolling that same afternoon. Patrol Sunday and Monday. Develop sources. Waiters, chambermaids . . .'

'So they still meet in hotels?' I said.

'Yes, sir,' said Jim. 'The chambermaids will be gun-shy at first. They'll know something big and spooky is going on, but they won't know what. But then they'll begin to realize that whatever's happening at their hotel is evil. And that's when they'll open up.'

'So what else will we do on the Sunday and Monday?'

'Scout around the resort,' said Jim. 'Figure out ways to penetrate.'

'Scout around looking for what?'

'Where the short wall is,' said Jim. 'Where the big drain-pipe is.'

'So we'll actually be climbing up drainpipes?' I asked.

'Climbing up drainpipes,' said Jim, 'trying not to sneeze or cough or step on twigs. Trying to avoid the guard dogs.'

'What's the name of the hotel?'

'I've – uh – got it written down here somewhere,' said Jim. He rifled through his pockets. 'Here it is. The Caesar Park golfing resort, Sintra, Portugal.'

I looked quizzically at Jim.

'Are you *sure* about all of this?' I asked.

'They are evil and their evil occurs in the dark shadows,' said Jim, emphatically. 'Behind closed doors. Ruling the world from a room. Imagine that. Let's get a drink.'

Jim took me to the Men's Bar upstairs at his club. We drank beers and watched sports on the TV above the bar. Framed front pages of big news stories of days gone by lined the walls.

'War in the Persian Gulf!'

'Thatcher Resigns!'

Jim said that both acts were orchestrated by Bilderberg.

'Margaret Thatcher is one of the good guys,' said Jim. 'Bilderberg ordered her to dismantle British sovereignty but she said no way, so they had her sacked.'

Big Jim said he once found himself at a drinks party with Margaret Thatcher and he took the opportunity to sidle up to her.

'How does it feel to have been denounced by those Bilderberg boys, ma'am?' he growled. She whispered back that she considered it a 'great tribute to be denounced by Bilderberg'.

*

98

I considered the significance of the endeavour we were about to undertake. For the other people I had met, Bilderberg was an inviolable almighty. Big Jim was the first man to have the tenacity to discover the address, and to plan on *going in*, and damn the consequences. This could change everything.

Jim wouldn't tell me how he discovered the room's whereabouts, but a few moments later as we sat at the bar, a tall man with a moustache bounded over and cheerfully introduced himself to me as Jim's mole from inside Bilderberg.

'I'm an accountant,' he explained. 'Some very big clients use our firm. One guy happened to mention to me that he was on his way to somewhere near Lisbon in June for a very private meeting.'

Jim appeared a little annoyed by his mole's instantaneous candour, but then he shrugged and joined in with the story.

'We know,' said Jim, 'that the Bilderberg Group always meet in May or June.'

'So Jim,' said the mole, 'started telephoning every five-star hotel near Lisbon.'

'They always meet at a five-star hotel with golfing facilities,' explained Jim.

'Always golfing facilities?' I asked.

Jim picked up on my subtext at once.

'Believe me,' he said, 'they're not there to play golf. They're too busy starting wars.'

'They may play golf when they're *there*,' clarified the mole, 'but they're not *there* to play golf.'

'OK,' I said.

'So,' said Jim, 'I finally got around to calling a hotel up in the hills, and I said to the receptionist, "I've been invited to the Bilderberg conference in June but I'm afraid I've been very silly and lost my invitation. Could you confirm that this is the correct venue?" And she said, "Why of course, sir. Oh yes, sir. This is exactly where you're supposed to be, and we're very much looking forward to serving you." '

Jim and his mole laughed. A nearby barfly heard their laughter and he came over to join us. Jim and his mole stopped laughing. They turned their backs on the new guy and myself. There was a moment's awkwardness.

'So what's all this about?' asked the new guy.

'Well,' I whispered, 'that big old man in the trilby has tracked down the tiny group of people who rule the world in secret. Anyway, the two of us are going to Portugal next week to confront them.'

'Oh, right,' he said. He seemed unimpressed. 'What do they do, these secret rulers of the world?'

I shrugged. 'Everything, I guess,' I said. 'They're called the Bilderberg Group.'

'Can't say I've heard of them,' he said.

'Jim's dedicated his life to exposing them,' I said.

'It's not so surprising that I've never heard of them,' said the new guy. He scanned the room. Every bar stool was occupied this afternoon. Retired newsmen in suits stared into their beer glasses. The Men's Bar seemed to be where the Washington press corps went when there were no more deadlines, no stories left to file.

'It's not so surprising,' he said. 'Pretty much everyone

here has dedicated his life to something or other that no-body's ever heard of.'

The next morning, Jim took me to the office of his news-paper, the *Spotlight*, which is just around the corner from Capitol Hill. It is pristine from the outside, gleaming white, on a lovely tree-lined street. But it is dark and dusty on the inside, and there are boxes everywhere. He introduced me to Andy, his editor. We sat in the courtyard and drank iced tea.

'Jon,' said Jim to Andy, 'thinks those Bilderberg boys are just playing pinochle in there.'

'Well, first off,' said Andy, impatiently, 'you get a lot of people, including newspaper editors, who say there *is* no Bilderberg Group, that it doesn't even *exist*.'

'They've kept the vow of silence like they're going to nun school,' said Jim.

'This is after you've had Prince Charles attend,' said Andy. 'This is after you've had Bill Clinton attend. And still people say it doesn't exist. Not that it's just a social meeting, but that it doesn't *exist*.'

'If they're just going to play golf and swap lies and chase girls,' said Jim, 'why the armed guards? Know what I'm saying?'

'They exist all right,' said Andy.

'Prince Charles and Bill Clinton,' explained Jim, 'are small fry. The rulers of the world are the ones who *do* the inviting. The steering committee. Clinton was just a small fry from somewhere called Arkansas when he got his invitation back in '91. Yeah, they had big plans for that boy.'

'You be careful,' said Andy. 'You're dealing with dangerous forces.'

'Mother,' said Big Jim Tucker, 'your dutiful son is playing hunt the macaroon at the Paris Hotel, Portugal, Monday morning, 10.30 a.m., thank you.'

It was a week later, and our first working day in Portugal. Our plan was to scout the target five-star golfing resort situated six miles north, develop sources and look for the short wall and the big drainpipe in preparation for the midnight penetration later in the week.

Jim placed the telephone back on its receiver and he lay back on his bed. Our hotel had been built on a busy roundabout. The ocean glistened in the distance, beyond a railway track and a couple of main roads. Even up here on the sixth floor you could hear the never-ending roar of the traffic.

'Unlike the Bilderberg luminaries,' said Jim, ruefully, scanning the dirty walls of this bad hotel, 'some of us are working on a tight budget.'

Jim lit an unfiltered Camel. He is a large, elderly man, and I am not athletic. Our agility levels were impeded by our smoking habits and we wheezed in the Portuguese heat. I was unsure as to how successful the two of us would be in climbing up drainpipes. I pictured slapstick scenarios that would be hilarious to onlookers but not to us.

Jim was acting breezily, but I could sense his nervousness.

'I'm a quarterback,' he said, 'gearing up for the Superbowl. Apprehension? Yes. You don't know what you're going to get with those Bilderberg boys. But am I so nervous as to want to take a spare pair of underpinnings in case of leakage? No.'

By Jim's reckoning, the Bilderberg Group was not scheduled to arrive in Portugal until Wednesday night. He said he had heard reports that their private security guards had already set up camp at the Caesar Park and were planning to operate a shoot-to-kill policy for all penetrators. This somewhat diminished the potential for slapstick hilarity. I was not feeling cocksure.

We had that morning fruitlessly scanned the news-stands for references to the meeting.

'Surprise, surprise,' growled Jim. 'Media black-out.'

There was, however, one notable exception, buried away in the special-interest sections. The *Weekly News*, a tiny English-language parish newspaper for Algarve tourist workers and regular English visitors such as Sir Cliff Richard, circulation 8,000, had gone big on the story.

Very big.

AS SPECULATION ON THE INTERNET RUNS RIFE, THE NEWS CHECKS IT OUT AND IT DOES SEEM THAT . . .
SECRET WORLD GOVERNMENT GROUP IS MEETING HERE!

The *Weekly News* made me feel less vulnerable down here on the ground. Jim said he wanted to touch base with their editorial team later in the week.

'If the *Weekly News* boys can help us expose those Bilderberg jackasses,' he said, 'I'm all for pooling information.'

*

I had rented a car from Budget. We drove into the mountains, away from the boisterous good-time package-tour Estoril, towards the more serene and ancient pastures of Sintra, seven miles up the road. On the way, we discussed cover stories in case we incurred suspicion while we were on our covert patrol. We elected to be holidaymakers, getting a drink at the poolside bar because we'd heard so many good things about the resort, which was undoubtedly the finest around.

The Caesar Park is situated three miles from the main Estoril–Sintra road – two and a half miles down a narrow country lane, through the wilderness of a national park, followed by another half-mile private driveway.

It became evident, as we approached the big peach gates that led into the resort, that the midnight penetration would be an even more formidable task than we had anticipated. The hotel is surrounded on all sides by dense undergrowth and sheer mountains. Jim silently pondered these obstacles from the passenger seat. He photographed the mountains. We drove through the gates (the gatekeeper let us in with a wave) and down the half-mile long driveway. And then the hotel appeared – a modern peach-coloured five-star resort of purpose-built luxury.

'The civilians haven't been shifted out yet,' muttered Jim, as we left the car and wandered towards the colossal marble reception area. The civilians were the holiday-makers. Jim whipped out his camera and photographed the tourists. These photographs would later appear in the *Spotlight* as 'unaware civilians'.

We were not inconspicuous, Jim and I, strolling around the Caesar Park in our open-necked shirts. We were, in fact, an unlikely holidaymaking duo. At a very big push, Jim could resemble a benevolent wealthy southern sugar daddy and I his gawky early-thirties toy-boy. But I doubted the persuasiveness of the scenario.

'I don't think,' I murmured, as we wandered out to the swimming pool, 'that the holidaymaking cover is a convincing one. I think we should think of something else.'

'We're salesmen,' said Jim. 'We're just salesmen getting lunch.'

'What do we sell?' I asked.

'We don't like to talk business when we're having lunch,' said Jim.

'Surely every undercover journalist claims to be a salesman,' I said. 'It's like calling yourself Mr Jones.'

'Calm yourself,' said Jim.

We sat on stools at the poolside bar. Unaware young women sunbathed in bikinis.

'Ma'am,' said Jim to a young passing waitress, bowing slightly, his newshound trilby now replaced by a tourist's straw sun hat, 'I'm a little confused. I tried to book a room here for Thursday and they told me that the whole hotel had been closed down for some big meeting. Must be a pretty damn big important meeting if you ask me . . .'

The waitress shrugged.

'I don't know,' she said. She smiled slightly and left us. Jim got out his notepad. He wrote notes and then he read them out to me:

Dateline Portugal.

Tension filled the air inside the posh Caesar Park resort on Monday. At the poolside bar, the pretty barmaid's face filled with tension when asked to speculate on the big important meeting taking place from Thursday. She shrugged her shoulders and feigned ignorance, but the tension on her face spoke volumes.

Jim put down his notepad.

'Is that accurate?' he said.

'I don't know,' I said. 'It's hard to confirm.'

'Why?'

'Well,' I said. 'We may be imbuing her with our own feelings of tension.'

'Still,' said Jim, finishing his iced tea, 'now we know what the drinks of the rich taste like.'

We paid and patrolled the resort some more. I was disappointed with the Caesar Park, its Eurotrashy aircraft-hangar spaces, its cold approximation of luxury. It was a neo-palace. The lobby shops have names such as 'Fashionable'. I would have assumed that Bilderberg would meet somewhere classier. I told Jim my thoughts on this matter, and he explained that I still hadn't quite got it. They are not there for classy holidaying. They are there to start wars.

Also, Jim said, there is a finite number of international hotels that can transform themselves into walled fortresses, that have their own helicopter pads and nearby military air bases. And, for reasons of security, Bilderberg never meet in the same place twice, so their choices of location must be running out.

Jim and I split up. I looked at the prints on the wall of the lobby outside the upstairs bar. A half-hour passed. I wandered aimlessly through the lobbies and the bars. There were other aimless wanderers too, a woman in a red dress and a man in his thirties wearing a tweed jacket.

It struck me that we all seemed to be wandering aimlessly in some kind of unison, but it didn't cross my mind – right up until the moment that the man in the tweed jacket marched across the room and began questioning me in an angry whisper – that I was being tailed.

'We've watched you for an hour. I'm the hotel manager. You take pictures. You ask questions about some big important meeting. Who are you?'

'I . . .' I paused. Then I clumsily announced, 'I'm from England.'

It was the only thing I could think of. This works of course in other circumstances abroad. But it didn't work here.

'What do you *want*?'

I stared blankly at him.

'What is your *business* here?'

I continued to stare blankly. And then another man appeared.

This new man was older, with a tan, and he spoke with a smooth European accent.

'It's OK!' he laughed. 'Everything's fine! There's no problem!'

He gave the hotel manager's shoulder a little squeeze.

'I am your servant,' he said to me. 'If there's anything you'd like, please be my guest. Think of this hotel as your home. If I can be of any service to you, any service whatsoever, don't hesitate to ask.'

I glanced over with anxiety at the hotel manager who

was now standing a little way off; overruled, slighted, and silent.

'I mean,' he smiled, 'what could you possibly be doing here that could cause any harm to anybody?'

'Are you . . .' I paused. There was something indistinctly alarming about the things he was saying to me. I could not imagine that he really did want me to think of this hotel as my home. So why did he say that?

I presume, in retrospect, that the message he was sending to me was: 'We have noticed you, you are not welcome, but we are allowing you to leave without incident just so long as you don't come back.'

At the time, however, the message I picked up was: 'I am extremely sinister and powerful. This is so evident that I can afford to feign generous subservience, a charade which is, of course, intended to make me seem all the more menacing.'

Jim Tucker was standing to one side, his arm draped over the balcony, watching this exchange with a lazy amusement, in contrast to the dread that was now swelling within me.

'Are you with the Caesar Park?' I asked the charming man.

'Oh no,' he laughed. 'No. I am not with the hotel. So, as I say, think of this hotel as your home. Really, everything's fine and there's no problem. What problems could there be?'

What problems could there be? I wanted the young hotel manager to intervene. I suddenly felt that he could be my ally in this situation. But he remained impassive.

'Don't feel as if you have to go,' said the charming man,

his arms outstretched. 'Stay as long as you like. Enjoy the facilities. Have a swim!'

'So if you're not with the hotel,' I said, 'who are you with?'

'I am with' – he paused – 'another organization.'

'Which is called . . .?'

He laughed and looked at the ground. He said nothing. Then he clapped his hands together.

'Enjoy your afternoon,' he said.

He shook my hand, and gave me a bow. Then he wandered idly towards Jim.

'I don't want any trouble,' I said to the hotel manager.

'Yes,' he smiled, coldly.

I waited for Jim down in the lobby, right by the revolving doors that led outside to the car park. The hotel manager stood nearby, watching me with a constant, even gaze. After five minutes, Jim ambled towards us. When he noticed the hotel manager, he slowed his gait to the laziest of strolls – a little gesture of southern gentlemanly defiance. We walked outside together. I hiked. Jim ambled.

There was something new in the car park now, a dozen police motorcycles lined up by the revolving doors.

'The big shut-down is beginning,' whispered Jim. He pulled out his camera and photographed the police. 'We're lucky,' he said. 'An hour later, we wouldn't have gotten near the place.'

'What did that man say to you?' I asked.

'Oh,' said Jim, 'he would just love to be of service and provide any help I needed, blah blah blah.'

'How can you say blah blah blah?' I said. 'That wasn't blah blah blah. That was actually fucking sinister.'

'Those Bilderberg boys can be pretty sinister,' said Jim.

We climbed into our car. I started the engine.

'So I told him that I didn't need any help wandering around the hotel, thank you all the same,' said Jim. 'Then he asked where we were staying—'

'*Did he?*'

'And I said, oh, just some flea-pit down the road.'

I looked over at Jim.

'They're going to have some pretty good photographs of us by now,' he said. 'I hope you've been smiling pretty.'

That evening, when I went for dinner, I put a sliver of paper in the crack between my hotel room door and the frame, as I had seen done by James Coburn in *Our Man Flint*. Actually, James Coburn put a single hair in his door. But my door crack was too large for single hairs and they kept falling onto the floor and disappearing into the carpet. I was standing there in the corridor tugging my hair out. So I switched to a sliver of paper. When I returned from dinner, the sliver was still there. There was always a possibility, of course, that they'd taken a look around and put the sliver back where they'd found it. I slept fitfully that night, but nothing happened.

4. *Bilderberg Sets A Trap!*

'Mother.' It was Tuesday morning. Jim was leaving his regular answerphone message with his friend back in Washington, DC to confirm he had not been murdered during the previous twenty-four hours. 'Your dutiful son is playing kick the can in Portugal. Thank you very much.'

This was supposed to be an easy day. Jim simply wanted to verify that the complete shutdown of the Caesar Park had been accomplished. We would drive up there and be turned away at the gate. Jim would ask why, for the record, and document the response in his notepad. Then we would turn around and drive back to our hotel for a leisurely afternoon by the pool and in the bar.

But this was not to be. We arrived at the Caesar Park to discover no police, no cordon, no shutdown. The gate-keeper lifted the barrier and waved us on with a cheerful smile. For the first time, Jim appeared sidestepped.

'That's surprising,' he admitted. 'That's surprising already.'

'Do we drive in?'

'I'm confounded,' murmured Jim. 'We saw the shutdown begin yesterday. We saw it with our own eyes. And now no shutdown. This is not what's supposed to happen.'

'What should we do?'

Jim faltered. The gatekeeper approached the car.

'Just drive in,' said Jim urgently.

Impulsively, I took my foot off the brake and we cruised up the drive. This was a disconcerting new twist. We were venturing into a place where it had been made perfectly clear that we were not welcome, and we didn't even want to be there. We were accidental *agent provocateurs*, propelled on by circumstance, simply because we had been waved on at the gate.

'The hotel is deserted,' I said, as we pulled into the car park. 'We're the only people here.'

'Let's get lunch,' said Jim. 'Just two guys getting lunch.'

We wandered through the now-deserted marble lobby. There were no more civilians. We walked out into the silent grounds and sat at the poolside bar, the only two customers in a hotel designed for thousands. A young waitress appeared.

'Ma'am,' said Jim, raising his trilby.

'Sir?' she said.

'What time do you get off work?'

The question seemed to startle her.

'Nine o'clock,' she said, cautiously.

'And what bars do you like drinking in?' said Jim.

'There are some nice bars in the village near the cathedral.'

'Any bars in particular?' Jim laughed. 'Don't worry. I'm buying.'

'Just lots of nice bars in the village,' she said, evenly.

'That's good information,' said Jim. 'Thank you, ma'am,' he called after her.

He turned to me. 'Now we know where the waiting staff drink. Could be good contacts.'

'So,' I said. 'Shall we try the bars near the cathedral?'

'Sure,' he said.

'Will we go then?'

'OK,' said Jim.

We walked back to the car and began driving the half-mile towards the exit. I glanced into my rear-view mirror. A dark green Lancia had pulled out behind us.

'Jim,' I said.

'Mmm?'

'I think we're being followed.'

Jim turned around.

'No shit,' he grinned. 'Don't worry. Once we're on the public highway they'd be pretty foolish to try anything.'

'OK,' I said.

'They're not going to want to have a fat old dead reporter on the side of the road,' said Jim. 'That's too big a news story.'

'OK,' I said.

'But here they could say, "Oh, we thought they were armed. They looked threatening. We told them to stop but they didn't stop." Bango!'

'I get the picture,' I said.

A flock of geese wandered idly up the drive in front of me. I honked my horn. We finally reached the peach gates.

'You watch,' said Jim. 'He'll turn around now. He's done his job. Poor fool.'

But the Lancia didn't turn around. It began to follow us down the deserted lane.

'Uh oh,' said Jim.

'British Embassy.'

'OK,' I said, 'I'm a journalist from London. I'm calling you on the road from Sintra to Estoril—'

'Hold on.'

'Press office.'

'I'm a journalist from London,' I said. 'I'm calling you on the road from Sintra to Estoril. I'm being tailed, right now, by a dark green Lancia, registration number D4 028, belonging to the Bilderberg Group.'

There was a sharp intake of breath.

'Go on,' she said.

'I'm sorry,' I said, 'but I just heard you take a sharp breath.'

'Bilderberg?' she said.

'Yes,' I said. 'They watched us scouting around the Caesar Park Hotel and they've been following us ever since. We have now been followed for three hours. I wasn't sure at first, so I stopped my car on the side of a deserted lane and *he stopped his car right in front of us.* Can you imagine just how chilling that moment was? This is especially disconcerting because I'm from England and I'm not used to being spied on.'

'Do you have Bilderberg's permission to be in Portugal?' she said. 'Do they know you're here?'

'No,' I said.

'Bilderberg are very secretive,' she said. 'They don't

want people looking into their business. What are you doing here?'

'I am essentially a humorous journalist,' I explained. 'I am a humorous journalist out of my depth. Do you think it might help if we tell them that?'

From the corner of my eye, I saw Jim wind down his window. He leant his head out and blew an antagonizing lady-like kiss at the Lancia.

'Hold on a second,' I said.

'*Jim!*' I said, sternly. 'Please stop that.'

I lowered my voice.

'I'm here with an American,' I said, 'called Big Jim Tucker. He's an *agent provocateur*. That might be the problem. Perhaps you can phone Bilderberg and explain that I may be in the car with Jim Tucker, but I'm not actually *with* him.'

'Listen,' she said, urgently, 'Bilderberg is much bigger than we are. We're very small. We're just a little embassy. Do you understand? They're way out of our league. All I can say is go back to your hotel and sit tight.'

'I'm actually just pulling into our hotel car park right now. The Paris Hotel in Estoril. He's right behind me. He's pulling up on the street right next to the hotel. He's getting out of his car . . .'

'Sit tight,' she said. 'I'll make some phone calls. Whatever happens, don't incite them in any way. Don't fan the flames.'

Before the chase had begun, Jim was lumbering and supine. Now he jumped out of the car with the agility of a young deer. The man from the Lancia climbed out of his car and took up a position behind a tree. He was young, in his thirties, with short black hair. He wore sunglasses and a dark green suit.

'I can see you!' sang Jim. 'You're behind the tree. Peek-a-boo! Smile pretty for my idiot-proof camera.'

'Jim,' I said, 'will you *stop* that.'

But everything was beyond my control. It was as if the invigoration of the chase had transformed Jim into a sprightly teenager.

A one-sided game of peek-a-boo ensued, during which the chaser maintained a steely expression behind his sunglasses, Jim performed a little ballet dance, and I sidled towards the swimming-pool area, attempting to distance myself from the unfolding crisis. Jim wandered over to me.

'Am I being paranoid,' he said, 'or did Bilderberg set a trap for us? No, listen. Yesterday, we saw the shutdown begin. We saw it with our own eyes. Today, surprise surprise, no shutdown. They let us in with a smile . . .' Jim trailed off.

'But they weren't going to keep the entire resort open on the off-chance that the two of us might . . .' I trailed off and looked over to the tree.

'Whatever,' said Jim. 'It looks like we have ourselves a waiting game.'

He smiled and blew a cloud of smoke from his nostrils.

'I consider it a great honour to be followed back to the hotel by those Bilderberg boys,' he said.

Jim said he needed a lie down. He may have twisted something when he leapt out of the car. He retired to his bedroom. I sat by the pool. The man behind the tree shrugged and paced around and adjusted his tie and busied himself there behind the tree. Holidaymakers splashed all around us. From time to time I made eye contact with the chaser, which meant, 'Can I come over and tell you who we are and what is going on?' But he waved me away with a flick of his hand.

Sandra from the British Embassy called me on my mobile phone to inform me that she had spoken to the Bilderberg office at the Caesar Park and they said that nobody was following us and how could they call off someone who didn't exist?

'He is,' I said, in a staccato whisper, 'behind the tree.'

'The good news,' said Sandra, 'is if you *know* you're being followed, they're probably just trying to intimidate you. The dangerous ones would be those you don't know are following you.'

But this was scant comfort. What if these men were the dangerous ones, and I just happened to be naturally good at spotting them? What if I was adept at this?

'But that isn't logical,' I said. 'Big Jim Tucker is obviously not intimidated. I don't think they'd waste their time trying to intimidate us when it is quite obviously failing.'

'*You* sound a little intimidated, if you don't mind me saying,' said Sandra.

'Perhaps so,' I said, 'but I am not behaving in a *visibly* intimidated manner. From across the car park I do not *seem* to be intimidated.'

Two hours passed. Jim and I reconvened at a hotel bar down the road. As I wandered through the lobby, two men in dark suits immediately grabbed brochures and began scrutinizing them. I found Jim some yards away staring into his beer glass.

'There are two men by the door,' I said, 'reading brochures.'

'I see them,' said Jim.

'They are only pretending to read brochures.'

'How do you know?' said Jim.

'You can tell by their demeanour,' I said.

'Here's the plan,' said Jim. 'We leave the bar together. When we get within earshot of the chasers, I say, "I'm gonna meet my Bilderberg contact at the Tiny Bar." You say, "Shhh." Say it urgently as if you don't want them to overhear. Feed them disinformation.'

'I'm not going to do that,' I said.

Jim and I left the bar together.

'JON,' said Jim loudly, 'I'M GONNA MEET MY SECRET BILDERBERG CONTACT AT THE TINY BAR.'

I scowled and said nothing and marched ahead.

'Very good,' murmured Jim outside.

We split up. I walked down to the beach and found a seafood restaurant. I do not think I was followed there (unless, of course, I was being followed by the people who didn't want me to know they were following me – perhaps an elaborate tag operation was in place involving Portuguese pensioners, a man painting some railings and small boys in bathers, but on balance I do not think so).

When I returned some hours later to the bar of the Paris Hotel, Jim was drunker than any man I've ever seen. He was surrounded by four Danish ladies and they were all singing 'Yes, We Have No Bananas'.

'Jim,' I said, urgently, 'are you still being followed?' I coughed. 'Sorry, ladies,' I said.

'Excuse me, ladies,' said Jim, bowing graciously. He turned to me.

'So what happened?' I said.

'I went to the Tiny Bar,' he said. 'They call it the Tiny Bar because it *is* a tiny bar.'

'And did they follow you there?'

'. . . *We have string beans and onions/Cabbages and scallions* . . .'

'I'm a superstitious old boy,' said Jim. He paused. 'Abe Lincoln was a good man. Shame he was an abolitionist. Well, I guess nobody's perfect. I've lost my train of thought.'

'You went to the Tiny Bar . . .' I prompted.

'They call it that,' said Jim, 'because it is a *very* tiny bar. So I'm a superstitious boy and I never sit with my back to the door. Don't want to end up like old Abe Lincoln. But I didn't want them to know, see, that I knew they were there.'

'And were they there?'

'I don't know,' said Jim. 'I had my back to the door. Ha ha ha ha ha!'

Jim nearly fell off his chair laughing.

'Jim,' I said, sternly, 'when you left, were you followed?'

'Who'd want to follow an old boy like me?' said Jim. 'The amount of pills they make me take for my plumbing, anyone would think I was F.A.G. Positive.'

'Jim!' I said, startled. 'That's a terrible thing to say.'

'I'm a Neanderthal,' said Jim. 'Grrrrr.'

*

Early the next morning, a Do Not Disturb sign hung on Jim's door, and sounds of typing echoed down the corridor. At 2 p.m., Jim let me in to read me his report.

Dateline Portugal.

Bilderberg Sets A Trap! Was that car following them or was paranoia setting in?

Tucker climbed several steps to the swimming-pool area and poked his camera between tree branches. Chaser took up position behind tree and played peek-a-boo.

'Come on, smile pretty,' Tucker ordered. Chaser struggled against it but for a brief moment his grim expression turned to an involuntary grin, then was reset.

Hours later by pre-arrangement, Tucker went to another hotel bar a block away. Chaser's car was gone so the stalking was over, right? Wrong. When Ronson joined Tucker he reported two new stalkers in the hotel lobby. How did he know the two men were stalking them?

'You can tell by their smell,' Ronson said.

'I did not say *that*,' I interrupted with indignation.

'You didn't say that?' said Jim. 'I thought I heard you say that.'

'I'm not the sort of person to say something like that,' I said.

There was a doubtful expression on Jim's face.

'Their demeanour,' I said. 'You could tell by their *demeanour*. Change it to demeanour.'

'You can tell by their . . . demeanour,' amended Jim, reluctantly, with a red pen.

There was a chilly pause.

'You said "smell",' said Jim. 'You just forgot you said it.'

'I did not,' I said, 'say smell. I have never in my life said that anybody could be told by their smell.'

A frosty atmosphere had developed between Jim and myself this past day or so. The tension was driving us apart. I was ready to sell Jim out to save my own skin, and I felt that Jim, invigorated by the chase, was grabbing my hand and jumping blindly into dangerous waters.

'OK,' said Jim softly, 'if you want to have said demeanour, you said demeanour.'

'I didn't say smell,' I said.

We had an appointment with Paul Luckman, the editor of the tiny English-language *Weekly News*, the Algarve parish newspaper that had stuck its neck out and gone big on the Bilderberg story. Paul's was the only newspaper in Portugal – indeed the only newspaper in the world, as far as I could tell – that was reporting the Bilderberg story.

Paul is an ex-pat from England, fifteen years an Algarve resident. He is not a journalist by trade. He runs a small telephone company. The *Weekly News* is a hobby for him and his wife, Madeline, and their two friends from church, Fred and Brendan.

Paul told me he was perplexed that their parish journal had stumbled into a world exclusive on this explosive, baffling story.

'I do not consider myself one of the world's greatest thinkers,' he said over the phone, 'but it doesn't take much to work out that this is something genuine. And no other newspaper will *touch* it. Nobody. The conversation dies as soon as you say the word Bilderberg. I mentioned it to an editor on the *Daily Express* yesterday, and he immediately changed the subject. I said, "Did you hear what I said?" "Yes." "Do *you* know about Bilderberg?" "I've, uh, *heard* of them." And that was it. The conversation died.'

'How did *you* hear about Bilderberg?' I asked him.

'From a little newspaper on the internet called the *Spotlight*,' he said. 'Have you heard of them?'

'I'm actually here in Portugal with Big Jim Tucker,' I said.

'Oh!' said Paul. 'He's a hero! Bring him along.'

Paul has a little office in a modern glass building in central Lisbon where he conducts his telephone business. He's a committed born-again Christian. Church posters decorate the walls.

'I find myself out of my depth,' he said, twisting an elastic band around his fingers. 'If what they're up to is perfectly innocent, why don't they say what's going on? But they don't. Not even a little bit. Not even a hint. Nothing.' Paul paused. 'Maybe my head's gone,' he said, 'but the Book of Revelation speaks of a one world order, one financial order, a one-world religion. There'll be a sense of disorder, of children not respecting their parents, and then a very powerful group will form. So it *does* all fit together.'

'I know they're bad guys,' said Jim, 'and I hate them, but I don't believe they're satanist.'

'I believe that Paul's not saying they're satanist,' I said. 'He's saying they're actually Satan.'

'You think that this is some kind of biblical prophecy being fulfilled?' said Jim.

'All I'm saying is this is the strangest thing I've ever known,' said Paul.

The next morning, Paul sent Fred and Brendan, his fellow *Weekly News* editors, to meet Jim and me outside the gates of the Caesar Park.

This was the day Jim said the limousines and the helicopters would arrive. If any of us still had doubts, Jim said, if any of us still didn't believe, today was the day we would realize that the world was nothing like we had been told it was, that it turned on a sinister axis.

The four of us waited out in the heat. A gypsy caravan trotted past, a few hikers. An hour trundled slowly by and we filled in the time with small talk.

'So Paul thinks Bilderberg represents the fulfilment of the Book of Revelation,' I said to Fred.

He chuckled. 'Well *that's* where Paul and I part company.'

We both laughed.

'You see,' said Fred, 'I believe that all the prophecies have already been fulfilled.'

There was a small silence.

'Oh,' I said.

Another hour passed. We ran out of mineral water. We kicked the gravel.

'They'll be here,' said Jim, but now even he seemed unsure. He wiped the sweat from his forehead with a silk handkerchief. Our shirts were soaked. We stopped talking to each other and just stood there.

Portugal is not an eventful country. There is tourism and there is football and there are golfing tournaments. It was, then, all the more extraordinary that at around four o'clock many of the world's most powerful people really did begin to roll past us in taxis and anonymous town cars.

There was David Rockefeller, net worth $2.5 billion, chairman of the Chase Manhattan bank, huddled into the back of a local cab.

'Good afternoon, Mr Rockefeller,' murmured Jim.

The gatekeeper bowed and lifted the gate. David Rockefeller waved, and the taxi disappeared up the drive.

Then came Umberto Agnelli of Fiat, Italy's *de facto* royal family, net worth $3.3 billion, barely noticeable in the back seat of some old sedan.

'Big Bilderberg family,' said Jim. He was trying to remain matter-of-fact, but pretty soon he was grinning broadly.

'Jim!' I said.

'Damn right, soldier,' he beamed. 'Pretty overwhelming, huh?'

There was Vernon Jordan, Bill Clinton's closest friend, his unelected unofficial adviser and golfing partner – Vernon Jordan, who plucked the President from Arkansas obscurity and nurtured him to the White House, and who is widely credited with pulling strings to get James Wolfensohn his job as president of the World Bank.

There was James Wolfensohn, president of the World Bank.

'Incredible,' murmured Fred. 'Unbelievable.'

And there was Henry Kissinger, possibly the most powerful individual the post-war world has known: Dr Kissinger, who sanctioned the secret bombing of Cambodia and later won the Nobel Peace Prize, who revealed to the press his heart attack with the words, 'Well, at least that proves I have a heart,' – and here he was trundling up the drive of the Caesar Park in the back of an old Mercedes.

'I'll tell you one thing, I bet you didn't know about Henry Kissinger,' said Jim. 'His accent is as American as mine. Creep up on him at a bar, as I once did, and whisper that you know *exactly* what he's up to, and he'll splutter and shout at you in an accent as American as Mom's apple pie.'

I attempted, for a moment, to judge rationally whether there was any truth to this startling claim – whether Henry Kissinger really had throughout his life adopted a fake European accent to camouflage his American one. But I couldn't. My rationality had suffered a tremendous blow, and I now no longer knew what was possible and what was not.

The taxis kept coming. There were CEOs of pharmaceutical giants and tobacco companies and car manufacturers, the heads of banks from Europe and North America. Some, like Richard Holbrooke, America's United Nations representative, gave us friendly smiles, which Jim returned with a glare of undisguised loathing.

'Who *are* these people?' said Fred. 'Why does nobody want to *know*?'

'They're the masters of the Universe,' said Jim. 'The rulers of the world. You know their names now.'

There was Conrad Black, the world's third biggest media magnate, the owner of the *Daily Telegraph* and the *Jerusalem Post* and the *Chicago Sun-Times* and 40 Canadian dailies and 447 other newspapers around the world. Conrad Black, who when asked what epitaph he would like replied, 'Just my name and dates. The more exalted a person, the less is written on their tombstone. Charles de Gaulle just has his name and dates, Winston Churchill has the same, Otto von Bismarck has only his last name, and Napoleon Bonaparte has only the letter "N" with no dates at all.' This was a man sure of his place in history, and now I felt that perhaps I understood why.

Fred and Brendan stared in horrified awe. Like Paul, their fellow editor back in the Algarve, these two men were taking an evangelical stance on Bilderberg, presuming its existence confirmed the prophecies laid out in the Book of Revelation. They looked as if they were witnessing the Devil himself ride past.

An old bus cruised up the drive. I paid it little attention, assuming it was full of hotel workers. Only Brendan scrutinized the occupants. I glanced over. Brendan seemed frozen to the spot.

'Brendan?' I said.

'Brendan!' said Fred, sharply. 'What is it?'

'I looked through the window,' he explained, finally, 'and I focused on one person, and he was staring back at me. I was standing with my camera in hand, and this person . . . just stared.'

'What kind of stare was it?' I asked.

'It was a strange stare,' he said. 'It was a different type of stare. Yes. He looked *down* at me. As if he was staring right through me.' There was a pause. 'I couldn't even lift my camera.'

'And who was it?' I asked.

Then Brendan said, softly, 'It was Peter Mandelson.'

There was a long silence.

'Peter Mandelson?' I said.

'I've never seen a stare quite like it,' said Brendan.

'Who's Peter Mandelson?' said Jim.

There was nothing left for us to do, so we got lunch. We lavished praise upon Big Jim, who grinned with satisfaction. He had, indeed, uncovered something extraordinary. Fred half-joked that Jim should win a Pulitzer, except Pulitzer was probably in Bilderberg's hands. We went back to our hotels to freshen up, and after a while Jim called to ask, if I had a moment, would I mind meeting him in his room?

There seemed to be something on Jim's mind.

'We can only wonder what evil things they're doing in there right now,' he said, lighting a cigarette.

'They've only just arrived,' I said, lighting one too. 'They're probably showering.'

There was a pause.

'So what is it, Jim?' I said.

And then Jim dropped his bombshell – he was calling off the midnight penetration.

'When I was at the Tiny Bar last night,' he explained, 'I

met this taxi driver. Local guy. Knew the terrain. I said I'd give him a hundred dollars to escort me through the undergrowth and up the drainpipes. "One hundred crisp American dollars," I said to him. "Buy the wife that red dress she's always wanted." '

Jim paused to cough. He had a coughing fit. He lit a cigarette. I lit one too.

'Anyway,' resumed Jim after he had drunk a glass of water, 'the taxi driver called just now. He said his wife wasn't going to let him go. Too dangerous, she said. She didn't want him killed. Poor fool.'

Jim looked out of the window.

'I'm sorry,' he said.

Jim gazed out at the traffic and the ocean beyond. He pulled on his cigarette. As I watched him, I considered the cancellation of the midnight penetration. Jim was never without a cigarette. He didn't like to admit it but his lungs were shot. His health was no longer a match for drainpipes and guard dogs and armed security. Bill Clinton's best friend Vernon Jordan was there, thirteen years a director of America's second-largest cigarette manufacturer, RJR Nabisco. I was sure that it was Jim's rattling, cigarette-induced emphysema that had put paid to his midnight penetration.

I went back to my own room and lay on my bed. I drifted off for a while, and then I was woken by the telephone. It was Fred from the *Weekly News*. He said he had something of great importance to tell me. Could I meet him at once at his hotel?

'Just come as fast as you can,' said Fred. 'I'll meet you by the pool. And don't bring your friend Jim Tucker.'

*

At the poolside of the Hotel California, Fred held a document. The document was screwed up in his hand and damp with sweat. Fred said that he had discovered something terrible in the hours that had passed since our lunch.

'OK,' said Fred, 'I returned to my hotel and I had a swim and then I went to my room and began surfing on the internet. And after a while I found this . . .'

Fred passed me the document. I uncreased it and laid it on the table.

Bilderberg material is fascist hoax!

Dear friends,

I am writing to you urgently to warn you about material being circulated about a 'Bilderberg Conference' due to take place in June in Portugal. The Washington-based journal Spotlight *is quoted as a source of information on the Bilderberg Conference.* Spotlight *is published by the fascist Liberty Lobby. The purpose of the material appears to be to make people imagine there is a sinister Jewish conspiracy that is trying to dominate the world. You may find much information on* Spotlight *by contacting any major anti-fascist organization.*

Against fascism and against capitalism,
Lisa Taylor

(International Solidarity with Workers in Russia).

'What do you think about that?' said Fred.

There was a long silence.

'Well,' I said. 'I should tell you that the other night Jim

told me it was a shame that Abraham Lincoln was an abolitionist.'

'Did he?' said Fred, clearly startled.

'But I can't really think of anything else Jim said that might be construed as . . . oh – he did say that with the amount of pills they make him take for his plumbing anyone would think he was—'

'We're getting all our information from neo-Nazis?' interrupted Fred. 'We're publishing a newspaper all over Portugal and our sources are neo-Nazis?'

'You might be,' I said. 'But that doesn't mean . . . ' I paused.

Fred looked out at the pool. Children were splashing around. It was a lovely day. He put his head in his hands.

'What,' he said, 'have we got ourselves into?'

5. *The Middle Men In New York*

ONE OUT OF EIGHT AMERICANS
HAS HARD-CORE
ANTI-SEMITIC FEELINGS

I was back once again inside the New York offices of the Anti-Defamation League of B'nai Brith, for ninety years the world's most influential monitors of anti-Semitism.

This poster, part of the ADL's ongoing publicity campaign, was framed on a wall in a corridor outside Gail Gans's office. Each time I saw it I felt it bore testament to the ADL's tireless work. What they must have done to find that out. But I also wondered how the terms had been defined. What is *hard-core*? What are *feelings*? The small print offered no clues. It was just a statement of fact.

When Gail Gans had given me fact sheets proclaiming Randy Weaver and Jack McLamb and Bo Gritz to be far-right extremists, I considered it to be an overstatement – particularly because I couldn't think of anything they had said to me that could have been interpreted as being anti-Semitic. I had raised this point with Gail, and she had explained to me about their use of code words.

It was Jack McLamb's contention that the ADL are *part* of the conspiracy, acting as a hugely influential crack team of character besmirchers who spring ruthlessly into action and accuse anyone of anti-Semitism who gets too close to the truth.

Now Gail said to me, 'the *Spotlight*, James P. Tucker's newspaper, is *the leading* anti-Semitic hate propaganda newspaper in America.'

Oh yeah, I thought. Here we go again.

(I had not, at this point, become one of *them*. I did, however, believe that the ADL might be guilty of utilizing a scatter-shot approach which seemed designed to label *any* anti-government radical as an anti-Semite, rather than fulfilling their public remit which was to protect the Jewish people from anti-Semitism.)

Then Gail handed me her *Spotlight* file. With eyebrows dubiously raised, I picked it up and glanced through it, immediately to discover, with alarm and embarrassment, articles denying the Holocaust, tributes to neo-Nazi skin-heads, books written by *Spotlight* editors dedicated to Adolf Hitler, and on and on. These were articles from some years ago, before the *Spotlight* began to utilize code words (phrases such as 'International Bankers' and 'International Financiers').

'Bloody hell,' I said. 'You're right.'

Gail looked at me quizzically, as if to say, 'Why had you even thought that I might be *wrong*?'

I was left in no doubt that I had been hoodwinked by

racists, that Big Jim Tucker's newspaper was every bit as despicable as Gail said it was.

But what about the others? Back in Waco, Colonel Bo Gritz had described himself as being 'right of Attila the Hun'. He said this while he was squeezed underneath Mount Carmel, the rebuilt Branch Davidian church, this huge man crammed into a tiny space between the floor and the earth, hammering in some lattice work.

'*Early in the morning when the sun don't shine . . .*' he sang, hammering away.

'What do you think of the ADL?' I had asked him back then. (I was squeezed in there too.)

'They are a bunch of bastards and wild dogs,' he growled.

Bang! Bang! He hammered away with a renewed vigour.

'They are vicious,' he said. 'You're not going to use that out of context, are you?'

'No, no,' I said.

(Why was everyone so afraid of the ADL? Even Bo Gritz, the most decorated Green Beret in the Vietnam War, who told me countless stories of how he carried mortally wounded comrades through enemy lines, and so on. And Alex Jones, the Austin radio talk-show host – one of the most outwardly fearless people I had ever met – even he seemed afraid of how the ADL might respond if I quoted his line about them being the 'scum of the earth' out of context.)

'I am an honorary member of the Jewish Defense League,' said Bo. (The JDL is a militant Jewish organization whose members have murdered Palestinian activists and suspected Nazi war criminals with pipe bombs. Bo's friend Jack McLamb was an honorary member of something called Jews for the Preservation of Firearms. I had no idea that there were so many crazy Jewish organizations out there and that they counted so many suspected anti-Semites amongst their roll of honour.)

'The JDL get their hands dirty,' said Bo. 'They don't sit behind their desks. I respect that. The ADL don't care if they are right or wrong. They will take advantage of any situation to make headlines and to put more jingles in their coffers.'

Bo hammered away some more.

'The ADL will bite their own,' he said. 'Watch out! They are vicious.'

I thought about Bo's warning as I sat with Gail. She mentioned that the ADL was always on the look-out for turncoat Jews, self-hating Jews, and I was afraid she might consider me to be one of those. I had, much to her bafflement, attempted to defend the honour of suspected anti-Semites to her. It was not a pleasant feeling. I had spent so much of the past few years with enemies of the Jewish people, and the only time I felt fearful and tongue-tied was when I was with my own representatives. I suppose the thing is this: the anti-Semites may possess the irrational and hateful belief that we Jews control the world, but we've got something even more potent. We've got the resources.

I did not want to get on the wrong side of the ADL. So I changed the subject. I asked Gail about the Bilderberg Group.

She chuckled and said, 'Oh! They're just a group of good citizens who like to discuss broad issues such as global economics and emerging markets without anti-Semites trying to break in and cause havoc. the *Spotlight* just loves its Jewish conspiracy theories. That's a big one for them. They also believe that putting fluoride in the water softens our brains. And that the weather is controlled by the government. They think those are Jewish conspiracies too!'

She laughed, to indicate that the Bilderberg conspiracy theories are as crazy as the ones regarding the fluoridation of the water and the control of the weather.

And then, using almost exactly the same words as Big Jim Tucker had back in Washington, Gail portrayed the events that occurred in Portugal as a battle between good and evil. Except that in her version, the man in the dark glasses behind the tree was not the dangerous one. The evil man was sitting right next to me in my hire car.

Gail's point was that Jim didn't hate Bilderberg, per se. Bilderberg was *us* – Western liberal global capitalists. What he hated was *our* way of life. Gail didn't say it, but I think she felt I had been to a dark place. I had allowed myself to be beguiled by racists, to see our world from their eyes.

Gail said that of course there was no media cover-up. Why would newspaper editors want to run stories concerning a bunch of dull CEOs sitting around discussing globalization? Who'd be interested in that? Come on, Gail said, David Rockefeller is hardly Michael Jordan.

She sighed. Then she said, 'The Anti-Defamation League is very concerned about code words.'

*

As I left Gail's office, my mind flitted manically between the two versions of what had happened in Portugal, attempting to marshal whatever insubstantial facts and partial truths I felt I knew, before finally and comfortably settling on Them against Them, with me doing the driving. My worryingly paradoxical thought process could be summarized thus: Thank God I don't believe in the secret rulers of the world. Imagine what the secret rulers of the world might do to me if I did.

The following two relevant pieces of information (unmistakable facts which I learnt long after the events) should, I hope, offer some kind of skewed clarity.

The first is a wire report from the *New York Times*, dated 12 March 2000:

> Lawyers for the Anti-Defamation League in Denver are appealing a $10.5-million judgement against the organization for defaming a couple the ADL publicly accused of being anti-Semitic. On April 28, a US District Court jury decided the organization had gone too far in accusing an Evergreen, Colo. couple of anti-Semitism.
>
> The jury concluded those statements were defamatory and 'not substantially true'.

The second is a newsletter Colonel Bo Gritz had produced back in 1988, shortly after announcing his candidacy for the office of President of the United States:

The number of the anti-Christ system is 666, a six within a six within a six. Six sides, six angles, six points. The six-pointed star of Judaism.

6. There Are Lizards And There Are Lizards

In a meeting room in a community centre in Vancouver, a blackboard said 'Strategy' and leaflets said 'Bigot Alert'. A coalition of prominent anti-racist organizations shook hands and took their seats, notepads at the ready.

A leading racist was about to land in Canada on a speaking tour. TV and radio stations were vying to secure chat-show bookings. There would be celebrity appearances, meet-and-greet the fans sessions and high-profile book signings.

This was, the coalition felt, an unusual and disquieting turn of events. The media do not, as a rule, scramble to book racists for celebrity appearances. But this was an unusual racist.

'Above all,' began the chair, 'David Icke represents a political threat. His writings are anti-Semitic. David Icke states that the global elite, the Illuminati who dominate every aspect of our lives, are genetically descended from an extraterrestrial race of reptiles who came to earth some

138

time ago in the form of humans, who are capable of changing their shape, who engage in ritual child sacrifice, who drink blood . . .'

The coalition shook their heads wearily. In terms of code words, they had now heard it all.

'What is this crap, this metaphorically hidden language?' said a member of Anti-Racist Action, a visiting scientist from Somalia. 'Who is a lizard? It's bullshit. Bullshit! As a human being you have to use proper language.'

'What do these words imply?' I asked him.

'What do you *think* they imply?' he replied. 'Lizards? Reptiles? Cockroaches? Amphibians? They imply hatred. Racist hatred.'

'Do you think that when David Icke says lizards he means Jews?' I asked.

'Of course!' he said. 'What is lizard? What is amphibian? It is a pile of rubbish. Why's he using those terminologies such as lizards? This vile language. Vile bullshit. I'm totally culturally shocked.'

'So,' said the chair, 'what are we going to do about this?'

Wheels had already been set in motion. The Canadian Hate Crimes Unit had been alerted. So had the media. The coalition had also written to ex-Canadian Prime Minister Brian Mulroney to inform him that David Icke was accusing him of being a reptilian child-sacrificing paedophile. But so far, to their bafflement, Brian Mulroney had declined to initiate legal action.

Indeed, every individual accused of reptilian paedophilia by David Icke had so far failed to sue, including Bob Hope,

George Bush, George Bush Jr, Ted Heath, the Rothschild family, Boxcar Willie, the Queen of England, the Queen Mother, Prince Philip, Kris Kristofferson, Al Gore, and the steering committee of the Bilderberg Group.

'Why do you think that is?' David Icke had asked me when I interviewed him about this matter in London. Then he turned to my notepad and thundered, 'Come on, Ted Heath! Sue me if you've got nothing to hide! Come on, George Bush! I'm ready! Sue me! I'm naming names! Come on, Jon? Why are they refusing to sue me?'

There was a silence.

'Because they are twelve-foot lizards?' I suggested, smally.

'Yes!' said David. 'Exactly!'

'Keep in mind that this is not a meeting to debate what David Icke stands for,' announced the chair in Vancouver. 'This is a meeting for people who are opposed to David Icke's presence in the community. I would like to know if any people here consider themselves supporters of David Icke?'

There was a silence.

'I . . . uh . . . haven't made up my mind yet,' said a man in a beige jacket whom nobody recognized. 'I don't know what David Icke stands for. I have been fighting Nazis for twenty years, but sometimes it is difficult to tell who the Nazis are.'

This man was unshaven. His blond hair was long and lank. Anti-racists shared quiet glances. Strictly speaking this man had – by failing to have made up his mind –

contravened the stated rule. This meeting was for people who *had* made up their minds. But the tacit consensus was not, at this stage, to demand his removal from the room.

'David Icke is opposed to community values,' explained the chair patiently. 'The purpose of this meeting is to organize against David Icke. If that is not your purpose you might want to reconsider whether this is a meeting you want to be at.'

A beat allowed this thought to linger, and then the subject was changed.

'He's clearly out to act as a conduit to the patriot movement,' said Tony from the British Columbia Socialist Caucus, 'the far-right anti-Semitic racist militia movement.'

It was at this moment that the stranger in the beige jacket made a startling announcement.

'I have been in the militia movement of the United States for four years,' he said, 'and I only ever met one racist there.'

The action that followed this declaration was swift and lethal.

'I think at this point it may be unproductive if you continue to remain in the room,' said the chair. He enunciated every word.

The militiaman looked shaken by this rapid response.

'If you ... uh ... want to rule me out, fine,' he stammered, 'but I just wanted to see if I could do anything to help.'

'I think that people are uncomfortable with you sitting at the meeting.'

'I came to hear what David Icke was about and whether I could help,' he said. 'Could I just ask two questions?'

'But this isn't a debate,' smiled the Chair.

'OK. OK. I'll go. But could I just ask—'

'Please, no.'

'I'm gone,' he said. 'I'm gone.'

And he left.

A break was called. Informal suggestions were thrown around over cigarettes in the car park by the younger and more rebellious activists. Someone offered to launch a physical attack on David Icke at his hotel.

I suspected a giant misunderstanding was in danger of spiralling out of control. Knowing what I did about David Icke's past – specifically his startling announcement on the Terry Wogan chat show on BBC1 in 1991 that he was the Son of God – I guessed that when he said that twelve-foot lizards secretly ruled the world, he really *was* referring to lizards. But what did I know? The code words *did* seem to be increasingly abstruse. I elected to remain an impartial observer to the unfolding events in Vancouver in the hope that some clarity might develop in the days ahead.

Wogan.

The blue comedian Jim Davidson was the top of the bill that night (this was prime-time BBC1, the autumn of 1991) but most of the viewers had tuned in to see Terry Wogan's first guest.

There had been rumours in the tabloids all week that something unexpected had happened to David Icke, the

popular BBC sports personality, once a professional football player, now the host of *Grandstand* and a household
name. The tabloids said that David Icke had started
wearing only turquoise, that he was predicting cataclysmic
flooding and earthquakes – and he was claiming to be the
Son of God.

I had watched a videotape of this broadcast before
leaving London for Vancouver. It was startling to see how
David Icke looked, how haggard and exhausted and terribly nervous – so unlike the genial BBC soccer and
snooker correspondent the British public had come to feel
so comfortable with – and dressed from head to toe in a
turquoise shell suit (turquoise being a conduit of positive
energy) as he stepped out onto the stage.

'Why *you*?' asked Wogan with an incredulity that
reflected the mood of the land. 'Why have *you* been
chosen?'

'People would have said the same thing to Jesus,' he
replied. 'Who the heck are you? You're a carpenter's son.'

'When might we expect tidal waves, eruptions and earthquakes?' asked Wogan.

'They will certainly happen this year,' said David.

This conversation took place amid howls of laughter
from the studio audience.

'Why should we believe you?' said Wogan.

'I'm saying that these things are going to happen *this
year*,' said David, 'so we'll see, won't we?'

'And what will happen to you if they don't happen?'
asked Wogan.

'*They will happen*,' said David.

He said this with such ferocity, such conviction, that the

audience stopped laughing for a moment. However wise and modern we are, this kind of thing can still shake us up. You could feel it sweep across the television studio, sweep across the land, a stirring of some primordial paranoia. Could David Icke actually be a soothsayer? At that moment, I think the nation looked to Terry Wogan for guidance. How would he respond? Which way would this go?

'The best way of removing negativity is to laugh and be joyous, Terry,' said David. 'So I'm glad that there's been so much laughter in the audience tonight.'

There was a small silence.

'But they're laughing *at* you,' said Wogan. 'They're not laughing with you.'

There was a gasp, followed by rapturous applause.

So the Canadian coalition was unaware of the moment that David Icke's career had crashed so dramatically in Britain. Had they known, would they have felt differently about the reasons why he said that giant lizards secretly ruled the world?

Furthermore, the coalition seemed to have disregarded the fact that many of the lizard-people Icke had publicly named and shamed were not Jewish.

I had felt a similar sense of bafflement when Gail at the ADL had told me that 'Bilderberg' was a code word for Jews. (Again, very few of the Bilderbergers who had whisked past me into the gates of the Caesar Park were Jewish.) One would presume that this would pretty much disqualify them from being, by anyone's reckoning, a Jewish conspiracy.

Why did nobody consider this important enough to bring it up?

Surprisingly, the only group I discovered that had addressed this complex issue head-on was Combat 18, Britain's fearsome neo-Nazi outfit. They recently published a fact-file entitled 'What Is ZOG?' It reads:

> ZOG is Zionist Occupied Government. Not all the controllers of ZOG are Jews. ZOG is 'Zionist' because their agenda seeks to realize their conviction that they are the 'Chosen People'. Their aim is to be the Masters of the World.

So there's the answer. In the absence of statistical substantiation, you need to put words in inverted commas. The Jews are metaphors now. You no longer need to be Jewish to be a Jew.

This is how things now stand: the Anti-Defamation League are searching for code words that have replaced the word 'Jew'; and for the anti-Semites the word 'Jew' has become code for non-Jews who meet in secret rooms, just as the anti-Semitic tracts of the late nineteenth and early twentieth centuries – the *Protocols of Zion* and Henry Ford's *The International Jew*, for instance – portrayed the Jews.

So perhaps David Icke *did* mean Jews when he said lizards. There were, in fact, two pieces of compelling evidence that support this view:

1. Combat 18 had once attended a David Icke lecture in London and had given him a glowing review in their newsletter:

Icke spoke of 'the sheep' and how ZOG, sorry, the Illuminati, uses them for its own ends. He is always clever enough not to mention what all these people have in common. (Salt beef sandwich anyone?)

So the anti-racist left was not alone in believing that when David Icke said lizards he meant Jews. But David had been mortified by Combat 18's enthusiastic critique, coming as it did from Britain's most menacing neo-Nazi unit. His response was to accuse Combat 18 of being a 'front for the sinister Anti-Defamation League'. He wrote:

The United States arm of Mossad – the Israeli Roths-child secret service – the ADL has been operating in Britain since 1991. Their role is to brand as anti-Semitic anyone who's getting close to the truth. What better way to discredit an investigator than to have Combat 18 praise him?

And:

2. Buried somewhere in the middle of David Icke's hundreds of thousands of published words is a short paean to the *Protocols of Zion* – the absurd nineteenth-century Tsarist forgery proclaiming to be the minutes of a meeting of the Jewish secret rulers of the world:

Protocol 9: The weapons in our hands are limitless ambition, burning greediness, merciless vengeance, hatred and malice. It is from us that all-engulfing terror proceeds ... We will not give (the people of the world) peace until they openly acknowledge our international Super-Government.

It is incredible that this document, which portrays my people as cackling villains from a Saturday matinee, formed the template for contemporary anti-Semitism. It is so obviously a fake. Even if some of us do possess 'limitless ambition, burning greediness, merciless vengeance, hatred and malice' (and I know I do), we'd never come right out and admit it to our peer group. There are appearances to uphold.

But then David Icke has declared that the *Protocols of Zion* is evidence not of a Jewish plot, but of a *reptilian* plot of Illuminati lizards. And nobody would be concerned about David Icke if it wasn't for the fact that his career is now a global sensation; that he lectures to packed houses all over the world, riveting his audiences for six hours at a time with extraordinary revelations; and that pop stars and movie stars request private audiences, with both P. W. Botha and Winnie Mandela happy to declare themselves fans. Indeed, in terms of the size of his following, he is the most influential racist on the lecture circuit – if, that is, he is a racist.

The airport.

Two Canadian immigration officers discreetly scanned the queue at passport control. They were holding clipboards. One turned to the other and murmured, 'That's him.'

Although David Icke had overheard this exchange, and was preparing himself for the worst, he feigned breezy innocence by humming 'Que Sera Sera'. He looked different now. The turquoise was long gone. He wore a comfortable sweater. His eyes were messianic-blue, and his grey hair was guru-long. There was little ridicule in his life now.

'Good evening!' he sang, handing over his passport. It was swiped through the scanner, and two words immediately appeared on the screen: 'WATCH FOR'.

At this, David Icke's composure was shattered.

'So this is life in the free world?' he boomed. 'It's pathetic! Simply pathetic!'

He was quickly bustled towards a holding room, protesting his innocence along the way.

'I am not an anti-Semite! I have a great respect for the Jewish people. Is this a Jewish plot? No, no, no!'

The authorities eyed him with some distrust. When David Icke said he didn't believe it to be a Jewish plot, was this code? Did he really mean that he *did* believe it to be a Jewish plot? What, exactly, was he thinking?

I was, of course, not there to witness what happened to David inside the holding room. But from his own description of the events relayed to me later, I have attempted to piece the scene together.

A man in rubber gloves scattered the contents of his baggage across a table – his clothes and toiletries and reading matter – and began to scrutinize them for some tangible evidence of anti-Semitism.

'Yes,' clarified David, 'the families in positions of great financial power obsessively interbreed with each other. But I'm not talking about one earth race, Jewish or non-Jewish. I'm talking about a genetic network that operates through *all* races, this bloodline being a fusion of human and reptilian genes.'

He threw up his hands.

'And now, suddenly, the idea is that I'm saying it is a gigantic *Jewish* plot. But let me make myself clear. This does not *in any way* relate to an earth race.'

David Icke's line of defence was clear. When he said lizards, he really was referring to lizards. He was not talking about cockroaches, or amphibians in general, contrary to suggestions mooted at the meeting in Vancouver, but Annunaki lizards, specifically, from the lower fourth dimension.

The immigration officers glanced at each other, attempting to square this denial with the memo they had received from a coalition of respectable and trustworthy anti-racist groups, accusing David of anti-Semitism.

Finally, after four hours of questioning, they concluded that when David Icke said lizards, lizards was what he meant. He was free to enter the country. There was no law against this. How could the lawmakers anticipate that sort of thing?

David Icke shook hands with the immigration officers, collected his things, and wandered outside to the concourse, where his entourage was waiting in a car to pick him up. It was 2 a.m.

'It is certainly not a misunderstanding,' said David, as we were chauffeured from the airport to the hotel. 'They are assassinating my character.'

'But why would they want to do that?'

'Because I am getting too close to the truth.' He looked out of the window. 'I miss my little boy,' he said. 'I cannot tell you the agony of being away from my little boy. But you've got to keep walking and talking.'

We reached the hotel, checked in, retired to our rooms for showers, and met again in the foyer.

David was jetlagged and downcast.

'Would I want to do other things with my life, something other than all this frigging travelling? God, yes.'

'What would you be doing if you weren't doing this?' I asked him.

'Something related to sport,' he said. 'I still love sport.'

'I guess you've burnt your bridges with the BBC,' I said.

'Oh, I'd never go back to that,' he said. 'The thought of presenting the same programme day after day, year after year. I think I'd have taken the pill by now. But do I want to go around radio station after radio station, book signing after book signing, interview after interview? No.'

We had breakfast and then we walked the three blocks to the studio of AM 1040 Radio One, where David was booked for a celebrity appearance on the morning show.

David was now more alert and cheerful. Smiling, he entered reception. We were greeted by the station manager, a small man wearing glasses and a friendly striped jumper.

'Hi!' he smiled, extending his hand. 'David Icke. I'm due to be on a programme at 10.15.'

'OK,' said the station manager. He coughed. 'I've reviewed the material that was submitted to us, and I've also reviewed the radio regulations of 1986 . . .'

'I don't believe this,' murmured David.

'. . . and I don't feel comfortable having you on.'

'Why?'

'I just don't feel comfortable. That's it. Thanks for coming in.' The station manager clapped his hands together. 'Thanks very much.'

'You invited me to your radio station,' said David patiently. 'I turned up on time, and now you stand here and say without any substance or explanation that you're not having me on?'

'Thanks for coming in,' said the station manager.

'You know what,' said David, leaning across the reception desk, their faces were now inches apart, 'it's *pathetic*. You say you believe in freedom? You couldn't spell it.'

He turned to me.

'*This*,' he said, pointing at the station manager, 'is one of the architects, unknowingly, of the destruction of our freedom.'

'You did say you were sick of doing radio interviews,' I offered.

'That's not the *point*,' said David. 'The information is being suppressed by unknowing, *frightened little men* like him.'

'Oh, thanks,' said the station manager.

'This is unbelievable,' said David. He was now addressing my notepad. 'Oh no, there's no conspiracy, no cover-up, no suppression, ladies and gentlemen of the world.'

'Please leave,' said the station manager.

That night, at Rosie's Bar in downtown Vancouver, David and some of his entourage drank mournfully until closing time. Word had just reached them that another media interview and a personal appearance in a bookshop had been successfully prevented by the coalition. There was only so much to be gained from being the maligned victim, the speaker of truth in a venal world. This was now becoming a serious problem. Book sales were at risk.

David's entourage attempted to buoy him up.

'At least this blows the myth of a free media in Vancouver,' said a quiet, bearded Austrian called Henrick. 'Clarity is good, right? At least this clarifies things.'

'Yeah,' said David, wearily.

I could not determine how Henrick fitted into the Icke camp. He just seemed to be there all the time, one of perhaps a dozen men and women in Vancouver who drove for David, picked up the hotel and restaurant bills, took him aside to whisper things that I couldn't hear, transported the books and the videos, organized the media engagements, kept the cottage industry rolling.

But the most surprising presence within David's entourage was that of Brian Selby, a veteran local journalist from the left and a one-time prominent Greenpeace activist. (The coalition was mystified by Brian's apparent defection to the far right. It had been the subject of much debate during their anti-Icke meeting.)

'I've been in this town fifteen years,' said Brian, 'and I've gotta say that this is the most twisted political cluster-fuck I've ever seen. You've got the weirdest coalition. You've got the draconian powers of the Canadian Jewish Congress. Then you've got people with a history of being progressive. The Seattle protesters . . .'

'Nobody does all this against one person unless there's something much bigger going on behind the scenes,' said David.

'You've got to have a lot of power to call up a radio station and get the plug pulled on a show,' agreed Brian.

'They're sending us a message. They're saying "Don't fuck with us now or forever more." '

There was a silence.

'Who is pulling the strings?' said David.

After David went to bed, Brian and Henrick elected to take matters into their own hands.

'We need to defuse this whole concept that David Icke is an anti-Semite,' said Brian.

'But how?' I asked.

Brian said he still had some friends inside the anti-Icke camp from his days as a leftist activist. He would use his contacts to initiate a meeting. But how to convince them of David's innocence?

Here, Brian and Henrick fundamentally disagreed. Henrick argued the coalition needed to understand that David Icke's lizard claims were 'politically relevant' (the lizards being the hidden hand behind corporate globalization) and that they had a 'factual core' (there was much talk here of archaeological evidence linking ancient cultures with reptilian invaders).

Brian, however, wanted to keep the lizards out of it all together.

'I mean it,' said Brian, severely. 'Don't mention the lizards. The lizards just confuse things. Jon?'

'The lizards muddy the waters,' I agreed.

'OK,' murmured Henrick, sullenly.

'So what's *your* argument?' I asked Brian.

'Two words,' he said. 'Noam Chomsky.'

'The Jewish intellectual?' I asked.

'David, at his most controversial,' explained Brian, 'is

saying nothing that Noam Chomsky hasn't himself written regarding, for example, the Zionist appropriation of the memory of the Holocaust for political purposes.' He paused. 'What do you think?'

'It isn't unconvincing,' I said.

'This is open and shut,' said Brian. 'Chomsky is the darling of the left. There's no way they can argue with that. Do you reckon?'

I shrugged.

'It will be interesting to see how they might argue with that,' I said.

The next evening, Brian and Henrick and I met Sam – the coalition's unofficial organizer – on neutral ground at a downtown bar. The stakes were high. More media interviews had been prevented by the coalition. Furthermore, the anti-racists seemed to be on the verge of convincing the Canadian Hate Crimes Unit that Icke's books should be seized and literally incinerated, and Icke himself deported.

'Hello, Brian,' nodded Sam, formally.

'Sam,' nodded Brian. 'This is Henrick.'

Henrick nodded formally.

'Jon,' nodded Sam.

'I'm just here as an impartial observer,' I said. 'I'm just going to sit here.'

'OK,' agreed the two camps.

The formalities were over and the discussion began.

'So,' said Sam, 'you say that Icke is not an anti-Semite.'

Brian held up his finger to say 'wait a minute' and he rifled through his briefcase. He retrieved a sheath of photocopies, which contained the writings of Noam Chomsky. Brian had marked passages which convincingly reflected his thesis – that David Icke was no more anti-Semitic than this respected Jewish scholar.

Sam studied the photocopies. He nodded thoughtfully.

'This might be true to an extent,' he finally agreed. 'But there is a very big difference between Noam Chomsky saying it and David Icke saying it.'

'Which is?' asked Brian, his eyes narrowing.

'Well, firstly,' said Sam, 'Noam Chomsky is Jewish. Secondly, Noam Chomsky is not mad. Thirdly, Noam Chomsky is, in fact, an intellectual. And, finally, Noam Chomsky is not an anti-Semite.'

Henrick shuffled uneasily in his chair. He clearly felt that Brian's modus operandi was falling apart before their eyes. Yes, Henrick had promised to leave the lizards out of the discussion, but these were desperate times, and they called for desperate measures.

Henrick shot me a glance.

'Go for it,' I mouthed.

'There is full documentation,' announced Henrick, 'which proves that twenty reptilian races have interfaced, intermingled and interbred with the human race, and are now controlling society from above.'

Brian stared daggers at Henrick.

'Twenty?' said Sam, leaning forward.

'Approximately twenty,' said Henrick. 'Certainly it is somewhere between fifteen and twenty-five.'

'Have you got the names of these reptilian races?' asked Sam, producing a notepad from his bag.

'Yes I have,' said Henrick, obviously pleased that Sam was showing an interest. 'OK. Firstly. Grays.'

Sam wrote down Grays.

'Next there are the Adopted Grays.'

Sam wrote it down.

'Then there are the Troglodytes.'

'They're the ones who live in caves, right?' said Sam.

'In caves,' confirmed Henrick. 'Then there are the Crinklies.'

'What do the Crinklies look like?' asked Sam.

'They are cuddly, pink, with old-looking faces,' said Henrick.

'Can I just point out,' interrupted Brian, sharply, 'this Chomsky passage regarding the oppressive subtext of the Talmud—'

'Then there are the Tall Blondes,' said Henrick.

'What do they look like?' asked Sam.

'Kind of like Swedes,' said Henrick. 'Next come the Tall Robots.'

'They're the ones covered in aluminium foil, right?'

'Right,' said Henrick. 'Then there are the Annunaki.'

'The Annunaki,' said Sam. 'They're the ones David Icke goes on about the most.'

'Exactly,' said Henrick. 'George Bush is Annunaki.'

Sam excused himself so he could step outside for a cigarette. He returned to discover that Henrick had taken the opportunity to grab his notepad and add further names of reptilian races to the list.

'The Elderbarians,' he had written. 'These are the crop circle makers. The Zebra Repticular. The Albarians. The

Interdimensional Sasquatch. The Goat Sucker or Goat Eater often found in Mexico.'

'Is there friction between these alien races?' asked Sam.

'Yes,' said Henrick. 'There is constant friction.'

'Do they actually fight each other?' asked Sam.

'Yes,' said Henrick. 'They are constantly battling for control of the fifteen dimensional portals. One is in Jerusalem. One is in Tibet. Nobody knows where the other thirteen are.'

'This,' said Sam, 'is a very interesting conversation.'

'That was *very* weird,' said Sam to me after Brian and Henrick had gone home.

'It was weird,' I agreed. 'You know, I've been trying to keep an open mind, but now I'm pretty certain that David Icke really *does* mean lizards when he says lizards.'

But the anti-racists were still not convinced.

'It's the hidden reptilian hand of Judaism coming to take over the world,' said a coalition member called Richard Warman. 'It's all about dehumanizing your enemies. How do we make Jews despicable, sub-human, and worthy of our condemnation? So, yes, I still believe that when David Icke says lizards he means Jews.'

It looked as if things could get no worse for David Icke. His supporters had pulled out all the stops to dampen hostility towards him, but even Henrick's intricate lizard dissertation had failed to convince Sam that David was not an anti-Semite.

Now he was a martyr. His fans started approaching him on the street, shaking his hand, sometimes even breaking into spontaneous rounds of applause, offering words of support.

'It's so terrible what those awful Jewish people are doing to you,' said one old lady.

'Little me!' David put his hand on his heart. 'This "nutter", as they call me. If I'm mad like they say I am, why don't they leave me alone? But ever since I started exposing the reptilian elite, the opposite has happened. Why *is* that?'

'The Jews are drawing their own parallels,' suggested one fan. 'Nothing that you have ever said could in any way be construed as anti-Semitism. They're just paranoid. It's not true. You are *not* an anti-Semite.'

'Jewish people have suffered as much if not *more* from this global manipulation as anyone else,' agreed David. 'Far from being the perpetrators of it, they are massive victims of it. And, in terms of racism, my own daughter's boyfriend is himself black.'

'You've changed my life,' said another fan. 'I used to be a sheep, I used to be like them, but you've changed my life.'

On Thursday, the anti-Icke camp suffered a public humiliation. VTV, Vancouver's popular local television station, decided to ignore the coalition's request to cancel David's scheduled TV appearance. Instead they put him on live – head to head with an eminent local psychology professor called Bill Bierstein:

HOST: Professor, why do you think Mr Icke has such a
    following when a lot of people would think his ideas
    are out of this world?

DAVID (*turning furiously to host*): What *research* have you done on that? Nothing! *Nothing!* Nonsense!

PROFESSOR: People like to enchant themselves. They want there to be grand conspiracies by superpowerful beings, rather than just a bunch of mistakes made by decent people—

DAVID: *Professor . . .! (To host)* Is he going to go on for ever?

HOST: Let's get Mr Icke to respond to that.

DAVID: Professor. Did you major in patronizing the people of British Columbia?

PROFESSOR: Well, there's no need for insulting comments.

DAVID: OK. Tell me about the Bilderberg Group.

HOST (*interrupting*): Let's talk about why—

DAVID (*thunderously*): Don't tell me what I'm going to say. Tell me about the Bilderberg Group!

HOST (*listening anxiously into her earpiece*): Mr Icke, we don't want to talk about that right now. Let's talk about—

DAVID (*a knowing smile*): I'm *sure* you don't!

HOST: Why are Jewish groups calling you anti-Semitic?

DAVID: Because I'm getting too close to the truth.

PROFESSOR (*laughing*): Don't get into these convoluted

paranoid fantasies that people are trying to shut you up—

This was, under the circumstances, the wrong thing to say. David could be accused of many things, but fantasizing that he was being censored was not one of them.

David smiled a little, and then he went in for the kill.

DAVID: I have had *three major interviews pulled this week*. I've had *book signings cancelled*. You wanna read the papers a bit more, *mate*!

The Professor faltered.

PROFESSOR: Well, uh, if you have nothing better to do than to insult me, then I'm sorry for your process of thought—

But it was over. The professor had blown it.

In the days that followed this TV debate, some of the coalition began privately admitting to me the whole thing was beginning to backfire. David Icke's fans were not, by and large, anti-Semites. It was more alarming than that. They were, in fact, the *coalition's core constituents* – liberals and anti-racists and left-wingers concerned with the perils of global capitalism. These people were beginning to look upon the *coalition* as the villains, as the hidden hand, as *them*.

When three representatives of the coalition appeared on a radio phone-in show to drum up support for a mass protest against David Icke, they received a volley of antagonistic questions. Why were they obsessed with denying freedom of speech to someone who clearly wasn't an anti-Semite? Who was *really* behind the coalition? What were they *hiding*? And so on.

The coalition hastily convened a meeting at a downtown coffee bar to discuss new tactics. Sam suggested producing a press release announcing that David Icke was suffering from some form of mental illness.

'To me he sounds schizophrenic,' he said. 'Hearing voices.'

'Having visions,' agreed Rob from Anti-Racist Action.

'The nutcase stuff,' said Sam. 'Do we want to hang him on that?'

But the others argued forcibly that the coalition should avoid these areas.

'We're not here to do a psychological analysis on him,' said a woman called Julia. 'Just leave it. Let's leave it.'

But as the evening wore on, the gathering began to seem more like a post-mortem than a strategy meeting. A young activist called Ali said she felt she had pinpointed the coalition's tactical error: they had made young people feel stupid.

'Young people are seeing this big task before them,' explained Ali, 'trying to combat economic global corporatization. And a lot of them have read David Icke and thought, "Hey! He's on our side. I'm looking for answers and he seems to have them." And we've made them feel *stupid*, like they've done something *bad* by getting sucked in.' Ali paused. 'And now they're saying to us, "*Don't tell me I'm stupid!*" What we should have said to them was, "You're *not* stupid. We *understand* why you thought he was OK." But we didn't. And now they think we think they're *stupid*.'

The next morning the Canadian Jewish Congress and B'nai Brith – the most powerful and respected groups within the anti-racist alliance – cut their losses. They telephoned Sam to say they were withdrawing their support.

This was a tremendous blow. Now, the only people left battling Icke were Sam and his young friends from Anti-Racist Action. On Friday night these tatters of the opposition met at the Havana Bar on Commercial Drive. It was a melancholy occasion.

'I guess it's over,' I said.

There was a silence.

'*No!*' said Michael. 'It *isn't* over.'

Michael is young and handsome. He had been pepper-sprayed in Seattle and trampled by Mounties in Vancouver. You could still smell the pepper spray on his bandana.

'Thousands and thousands of people,' said Michael, 'went down to Seattle, risked their *lives* to try and address the problems created by the evolution of global capitalism, and now this pompous wingnut, this buffoon has flounced into town . . .'

Michael didn't need to finish his sentence. We knew. David Icke had flounced into town with his lizard thesis on the dangers of international capitalism and he was cleaning up, winning the hearts of those Michael himself had hoped to convert by serious debate about global economics, swiftly followed by some kind of direct action.

Rational thought was being vanquished, and the lizards were winning.

'He can discredit the *whole movement*,' said Michael. 'I can see the World Trade Organization saying, "If you oppose us you're just scared of some . . . some . . . lizard conspiracy." And *that's* the most scary thing to me . . .'

I think that in David Icke, Michael was seeing an omen of the blackest kind. He was seeing the future of thought itself: a time when irrational thought would sweep the land, much as racism had done the previous century, when Washington, DC was a blaze of white, the white of a million Ku Klux Klansmen marching past a Klan-friendly White House and a Klan-friendly Capitol Hill.

Now Michael said, 'This ridiculous guru has blinded the people of Vancouver, and there's only one thing for it.'

'Which is what?' I asked.

'Icke needs his pomposity pricked in public,' said Michael. 'He needs to be humiliated, disgraced, he needs to become a laughing stock. Only then will his followers see him for what he is, a self-important, humourless clown.'

And, as we sat on the terrace of the Havana Bar, Michael understood how he could make that happen.

It was Saturday morning at Michael's house. Michael and Sam and a few of their friends were making the final preparations for today's physical assault on David Icke.

'Are you nervous?' I asked them.

'I'm getting butterflies,' said a woman called Linda. 'It's exciting. I just hope no militia wingnut acts in a hostile way.'

'Oh, it'll be just new-age flakes there,' said Michael.

'No it *won't*,' said Linda. 'Just look at Mr Militiaman

who turned up at the meeting last week. *He* was dangerous.'

'The point is,' agreed Tony, 'if someone is unstable enough to believe that lizards run the world, God knows what they might do to *us*.'

The plan was this: at 2 p.m. David Icke was scheduled to make a personal appearance at Granville Books in the centre of town. Sam and Linda would arrive first to create a distraction.

'Some chanting,' said Sam.

'Any kind of confusion,' said Michael. 'And then I'll just run in, get to the front of the queue, and smack the meringue pie right into Icke's face!'

'Excellent!' said Sam.

'A flaky pie for a flaky guy!' said Michael.

The anti-racists envisaged a devastating result. The mask would slip the moment Icke's face was publicly splattered with meringue. His self-importance would blow up into the most hilarious tantrum, and he would be seen for the pompous fool he was.

'We're going to ridicule the idiot,' said Michael. 'Are we ready, my fellow *les en tartiers*? Let's go . . .'

At 1 p.m. David and I walked the three blocks from the Rosedale Hotel to Granville Books. I was feeling terrible about my passive role in the impending pie attack. I believed that Michael was correct in his analysis of how David would respond to this public humiliation. But I had decided to remain an impartial observer, and so I gave him no clue as to what was about to happen.

David was in high spirits. He started reminiscing about the events of the early 1990s, the bad days that followed his appearance on the *Wogan* show.

'You know,' he said, 'one of my very greatest fears as a child was being ridiculed in public. And there it was coming true. As a television presenter I'd been respected. People come up to you in the street and shake your hand and talk to you in a respectful way. And suddenly, over-night, this was transformed into "Icke's a nutter". I couldn't walk down any street in Britain without being laughed at. It was a nightmare. My children were devas-tated because their dad was a figure of ridicule . . .'

David carried on walking and talking.

'You have to keep walking and talking,' he said.

In the aftermath of the *Wogan* show, David told me, he exiled himself from Britain. He took to travelling in the United States and South Africa – countries that knew nothing about his predictions of cataclysmic flooding. Their failure to materialize had damaged his credibility in Britain even further. Nonetheless, he began to blame the media for the ridicule he suffered at the hands of the general public.

'Yes, I said some pretty astonishing things back then,' he explained, 'but the media still managed to massively exaggerate them. And what I realized, with all the laughter and all the ridicule, was just how easy it is to get vast numbers of people to believe anything. You just have to print it in enough newspapers. So I started to look into who was in a position to orchestrate this kind of global manipulation. And that's how I learnt about the Bilderberg Group.'

David became an avid reader of Big Jim Tucker and the *Spotlight*. Blaming the global elitists, in part, for scheming the assault against him in the British media, he researched and wrote two books about the spider's web of secret societies that controlled the planet.

He wrote that the global elite are hopelessly drawn to strange rituals, that they run around in robes and burn giant wicker owls at a secret summer camp called Bohemian Grove in the forests north of San Francisco. Henry Kissinger and David Rockefeller are rumoured to be amongst the berobed.

(Jack McLamb too believed that Bohemian Grove was a hot-bed of global elite debauchery. He had suggested to me back in Idaho that the rituals undertaken at Bohemian Grove proved that the New World Order were witches and warlocks. It became increasingly clear to me that I should pay a visit to Bohemian Grove to see if I could witness any of their rituals with my own eyes, to clear this matter up once and for all.)

David came to believe that the global elite were not just stealthily influencing free-trade legislation so as to ease the way for complete global domination; they also operated, out of the White House, a harem of kidnapped and hypno-tized underage sex slaves.

Shocked by his findings, he looked to ancient times, hoping to find some validating evidence.

He discovered primitive cultures that had carved effigies of lizard-men descending from the skies. He put two and two together. This was the key. The reptilian invaders *were* the secret rulers of the world.

Now he was ready to publish.

It was a hit. His career went into turnaround. He was invited to speak all over the world.

'And you see,' said David, 'it all turned out all right. Now my children can hold up their heads and say, "That's my dad. You laughed at him. But look at him now." '

Granville Books was packed with fans and TV crews and journalists.

'Nobody's going to travel miles and hours just to come and see an anti-Semitic madman,' suggested a fan to me. 'Whatever Mr David Icke has to say is more than fascinating.'

David's entrance was greeted with whoops and applause.

'*You are one of the great thinkers of truth!*' yelled a lady from the back.

'Hooray!' responded the crowd.

'Thank you,' said David. 'Once we free our souls, the hierarchies of *all* religions, the Muslim hierarchy, the Jewish hierarchy – I call them "OppoSames" – can't touch us.'

This statement was greeted with cheers and spontaneous applause, and autographs were signed.

It was thirty minutes later that Sam and Linda entered the shop to create their distraction. They noisily elbowed their way into the middle of the crowd.

'*Tell us why you're against Jews!*' yelled Sam, the television cameras now on him. '*Tell us about the* Protocols of Zion . . .'

'*Don't care!*' screamed the supporters. '*Don't care! Get out of here!*'

Two old ladies grabbed Sam and pushed him – with unexpected savagery – against a display of new-age literature.

'Out!' they chanted with ferocity. 'Out! Out! Out! You're not welcome! *Get out!*'

Michael slipped into the shop. His face was hidden by a scarf, his pie buried beneath his trenchcoat. He noticed me and he winked.

I looked away.

Michael quietly walked towards the front.

' . . . OUT! OUT! OUT! . . .'

Fans and TV crews blocked his path. He hesitated for a moment. But then, miraculously, a gap appeared, a window of opportunity.

Michael opened his coat, retrieved his pie, and took aim.

The meringue pie flew through the air. It lightly brushed David's sleeve and continued its journey. It splattered, with a devastating thud, all over the children's book section.

'Well,' murmured David, brushing the pastry flakes from his jacket, 'that massively backfired.'

'We're just booksellers,' said the manager softly. 'You're wrecking the store.'

'Shame,' said some old ladies.

There were sad tuts of disapproval.

The manager produced a sponge and began gently to clean the children's books.

'Please leave,' he said.

And, as the anti-racists slipped quietly away, a few members of David's entourage grinned behind their hands.

Later, over dinner, I heard one of them murmur: 'Well,

the fat Jews fucked up.' David didn't hear this comment. When they saw that I had, they blushed and fell silent and said nothing like it again.

7. *The Klansman Who Won't Use The N-Word*

Somewhere in the middle of the Ozark Mountains, northern Arkansas, is an unusual white building. It stands surrounded only by trees and hacked-out clearings and dirt tracks. The road up here is strewn with chunks of rusted corrugated iron and abandoned pick-up trucks and shacks with brutal No Trespassing signs, illustrated with cartoons of giant snarling dogs, and I wondered who would dare to trespass all the way out here in conspiracy-theory country, armed-response country, Ku Klux Klan country. The signal on my mobile phone had failed along the way.

This unusual white building looked a little disturbing to me, as it is quite obviously inspired by the architecture of the Third Reich, using local timber and whitewash, with vast blood-red flags draped from roof to porch at either end. These strange flags are centred with thick black crosses in white circles. The dirt driveway is also marked out with these flags, a column of them in the darkness, illuminated by a nearby bonfire. This building, and all the odd neo-Nazi pomp surrounding it, seems incongruous out here in the deep forest. From high clearings, you can just about make out little distant specks of everyday global corporate life – strip-malls, NikeTowns, Marriott Hotels, Wal-Marts, Holiday Inns and Burger Kings.

The Ozark mountains make the news from time to time when neo-Nazi gunmen or abortion clinic bombers pursued by scores of FBI agents vanish into them. It is a hiding place, a labyrinth of forests and dirt tracks and compounds populated by an informal army of supremacists and separatists allied by a common purpose, which is to see the supremacists and separatists of a homeland where the white race can live in peace and separation and not be bothered by the government or the immoral liberalism that infects the United States via Hollywood and stems, essentially, from the Jews.

The homeland they dream of is, in fact, not unlike the Ozark Mountains themselves, where the FBI can rarely find their man, where there are virtually no black people, and even fewer Jews. I was probably the only Jew within a hundred miles or more, and I was doing my best to tone it down, sitting out here on the porch of the strange white building. I was consciously suppressing my hand gestures and attempting not to be overtly cosmopolitan.

This strange white building and the compound that it stands in, a hundred acres in total, is owned by Thom Robb, the Grand Wizard of the Knights of the Ku Klux Klan. Thom and I sat outside, as night was falling, and we talked for an hour. This was the night before the opening day of the Ku Klux Klan's annual National Congress. All the preparations had been made. The marquee had been erected. It was orange with white stripes. It looked like a tombola tent at a village fête. The Welcome banner flapped in the evening breeze. The words 'Ku Klux Klan' were surrounded by friendly red and blue stars.

I had come to see Thom Robb because he was undertaking an unusual task. Thom too believed that the New World Order, the Bilderberg Group, met in secret rooms to plot a planetary takeover. But unlike Omar Bakri and David Icke and the others, who seemed resigned to constrain themselves as boisterous outsiders, appearing at Speaker's Corner, theorizing about giant lizards, and so on, Thom Robb wanted to fit in. He wanted to slide into the mainstream. He wanted his own TV show, he said, with jokes and music, like David Letterman, or Regis and Kathy Lee with him as Regis and his daughter Rachel as Kathy Lee.

That was his number-one plan. But first he had to teach his members to stop saying 'nigger' when they were in public.

Some Klanspeople had already arrived from states across America, and they were standing in the darkness, their faces illuminated briefly whenever they took a pull from their cigars. Thom reminisced about a fateful day, 29 June 1996, when the Klan rallied in Chicago and got beaten up by Communist Negroes.

'I'm a little guy, huh?' said Thom. 'I'm not aggressive. You can see that. I'm not a violent man. But I beat this guy up pretty good. Yeah! I hit his fist twenty-nine times with my nose! Ha ha. Oh yeah, I beat his fist up pretty good with my nose. But I've got nothing against those black fellas. They should be proud of their . . . uh . . . skin. That's cool. There's my wife, Muriel. Muriel! Come and meet Jon!'

'Hi!' called Muriel from over by the bonfire.

Thom waited for Muriel to arrive before he said: 'You know, when I met Muriel, I knew she was Miss Right. I just didn't know her first name was *Always*! Ha ha! No, no. I'm just kidding.'

'Hi, Jon,' said Muriel. 'Would you like some peach cobbler?'

'Yes, please,' I said.

'Muriel and me,' said Thom, 'we're always arguing. I say to her, "We wouldn't fight so much if you'd just agree with me once in a while!" '

'Oh, Thom,' sighed Muriel.

Thom hunched his shoulders as he told his self-deprecating jokes. He is a friendly and cheerful man, with an amiable demeanour. Had he not been the Grand Wizard of the Knights of the Ku Klux Klan, I'd have described him as having the humorous demeanour of a Manhattan nebbish. The door was open for me, many times, to say to him, 'Oh, Thom! You're such a nebbish!' But that would have been a mistake. Still, it was surprising to find myself in a situation where I was toning down my Jewish character traits so as not to alienate myself from a Ku Klux Klan leader who reminded me of Woody Allen.

'What are your plans for tomorrow's National Congress?' I asked Thom.

'Well,' said Thom, 'Anna, my daughter-in-law, is going to . . . Anna! Come and say hello to Jon.'

'Hi!' said Anna, with a welcoming smile.

'Anna,' said Thom, 'is going to be holding an Individual Personality Skills workshop.'

'Really?' I said.

'That's right,' said Anna.

'. . . Nigger . . .' said somebody in the darkness nearby. Thom winced. There was a small, awkward silence.

'Well, you see,' said Anna, 'there are four types of personality. There are the Popular Sanguines, the Powerful Cholerics, the Perfect Melancholics and the Peaceful Phlegmatics.'

'I didn't know that,' I said.

'Right,' said Anna. 'And I bet you're asking yourself, what on earth does that have to do with the Klan?'

'Well,' I said, 'I was.'

'Well,' said Anna, 'you've got to think of the Klan almost like an orchestra. You've got the trumpets, which are like the sanguines. They keep everyone excited and they kind of set the pace for everyone. They kind of set the tone. The melancholics are more like the bass drums. They've got that steady beat, and they kind of keep everyone on track, keep everything the way it's supposed to be.'

'That's right,' said Thom.

'And an orchestra only works good when everyone's on the same page and everyone's working together,' said Anna. 'And that's kind of how you've got to think of the Klan. Everyone's got to be on the same page, and everyone's got to be working for the same goals. And then everything's gonna work out all right.'

'What personality are you?' I asked Thom.

'I'm a powerful choleric sanguine,' said Thom.

'Powerful choleric sanguines,' said Anna, 'make the best leaders.'

'Well,' said Thom, 'that's right. But all personalities are good.'

'You know,' I said to Thom, 'you are quite different to how I imagined the Ku Klux Klan's leader to be.'

'And I bet you got your impression of the Klan from all those Hollywood movies,' said Thom.

'I did,' I said.

'We do a lot of wonderful positive things,' said Anna, 'that you don't hear about on the radio or the TV.'

'. . . Nigger . . .' said somebody, somewhere.

'. . . Jew . . .' said somebody else.

There was a silence. Whenever this awkwardness occurred, these bad words drifting up to us from conversations between rank and file Klanspeople in the darkness, Thom and Anna and Muriel looked embarrassed. Nobody mentioned it. Instead, Thom told me that his intention to rejuvenate the image of the Ku Klux Klan was influenced for the most part by popular self-help books.

'Which titles in particular?' I asked him.

'*Successful Positive Mental Attitude*,' said Thom. '*Think and Grow Rich*, *The Magic of Thinking Big* by Fred Schwartz. *How to Win Friends and Influence People*. I'm not implying . . . you know . . . I respect these authors very much. So I don't want to imply that they're secret Klansmen, or that they support the Klan in any way. All I'm saying is that they continue to have a very positive influence.'

I was struck by Thom's choice of words. He respected the self-help authors so he didn't want to imply that they were secret Klansmen. This was an unusually self-deprecating position for the leader of the Knights of the Ku Klux Klan to take. I remembered Omar telling me that I should be proud to be a Jew, that assimilation was the worst thing of all, and I considered offering similar advice to Thom.

Instead, I said, 'In terms of your image makeover, I was wondering if you'd considered changing the name to something other than, well, Ku Klux Klan. The thing is, it carries baggage.'

'Good point,' said Thom. 'And don't think that I haven't considered that. But in this movement, it doesn't matter what name you go by. You can call yourself the Western Society To Preserve The White Race, it doesn't matter. The liberal media are going to give you the same label. They're going to call you Klansmen, they're going to call you Nazis, they're going to call you pigs. And the Klan is, let's face it, a very cost-effective way of reaching people. I can't buy the kind of advertising that I can get free by using the name Ku Klux Klan.'

I knew what he meant.

'Would you have come to see me if I was the leader of the Western Society To Preserve The White Race?' he asked.

I had to admit that I probably wouldn't have.

'So you see,' laughed Thom, 'the name benefits us all.'

The Knights of the Ku Klux Klan weren't always like this, of course. Thom's predecessor, Don Black – a handsome and brutal Klan boss from the 1980s – was not interested in self-help books or image makeovers or personality skills. His masterplan was to overthrow the government of Dominica, a tiny island in the Caribbean, and establish it as a homeland for white racists. He engaged a small army of ten mercenaries, and told the non-Klanspeople amongst them that they were taking part in a secret government operation to combat communism in the South Seas. Their plan was to set sail from a marina in Slidell, Louisiana, and anchor two thousand miles away at Dominica's capital, Roseau, where they'd attack the police station, depose the Prime Minister, and declare Dominica an independent haven for white supremacists.

As they climbed into their boat, however, FBI helicopters swooped down and arrested them all. Don Black was sentenced to two years in jail. While he was inside, Thom Robb held an emergency AGM. He got himself elected Grand Wizard.

Thom rode high for a while, leading the Klan into an era he called the 'Sixth Era'. I don't quite understand the 'Sixth Era', but I believe it to be not unlike the Age of Aquarius – only without the connotations of free love and hippie women in flowing dresses which presumably would not sit well with the Klan. He was America's number-one racist leader.

But then many Klanspeople began to desert him for more outspoken neo-Nazi leaders – leaders of rival Klan groups and organizations such as White Aryan Resistance – fearsome men who cared nothing about negative connotations. And some Klansmen were going it alone: they called it Leaderless Resistance. Timothy McVeigh, the Oklahoma bomber, was a one-time member of Thom's

Klan who became disenchanted with the image makeover and decided to go it alone.

The truth was many Klanspeople felt that without hatred there was no point in even having a Ku Klux Klan. Hate, they contended, was a pivotal Klan activity.

Furthermore, across America, Klan membership had fallen to an all-time low. Seventy years ago, there were three million Klansmen in America, with Klan friendly presidents and judges and movie directors. Today there were only a few thousand left. Thom's image makeover was his Unique Selling Point in a declining market. If this didn't work, his whole organization could crumble.

These were rocky times for the New Klan.

Early the next morning I arrived at Thom's compound just in time for Anna's Individual Personality Skills workshop. There were forty or fifty Klanspeople crammed into the orange-and-white-striped marquee. Some were dressed in old Klan T-shirts and baseball caps, some wore the Klan uniform, a white shirt and black tie. Stitched into their shirts was the Klan insignia, a black cross in a white circle on a red square. Thom's Klan insignia looked much like a swastika, which I felt was a mistake.

Anna was standing in front of a whiteboard marked with arrows and phrases such as 'Unemotional', 'Decisive', 'Goal Oriented', 'Artistic' and 'Witty'.

'You're probably wondering,' began Anna, 'what in the world does all this have to do with the Klan?'

There were nods from the audience.

'Well,' said Anna, 'first of all we want to see if any of you *have* a personality!'

She laughed. But the ice-breaker was greeted with a stony silence. It was an awkward start. Anna changed tack.

'OK,' she said, 'if I was to give one of you a million dollars to jump out of an airplane without a parachute, would any of you do that?'

Nobody raised their hands.

'For a million dollars?' said Anna, scanning the marquee. 'Mmm? Right. Nobody would.'

'Um,' said a woman in Klan uniform, raising her hand sheepishly, 'excuse me. What if the airplane was on the ground?'

'OK,' said Anna. 'That's right. OK.'

Anna consulted the printed notes that the Personality Test people supplied as a guideline for the examiners.

'OK,' she said. 'What if the airplane was on the ground? Well, then. Sure. Everybody would. You'd have to be crazy not to.'

There were nods.

'Well,' said Anna, 'that's what we're talking about today. You can't make an informed decision about something until you've got all the details. Right? You couldn't answer that question intelligently until you knew that the airplane was on the ground.'

The Klanspeople scrutinized the photocopies of their personality sheets. One or two of them began filling them in.

'No,' said Anna, sharply. 'Don't start until I tell you how to. OK?'

Anna smiled – a chilling cheerleader smile. The Klanspeople hurriedly put down their pens.

'A lot of times in dealing with people in the Klan,' said Anna, 'or in your marriage, we make decisions about people we really don't have all the information about. You might meet somebody and, well, he just rubs you the wrong way. And you just say "I don't like that person". But maybe they're having a bad day. You don't know the situation.'

There were nods.

'OK,' said Anna. 'Turn to your sheets. In each of the following rows with four words across, place an X next to the word that most applies to you. Are you ready? OK. Here we go. "Angered easily. Aimless. Argumentative. Alienated." '

The Klanspeople marked their sheets with an X.

' "Unpredictable. Unaffectionate. Unpopular. Uninvolved." OK? These are the weaknesses. We'll be getting to the strengths in a while. Place an X next to the word that most applies to you.

' "Too sensitive. Tactless. Timid. Talkative." '

Anna paused. She consulted her book. 'You want to know what "tactless" means?' she said. ' "Sometimes expresses himself in a somewhat offensive or inconsiderate way." ' Anna looked up. 'We don't have anybody like that in the Klan! OK-*ay*! "Wants credit. Withdrawn. Workaholic. Worrier." '

'Um,' said a voice from the crowd. 'Excuse me. In this one here, you've got down "Warrior". Well, I don't consider being a warrior to be a weakness.'

'Right,' said Anna, consulting her sheet. 'Sometimes a weakness can become a strength. For some people, being a worrier may be a weakness, but for others . . .'

'I think that being a warrior is a strength,' he said, emphatically.

His name was Fred. This seemed to be something of a stand-off. Fred was articulating what many Klanspeople were thinking. The Klan were Aryan Warriors, and Aryan Warriors should not concern themselves with personality skills.

'OK,' said Anna. 'Let's move on to the strengths. "Mixes easily. Mover. Musical. Mediator". . . '

Later, during the coffee break, I asked Anna whether she'd considered changing some of the weaknesses and strengths around, bearing in mind the Ku Klux Klan's particular perspective.

'What do you mean?' she said.

'Well,' I said. 'Take "mixes easily". For many people, that's a strength, but for you "mixes easily" must presumably be considered a weakness.'

'Right,' said Anna. 'OK. Good question. We're talking about mixing within groups of our own people. What we don't do is mix, in an inter-marital way with, you know, ethnic groups.'

Thom wandered over, along with Heidi and Kyle, two handsome young Klanspeople in uniform.

'Wasn't the personality test *great*?' Thom said.

'Yes,' I said.

'What were you?' said Thom to Anna.

'I'm a popular sanguine,' said Anna. She turned to Heidi. 'And you?'

'I'm a popular sanguine too,' said Heidi.

'Wasn't it great?' said Thom to Heidi.

'Well,' laughed Heidi, 'I'm a real compassionate person, but the test said I wasn't. So I didn't agree with that. But I do like to think I have leadership skills.'

Anna turned to Kyle.

'And what were you?' she asked.

Kyle looked to the floor and mumbled, 'Melancholic.'

Thom gave Kyle a little awkward pat on the shoulder.

'And you?' said Anna to me, brightly.

'I'm a peaceful phlegmatic,' I said, cheerfully.

'That's a *good* one to be,' said Anna.

'Thank you,' I said.

Some more Klanspeople joined us carrying coffee in styrofoam cups. We sat on a bench near the children's play area. The conversation turned to the subject of Islamic fundamentalism. This was in the news more than ever since Bill Clinton had declared Osama Bin Laden to be as dangerous as any state America faced.

'You've got to respect that guy,' said Thom. 'It takes some dedication to live in a cave, especially if you're a multi-millionaire.'

'We could work with those Islamic guys,' said Pat from Alabama. 'You know, when I see those Nation of Islam guys at rallies, I go right up to them and tell them I'm in the Klan, and most often they give me the thumbs up.'

'Do they?' I asked.

'Oh, yeah,' said Pat. 'They say, "You just keep on keeping on, and we'll just keep on keeping on." '

'We're certainly working for the same goal,' said Thom.

'Those Islamic guys,' said Pat, 'all feel the same way we do about who controls the world.'

Thom said there was something else that the white

supremacists and the Islamic militants have in common. Both had been accused of planting the Oklahoma bomb. (It was true that the newspapers had rushed to a judgement in the immediate aftermath of the attack. One British tabloid filled its front page with a photograph of a fireman cradling a dying baby. The headline read: 'In the Name of Allah'.)

Thom said everyone knew that government agents had really blown the building up, for the purpose of demonizing armed racists so as to implement gun-control laws. They needed to take the guns away in preparation for the day the world government would declare martial law and imprison Klansmen in secret internment camps hidden in rural America.

The coffee break was over and it was time for Thom's keynote speech. A bell was rung, and a cassette of bagpipe music was played through the public address system. The Klanspeople drifted into the marquee. There was a teenage girl wearing a Calvin Klein T-shirt. Calvin Klein, a New York Jew, represented on a T-shirt here at the Klan congress. I'd noticed the girl earlier. She'd been standing by the raffle stall, studying the prizes. One of the prizes was a collection of Walter Matthau videos.

Then Thom walked past me, grinning and hunching his shoulders in his nebbish-esque self-deprecating way that I guessed was unconsciously inspired by watching Jewish characters on TV. Jews make up just 2.5 per cent of the population of the US, but even out here in Harrison, Arkansas, even here at the Ku Klux Klan National Congress, we had quite a presence. I didn't feel quite so alone. We were doing OK.

Thom's speech lasted an hour. He spoke without cue cards, and at times his points were repetitive. But, for the most part, it was a mesmerizing speech, outlining his vision for the new, upbeat, happy and go-getting Ku Klux Klan.

Thom began, dramatically, by holding up a poster with the words: 'GET OUT NIGGER!' scrawled out in bold letters. It was an arresting moment.

Thom scanned the marquee.

'This is *stupid*,' said Thom, waving the poster in the air. 'This is stupid, stupid stuff.'

Thom's son, Nathan, handed out photocopies of the 'GET OUT NIGGER!' poster to the audience so they could scrutinize it further.

'When your grandmother sees this,' continued Thom, 'who is she going to support? Is she going to support you? No! So we don't want to call those black fellas the N-word, because the very people we're trying to reach, all they'll hear is the N-word. Right?'

Then Thom moved on to the subject of gender politics. Specifically, he spoke of how gender politics affected the image of the Ku Klux Klan. Thom began this portion of the speech by warning the audience that this was a compli-cated area, and he hadn't completely worked it out in his own mind, so we should bear with him.

'The masses,' said Thom, 'are *feminine*. In the area of politics, the masses are *feminine*. OK? And the feminine masses look to what? They look to the *masculine* for pro-tection. And who is the masculine? The government. So the feminine masses look to the masculine government for protection. OK?'

There were nods.

'So when the feminine masses see a Klansman on TV, or a militiaman running around with a gun, or a patriot wearing camouflage, what is she going to feel? She's going to feel that her *safety* is being what? She's going to feel that her *safety* is being *altered*. And she doesn't *want* her safety to be altered. So she's going to turn to who? She's going to turn to the *masculine* for protection.'

Thom paused. He said, 'I'm going to show you something else now.'

Nathan handed out a photocopy of a leaflet that read, alarmingly, 'You have been paid a friendly visit by the Knights of the Ku Klux Klan. Shall we pay you a *real* visit?'

'Do we want to go around threatening people?' said Thom, softly.

The audience shook their heads.

'*Come on!*' yelled Thom. 'We're supposed to be the *knights* on the *white horses* who ride into town and save our people! We're supposed to be the *good guys*! *Shining armour!* Do we want to go around *threatening* people?'

A gust of wind blew the photocopies across the marquee. There was a short break while they were retrieved and secured onto the lectern with a rock. Thom resumed.

'Truth,' he said 'is what we *perceive*. To the feminine masses, what they *perceive* is the truth. OK? So we, as individuals, and we as a corporate body, are two different things.'

Thom scanned the marquee. He looked at the individuals in the marquee.

'We as a corporate body,' said Thom, 'must have a corporate image. And that corporate image has to be projected to the feminine masses. So when a news team comes around and they want to find out what's happening in the racialist movement, they don't call on Jeff Moron Berry . . .'

Jeff Berry is the leader of the American Knights of the Ku Klux Klan, one of Thom's chief rivals. Jeff Berry is an occasional guest on the *Jerry Springer Show*. People throw chairs at him on TV and he throws chairs back. He growls wild-eyed into the camera, much like a WWF wrestler, and says 'nigger' freely in public.

'They don't call on those idiots,' said Thom. 'They'll come to us because we have carved out a *niche*. And all these other screwballs with all this garbage . . .'

Once again, Thom held up the 'GET OUT NIGGER!' poster.

'All this garbage,' said Thom, 'becomes meaningless. When I'm up in my lonely office late at night, with my candle twinkling, and I've got my pencil and paper and I sit and think of what we're facing, it all becomes so clear. There is nothing, nothing, nothing, more important than for us to win political power.'

Thom paused. He whispered, 'Nothing.'

Louder, he said, 'Nothing!'

Louder still, he said, 'What about my wife?'

Then Thom roared, 'NO! YOUR WIFE IS NOT MORE IMPORTANT THAN POLITICAL POWER.'

Quieter, he said, 'What about my kids?'

Then he roared: 'NO. YOUR KIDS ARE NOT MORE IMPORTANT THAN POLITICAL POWER! Because if we don't win political power, who does? The enemy. All I'm saying is, let's send out the right signals. And then . . .' Thom looked around. The audience were rapt.

'And then,' said Thom, 'we will have become the *voice*.'

It was dusk and time to erect the cross. Thom said that the liberal media routinely call it a cross *burning* even though they are fully aware that it's known as a cross *lighting*. The cross had already been built using, unusually, strips of plywood nailed together rather than one large log. It was an especially big cross. Thom had warned the Klansmen against building it too big because of the logistical difficulties.

This was a sensitive matter right now. A few weeks earlier, news of a chaotic cross lighting outside Chicago had been released by the FBI. One of the Klansmen present that night in Illinois was a covert federal agent. (This was not a big surprise. It has been estimated that 25 per cent of all Klansmen are undercover federal officers. I wondered which of Thom's Klansmen were secretly working for the government.)

The Illinois agent reported that the cross lighting was sparsely attended, as a result of dwindling membership. Furthermore, the Klansmen present were mainly senior citizens and were not able to deal with the physical exertion required. He wrote:

After starting an hour late, the Klansmen found the cross was too heavy for those present to lift. It took them three hours to chop it down to size and haul it into place. When they managed to erect the cross, however, they were unable to ignite it.

Fortunately for the Klan, the resultant bad publicity had been minimal. Very few of the papers had decided to run the story. This surprised me. I'd have thought that a Klan fiasco might have made a good news story. But it turned out that it wasn't. The big Klan news right now was Jeff Berry throwing chairs around on TV and saying the word 'nigger' unashamedly. In the light of this, I wondered what they would make of Thom's image makeover. Coming from a Klansman, Thom's positive message of love could be seen as puzzling, faintly disappointing and not easily soundbiteable.

Thom wanted to ensure that an Illinois-type scenario was avoided during his cross lighting. But the Klansmen wanted their cross to be big and special, so they didn't listen to him. It was wrapped in cloth. For now, it was lying in tarpaulin in a small field below the children's play area.

A dozen Klanspeople stood around it, debating how to proceed.

'Do we raise it and *then* soak it,' said Ed from Colorado, 'or soak it and then raise it?'

'Well,' said Ed, 'in the past, it's always been soaked and then raised—'

'. . . but,' said Joe, 'if we soak it before we raise it, we'll get kerosene all over our hands and our clothes when we raise it.'

Thom arrived at the cross.

'You know,' said Joe, 'we were just debating whether to soak it *before* we raise it or *raise* it before we *soak* it.'

'You can't raise it before you soak it,' snapped Thom. 'How you going to soak it after you've raised it?'

The Klansmen looked at the ground. Nobody said anything.

'We thought you'd have a ladder,' came a sheepish murmur from the crowd.

Thom looked over at me and he grinned apologetically. His look said, unmistakably, 'I'm sorry that my members are so stupid, Jon, and I'm sorry that you have had to witness such stupidity.' At this moment, Thom seemed actually to prefer *me* to his members, which didn't strike me as a very good leadership skill.

Somebody produced some kerosene cans and they began to soak the cross.

Pat from Alabama said that his robes and hood were in the boot of his car, and he invited me over to take a look. His friend Joe came too. Tonight was the only night in the year that Thom would give his members special dispensation to wear their robes (which had otherwise been banned as part of the image makeover). Pat was one of Thom's keenest supporters. He had a kind face. He was in steel. Instead of a business card, he gave me a pen, upon which was printed: 'Pat Minshew. Simply The Best'.

'The pens were a free gift,' said Pat. 'I'm not going to take them up on the offer. They leak. You'd better watch your pocket.'

Joe was taller. He was thin and drawn. He looked like Willie Nelson.

We made small talk on our way to Pat's car.

'Have you got any women over in England,' said Pat, 'who might want to marry me?'

'I'm not sure,' I said.

'It would be a good thing,' said Pat. 'Good for me, and good for the movement. You know, a fine woman is a good thing. But she's got to be someone who feels the way you do. A lot of women, they hook you, and the next thing you know they're saying: "You can't go to that there Klan rally! You've got to stay home!"'

'Well,' I said, 'the truth is, the women I know in England are probably more like that.'

We arrived at Pat's car. Pat opened the boot and pulled out his robes from a bin liner hidden underneath his spare tyre. Joe came over to scrutinize them.

'They're different to the ones we've got now, aren't they?' he said.

'I believe that the hood might be a little bit different,' said Pat.

'Silk or cotton?' said Joe.

'Cotton,' said Pat.

'We were using silk,' explained Joe to me, 'but we had problems getting them cleaned. You take them to the cleaners and the niggers'll lose them. But these cotton ones right here, you can wash them yourself.'

'I've put some cardboard into my hood to line it,' said Pat, 'to stop it from collapsing in the rain.'

'You've got to be careful how you wash them, though,' said Joe. 'One time, I washed them with some red stuff, and I got myself a pink robe.'

'Hold your hood up sideways,' said Pat to Joe. 'Mine's got a kind of shark-fin look. See?'

'Oh yes,' said Joe, 'you've got a different kind of lining. See? Mine's got a kind of scratchy lining.'

'They've both got that shark-fin look,' said Pat.

For a while, Pat and Joe held each other's hoods, feeling the lining, running their fingers with some tenderness along the shark-fin edge.

I guessed then that Thom had underestimated how much his members enjoyed wearing their robes.

Pat turned to me.

'You want to try it on?' he said.

There was a short silence.

'OK,' I said.

'You better take your glasses off,' said Pat. 'I don't think these things are designed too good for people with glasses.'

I took my glasses off. I slipped the hood over my head. Through the eye-slits, I could see Pat and Joe smiling and giving me the thumbs up. And how did it feel for me, a Jew, to be wearing a Klan hood? I found myself feeling a little sad, imagining the time in the future when Pat would inevitably discover my Jewishness and feel just awful about letting me try on his hood.

'You should send your mother a photograph,' said Pat. 'You look like a real Klansman.'

I took the hood off and I handed it back to Pat.

There were cheers and applause drifting down to us from the field. The cross had been successfully erected.

'Isn't that a great-looking cross?' yelled Thom. 'It's a perfect, perfect job!'

'Two thumbs up!' yelled Ed.

'White power!' yelled somebody.

A few others joined in. 'White power!' they yelled. 'White power!'

Night fell. Thirty or forty hooded Klansmen milled quietly around near the marquee. Thom appeared, also robed. There were eight black stripes on his robe. Pat whispered to me through his hood that Thom, as leader, was entitled to as many stripes as he wished, 'But he wouldn't want to look like a zebra.'

'And now,' announced Thom, 'we shall walk in line and in silence to the cross.'

The hooded Klanspeople walked down past the children's play area, past the car park, and formed a wide circle around the cross, as wide as the hedges would allow.

Thom said, 'We are gathered here for what is called a Cross Lighting ceremony. I know that sometimes people have called it a Cross Burning, but we know it to be a Cross Lighting.'

A man in black robes appeared from the darkness, carrying a flaming torch. Thom walked over to him. He lifted his own torch, and held it out to touch the flames. Now, Thom's torch was also lit.

'And it starts out small,' said Thom, through the darkness. 'And yet we realize that one torch of revival, touching a heart of one man, does not stop. And we will bow not in obedience to the government but only to our God.'

At this, Thom knelt at the foot of the cross, and he lit it with his torch. There was a whoosh, as the fire engulfed it. At first, the flames shot up vertically, as if it were a lit stake. It took five minutes or so for the entire cross to glow in a manner reminiscent of old archive news film of crosses burning on the lawns of Jews and blacks.

I had asked Thom about these frightening events that occurred on lawns. He said, 'You know, I've *heard* it goes on. But we've never done it. Stupid people do it. The people who do that, I don't call them Ku Klux Klan. I call them Ku Klux Clowns.'

The new Knights stepped forward and swore an oath to the leadership of the Klan. These new Knights, twenty in total, had taken a written test some days earlier to qualify them for their Knighthoods. There were sixty questions in the test, which included:

Do we hate Negroes? (No. We just love white people.)

Do we say the word 'nigger' in public? (No.)

So the Knights test turned out to be a public relations examination.

And we stood there, watching the cross burn. Photographs were taken. Fred, the man who had mistaken 'worrier' for 'warrior' during the Personality Skills workshop, cried when he was knighted. Twenty minutes after the cross was lit, the base burnt through and it collapsed dramatically to the ground with a whoosh and a thud.

'Whoa!' exclaimed dozens of Klansmen – and me too – as it fell.

The next morning, Thom spotted me trying to take a picture of the charred remains of the cross. He asked me not to. I asked him why not.

'It'll look like a hangover after a Saturday night party,' he said. He added, 'People will get the wrong idea.'

And now, as the cross lay glowing flat on the grass, Thom and his people wandered back to the marquee. They rounded off the night by watching the 1915 Hollywood movie, *Birth Of A Nation*, on the video.

Where were the positive images of the Ku Klux Klan in the movies nowadays? It all seemed so easy to Thom up here in the woods.

'Why not make the white supremacists the heroic leads?' he said to me. But no. It was impossible to imagine a pro-Klan film coming out of Hollywood today. But back in 1915, before the Jewish moguls arrived in Hollywood, D. W. Griffith had made *Birth of a Nation*, a paean to Klansmen.

On our way to watch the film, I asked Pat if he believed that the secret rulers of the world were deliberately disseminating anti-Klan material, in the form of Hollywood movies. Pat considered this for a time.

'Well,' he said, 'not all Jews, but we know the ones who are doing it.'

'How?' I asked.

'By the names,' said Pat. 'We all know those names.'

The truth of the matter, the statistical truth, is that Jews – who make up 2.5 per cent of the population of America – constitute 60 per cent of the leadership of the Hollywood studios. Thom didn't mention the word 'Jew' in his keynote speech, but he spoke of 'blood-sucking parasites' and 'the anti-Christ system', and I don't think I was being oversensitive when I guessed that he meant us. At least one knew where one stood with these code words.

We settled back in the marquee and the movie began.

'Shhh!' said some Klansmen to others.

The villain of *Birth of a Nation* is Silas Lynch, the leader of the Black Menace. Drunk with wine and power, Silas kidnaps the beautiful, white, Elsie Stoneman, so he can make her Queen of his Black Empire. The Ku Klux Klan arrive on horseback in the nick of time to save Elsie from Silas's clutches. They ride into town, knights on white horses, the good guys in shining armour – just as Thom had described the heroic Klan in his speech. A battle ensues, and the Ku Klux Klan are quite effortlessly victorious. In one scene, captioned 'Disarming The Blacks', two hooded Klansmen wander over to dozens of armed black rebels who take one look at them, hurriedly throw their weapons to the floor, and scurry away. White supremacy is restored to the South, and the blacks, crushed and disenfranchised, go back to knowing their place.

The movie ended. The Klansmen in the marquee cheered sleepily. It was now very late at night. Then they drifted off to their tents. Pat and I stayed around for a while, and we took a walk back to the embers of the cross. Watching *Birth of a Nation* had made Pat melancholy. Had it not been for the Jews arriving in Hollywood soon after the release of *Birth of a Nation*, Pat said, who knows? Racial segregation in America might today be considered healthy and normal.

Perhaps Pat was right. America was a gawky teen back in Hollywood's golden days, stomping awkwardly around, trying to decide which dream to believe in. Should they go down the *Birth of a Nation* road of chivalrous and highly armed Klansmen? Or how about this new and different kind of America – everyone waving to each other, black people being treated nicely, the little guy, the outsider making it big?

The dream that won out and got called the American

Dream was, of course, a Jewish dream, of sentimentality, of liberal harmony, of the immigrant becoming a success in business without prejudice.

The $50,000 distribution costs of *Birth of a Nation* were put up, by the way, by the twenty-eight-year-old movie novice Louis B. Mayer. The film was a smash hit, and Louis Mayer made a $500,000 profit. This single deal set him on the road to becoming a mogul.

So Jewish Hollywood was funded, in part, by the heroic positive images of the Klansmen in *Birth of a Nation*.

8. *Hollywood*

It was early in the morning on Sunset Boulevard. I had just been picked up from my hotel, the Chateau Marmont, by a long black limousine which now cruised towards Wilshire Boulevard. The limousine was equipped with seven telephone lines, a fax-modem, an ISDN line, a videophone and a friendly chauffeur. The limousine's licence plate read JEW1SH, which reflected the religion of the movie director sitting next to me in the back seat, who restlessly drummed his fingers on the walnut veneer.

'Goodwill,' the movie director murmured to himself. 'Goodwill. Goodwill.'

I gazed out of the window at the passing buildings – one-storey shells housing fancy Japanese restaurants, Lexus showrooms, cool bars, liberal synagogues – concrete boxes identifiable only by the interior design. Such is the homogeneity of these buildings, a bankrupt business could probably be replaced within hours by a small team of workmen carrying some prefabricated milieu.

I had travelled here to try to ascertain if there was any truth to Thom Robb's view that Hollywood is a crucial and knowing part of a global conspiracy. Thom envisages shadowy scenarios of a clandestine network of Jews making plans, subtly promoting the interests of World Jewry through movie plots, writing pointed stereotypes of buck-toothed white supremacists with bad social graces, ruthless Islamic fundamentalists blowing up office buildings – all this to pave the way for the day the New World Order will rise up and seize control of a world that will welcome them with open arms.

The movie director was Tony Kaye, and right now he was halfway through editing his debut film, *American History X*. This was 1998. New Line films, the producers of *American History X*, sent me a press release, which read:

> *American History X* is a profound and stirring drama about the consequences of racism as a family is torn apart by hate. A graphic examination of extremism in America, the film follows one man's struggle to re-form himself and save his brother after living a life consumed by bigotry.

> Produced by New Line films.
> Directed by Tony Kaye.

So this was it: a millionaire Jewish Hollywood director finishing off a movie about a psychopathic neo-Nazi who sees the light in jail when he pals up over laundry duties with a cheerful black inmate, leaves jail, renounces racism, and becomes a liberal.

This was everything Thom Robb was talking about. This was, for Thom Robb, the conspiracy in essence.

I sat back in the deep leather seat and put my hands behind my head. This was the life. It was great in the limousine. *These* were my people. Frankly, I deserved a break from Klan compounds, from Jihad training camps, from people telling me that the world was nothing like I thought it was like – that everything was a brilliantly contrived lie.

And the truth is, I fully intended to dispel Thom's myth of a covert Jewish conspiracy. Of course it was nonsense! I poured myself some juice from the limousine's decanter and enjoyed the ride.

And then I saw where I was, in a limousine with the licence plate JEWISH, me, a Jew in the media cruising through Hollywood with *my* people, out to deride Thom's beliefs, and I wondered – are *we* the New World Order? Is *this* the secret room, this limousine's interior, right now? Is it *us*?

'So how is the editing going?' I asked Tony Kaye.

'Right now it's good,' he said. 'And good is the enemy of great. My singular vision is on the verge of being diluted. My film must make a difference. The power of film is more immense than people realize and vastly wasted on triviality. Hang on a minute.'

Tony wound down his window.

'Excuse me,' he yelled to the passenger of another limousine that had pulled up alongside him at the lights. She wound her window down.

'What do you think about racism?' yelled Tony.

'I don't know,' she yelled back. 'It's bad.'

'Thank you,' yelled Tony.

Tony wound the window back up.

'You see?' he said.

The lights turned green. The two limousines cruised away.

'These are the questions I've been grappling with,' said Tony. 'What is racism? Are the Jews a race or a religion? Are we not all racists? These are the thought channels I've been led down since I started making *American History X*.'

During my negotiations to secure access to Tony Kaye and his JEW1SH limousine, I had no idea that *American History X* was in the midst of a crisis. But an ongoing dispute between Tony and his producers was spiralling out of control, and the limousine now was cruising towards the feud's climax, a breakfast meeting at New Line films.

The crisis was this: Tony had been editing *American History X* for a year and a half. His producers were demanding he give it up. They thought it was fine already. But Tony was refusing to hand it over.

'We're about to drive down Wilshire Boulevard to pick up Marty, my manager,' said Tony. 'Marty is worried about my standing within the Hollywood community. But Hollywood should be more concerned about being in *my* good books than me being in *theirs*.'

Tony paused for a moment. He drummed his fingers on his knee.

'So that's where we are,' he said. 'Did you notice my licence plate?'

'JEW1SH,' I said.

'I used to call this the Jewish Car,' said Tony. 'But now I'm thinking of calling it the Motherfucking Bigot Car.'

'Why's that?' I asked.

'Because we are all racists,' said Tony. 'Aren't we? Do we not need to accept that before we can move on?'

Tony Kaye is very tall and very thin. He is blessed with messianic good looks: a striking facial bone structure and shaved hair, which makes his head look even more like a skull, a skull hard at work, resting on some shoulders.

During the last few days, Tony had been thinking intense thoughts about his impending crisis meeting with Michael De Luca, the senior product president of New Line films. De Luca had thrown down the gauntlet. If Tony didn't hand over the movie, he was going to let Edward Norton, the star of *American History X*, release his *own* cut of the film.

This was to be the most important breakfast meeting of Tony Kaye's career. How could he convince De Luca to let him have more time? How could he convey in a metaphysical and spiritual manner the significance of his vision of *American History X*?

What could he do to make De Luca see it?

And then, in the middle of the night, it had come to him in a flash. The meeting needed a spiritual dimension – an actual spiritual presence.

At 3 a.m. Tony called up his personal assistant, Keeley. He told her to procure a Roman Catholic priest, a rabbi, a Tibetan monk, and, if available, a Muslim cleric. These spiritual people, Tony told Keeley, must attend the meeting also. Cost was not an issue. 'Get them,' he told her.

Keeley made some calls. The rabbi and the priest she secured were local. Unfortunately she couldn't find a Muslim cleric amenable to the cause. The Tibetan monk was being flown first-class all the way from Tibet.

They were all due to meet Tony in the New Line reception at 9 a.m.

'I've spoken to the spiritual people on the phone,' said Tony. 'I told them, You're not there to talk on my behalf. You're there to listen. If you want to write somebody a letter afterwards, by all means do it. If you want to say a prayer, or whatever, do it. You're there to make the meeting a more important, thoughtful and spiritual one.'

'Is Michael De Luca aware that the spiritual people are coming to the meeting?' I asked Tony.

'No,' he said.

'What about Marty?' I asked. 'Does he know?'

'No,' said Tony.

'How will Marty feel?' I asked.

'Marty will be very concerned,' said Tony.

The limousine pulled up outside Marty's office block. Tony's chauffeur telephoned Marty's personal assistant from one of the car's seven phone lines to inform him that the limousine was downstairs. Tony sat in the back seat, repeatedly whispering the word 'Goodwill' to himself.

Marty came out of his office. He climbed into the limousine. Tony got straight to the point with Marty.

'This is a very important meeting,' he said.

'That's right,' said Marty.

'And one of the ways I can make it even more important . . .'

'Make a left and go up Santa Monica . . .' said Marty to the chauffeur.

'Sir,' said the chauffeur.

'. . . I'm not into religion right now,' said Tony. 'It causes a lot of problems. Right?'

'Right,' said Marty.

'But when spiritual people are around, it makes the atmosphere more spiritual,' said Tony. 'Right?'

'Right,' said Marty, cautiously.

'So,' said Tony, 'I have a Roman Catholic priest. I have a, uh, rabbi, and a Tibetan monk. They're coming to the meeting too, and I refuse to go into this meeting without the spiritual people.'

There was a pause.

'I think it's inadvisable, but . . . uh . . .' said Marty. 'This is not the way I'd do it, but if you choose to . . .'

'Why do you think it's inadvisable?' said Tony.

'Michael wants a personal conversation with you,' said Marty. 'I think the monks will make him feel uncomfortable.'

Neither Tony nor Marty needed reminding that Michael De Luca had been having personal problems of his own lately, and the last thing he needed was more stress. A few months previously, Michael De Luca had recklessly received oral sex in view of important celebrities at the William Morris Agency's Oscar party. News of the oral sex quickly spread back to the New Line shareholders, and his position within the company was said to have become shaky for a while. Things were only just beginning to settle down.

'Look,' said Marty, 'I strongly recommend that you

leave the monks and the rabbi downstairs. That would be my recommendation.'

'I have to, I'm afraid, say that that's not the way I work,' said Tony.

'Do what you want to do,' said Marty, thinly. 'I've given you my advice.'

'I'll make it very clear to Michael that you had no idea about the spiritual people and you advised me against it,' said Tony.

'I'd appreciate that,' said Marty.

Marty and Tony turned their shoulders away from each other and looked out of their windows, as the limousine sped down Wilshire Boulevard. The silence didn't last long. Tony was unsettled.

'What do you think about all of this?' he asked the chauffeur.

'It's a bold move,' said the chauffeur.

'Yes,' said Tony. 'It has never been done before. Nothing like this has ever been done before.'

The limousine arrived at the offices of New Line Films. The chauffeur jumped out to open the door for Tony and Marty and me.

'Good luck,' he said.

'What do you think about all this?' asked Tony.

'It's a bold move,' said the chauffeur again.

We wandered into the office block. We called the elevator. When we got in, Tony pressed the fifth-floor button. Just as the lift door closed, a young woman rushed in and joined us. The four of us stood in silence for a moment, inside the elevator.

'Who are you?' said Tony to the woman.

There was a pause.

'I work here,' she said, cautiously.

'I've got a meeting with Michael De Luca,' said Tony, 'about my movie, *American History X*. And upstairs I've got a rabbi and a Tibetan monk and a Catholic priest, and they're all going to be attending the meeting also, so as to make the meeting a more spiritual one. What do you think about that?'

The woman stared ahead at the lift door. She didn't respond.

'Which floor do you want?' said Tony.

'Which floor are you getting out at?' she asked.

'Fifth,' said Tony.

'Then I'm getting out at any floor except for the fifth,' she said.

There was a silence. The lift door opened at the fifth floor. Tony and Marty and I got out of the elevator.

The rabbi had already arrived. He was sitting alone on a leather sofa. He was a nice-looking, elderly man. Tony rushed over to him. They shook hands.

Marty walked slowly over to the sofa. He took his seat at the far end, as far from the rabbi as the sofa would allow. He folded his arms and stared out into the middle distance.

'Marty?' said Tony, sternly.

Marty leant over and shook the rabbi's hand.

'Good to meet you,' he announced. 'I'm just going to . . . um . . .'

Marty stood up and walked away.

'I apologize for Marty's rudeness,' said Tony to the

rabbi. 'He's a little worried about me. You know how this town works.'

'Well,' said the rabbi, 'I'm thinking of getting into film production myself, so really I'm here to learn the rules.'

'OK,' replied Tony. 'Let me tell you a bit about my film. It's a film about racism. That is a tremendously important responsibility for the director of the film, which is me.'

The rabbi nodded.

Keeley, Tony's PA, arrived. She was here to drop off the Tibetan monk, who had just arrived from Tibet. Keeley made the introductions.

'This is Lama Lana,' said Keeley. 'This is Tony, and this is rabbi . . . uh . . .'

'I'm really sorry,' said Tony. 'You're going to have to excuse me.'

Tony rushed off to find Marty. Keeley followed. The rabbi and the Tibetan monk were left alone on the sofa.

'I'm pleased to meet you,' said the rabbi. 'Where do you come from?'

'Tibet,' said the monk.

'Very nice,' said the rabbi.

Out in the corridor, which was decorated with posters of recent New Line hits, such as *The Wedding Singer*, Keeley told me that she had been profoundly moved by the short time she had spent with the Tibetan monk riding in the limousine from Los Angeles airport to here.

'He's the most incredibly spiritual person I've ever met,' said Keeley. 'Honestly. He's the most amazing, amazing Tibetan monk. He's an oasis of calm.'

The Catholic priest arrived. Introductions were made.

Tony returned with the latest news from Marty, which was that Michael De Luca was prepared to allow the spiritual people into the meeting. The journalist from London, however, was to remain in the reception area.

The group stood up and walked into Michael De Luca's office. The door was closed.

I passed the time by pacing the reception area and thinking about Hollywood Jews. Far from actively advancing the interests of the Jews, as Thom Robb believes, the Hollywood moguls have often done the opposite. When Hitler raged, when reports of the Kristallnacht made it back to LA – 'The Night of the Broken Glass', when almost one hundred Jews were killed at random, and countless Jewish businesses were destroyed – the moguls hurriedly convened a meeting amongst themselves. What could be done about it? Should the movie industry wield its power to condemn the Nazis?

Their conclusion – do nothing. Don't rock the boat. Anti-Nazi movies might only give rise to more anti-Semitism. It would do the Jews no favours to advertise just who did, in fact, run this town.

Another meeting was hastily organized, in 1946, when the film *Gentleman's Agreement* was due for release. Some empathetic gentile movie makers, aghast that the Jewish moguls were doing nothing to combat anti-Semitism, elected to do the job themselves. *Gentleman's Agreement* – a film about a gentile who pretends to be a Jew and encounters anti-Semitism – was directed by a gentile. The moguls, fearing an anti-Semitic backlash, offered him one million dollars to suppress it.

So it seems that Jewish moguls do not meet in darkened rooms except for when they are planning ways to suppress pro-Jewish movies. We are notoriously prickly when it comes to identifying with our own. Imagine Harry Cohn, who founded Columbia Pictures in 1924, meeting in a darkened room – Harry Cohn, who was once asked to donate money to a Jewish relief fund, and roared: 'Relief *for* the Jews? How about relief *from* the Jews? All the trouble in this world has been caused by Jews and Irishmen.'

Or Louis B. Mayer – who changed his birthday to the fourth of July, who attended Catholic church (the very same church, in fact, that Harry Cohn attended), who wept with sentimentality every Christmas, who funded the distribution costs of *Birth of a Nation*.

And Irving Berlin, dreaming of a White Christmas and an Easter Parade. How about that for cleaning up some touchy dates in the Christian calendar? As Philip Roth said: 'After Moses, the next great Jewish genius was Irving Berlin. He took Easter, took the blood out of it, and made it about fashion. He took Christmas, took Christ out of it, and made it about the weather.'

I have a childhood memory of my parents taking me to our local cinema in Cardiff to spot the Jews amongst the movie stars. Some were easy, of course. Mel Brooks. Woody Allen. The Marx Brothers, possibly: Groucho and Harpo, no question. Chico, presumably Roman Catholic.

'Ernest Borgnine. He's a Jew.'

'Yes. Well. That's obvious.'

'He's a Jew. The one by the door in the hat.'

'Look at the face!'

'Paul Newman. He's a Jew.'

'Paul Newman is *not* a Jew.'

'He *is*. Never played a Jewish character in his life. In Hollywood! And nobody would guess.'

'Butch Cassidy. Does anyone know?'

And we'd whistle in admiration. Paul Newman (who is actually half Jewish but we'll take him), Lauren Bacall, these were credits to our religion: romantic leads and nobody knew.

Unfortunately, in our sunshiny attempts at mingling with the gentiles we have unintentionally helped to create the myth of a shadowy cabal: we Jews who camouflage ourselves. The camouflage is mistaken for scheming, as if we're concealing something sinister, when in fact we are just hopelessly in love with the camouflage.

Tony Kaye – his JEWISH limo parked outside – seemed to be breaking the unspoken golden rule, that Hollywood can be about Jewish values just so long as you keep the *Jewishness* out of it.

Forty-five minutes passed. Then Tony and the spiritual people emerged – Tony, lofty and thin, floating through the foyer, his head bobbing above the spiritual people who clustered around him and stared upwards, awed by whatever it was he had done in there. This vision resembled a bizarre re-working of some early Renaissance painting – Christ Exits Michael De Luca's Office, On The Road To Oblivion.

'You put your point across wonderfully,' said the rabbi, outside in the corridor. 'This is *your* vision. Remember that.'

'Right,' nodded Tony.

'I feel that if you can develop your vision better with more time, by all means do,' said the priest. 'Visions take time to develop.'

'Right,' said Tony. 'Right.'

'I'll be in touch,' said the rabbi. 'I'd very much like to talk with you at some point about my screenplay.'

'Right,' said Tony.

'You told the truth from your heart,' said the Tibetan monk. 'And that's beautiful.'

'Thank you,' said Tony, clearly moved by the monk's words.

'Thank *you*,' said the rabbi.

'You're welcome,' said Tony.

Keeley took the Tibetan monk off to a coffee shop because there was a little time to kill before his plane journey back to Tibet. The rabbi and the priest caught taxis back to their congregations. I asked Tony how the spiritual people had contributed to the meeting.

'You mean in terms of words?' asked Tony.

'Yes,' I said. 'Rather than just . . . you know . . .'

'Spiritually?' said Tony.

'Did they actually *say* anything?' I asked.

'Only the rabbi,' said Tony. 'He said something.'

'What did he say?' I asked.

'I can't remember,' said Tony. He paused. 'I just remember that it was something embarrassing. To tell you the truth, I wish he hadn't opened his mouth.'

*

Two weeks passed. I was back in London when I received the bad news over the telephone from Tony. The spiritual aspect of the meeting with Michael De Luca had proved to be fruitless. New Line were taking Tony's film away from him and releasing Edward Norton's cut. Now, Tony said, he was going to put as much effort into destroying *American History X* as he had to creating it. Tomorrow morning he was going to fly to Canada to meet the director of the Toronto Film Festival. His intention was to demand that *American History X* be withdrawn from their competition.

'Has this ever happened before?' he asked me over the phone. 'Have you ever heard about anything like this ever happening before?'

'Well,' I said. 'Hunter S. Thompson was going to fly to Cannes to protest against the screening of *Fear and Loathing* . . .'

'Oh, yeah,' said Tony Kaye. '*Writers*. Lots of *writers* go on about how crappy directors ruin their movies. But has anything like *this* ever happened before? A director flying to the Toronto film festival to stop his *own film* from being shown?'

'No,' I said. 'I don't think anything like that has ever happened before.'

'Exactly,' said Tony Kaye. 'Can you be in Toronto by tomorrow morning?'

'I can't . . .'

There was a long silence.

'Oh,' said Tony, softly.

'It's just because my wife is about to go into labour . . .'

'Oh,' said Tony.

'But, look,' I said, 'I'll phone you in a few days to . . .'

'And this is just the beginning,' interrupted Tony. 'I'm going to bribe projectionists across the world to destroy the prints of the film. I'm going to position private security guards outside cinemas to stop the audience getting in. New Line won't know what hit them.'

He paused.

'Bloody Hollywood,' he muttered. 'Bloody America. I flew to the Caribbean last week to speak with a very wise man, a Nobel Prize winner, and he said that America was so bloody . . . so stupid . . . could you hold on a minute?'

'OK,' I said.

I heard Tony place the telephone receiver down onto the table.

'I don't mean it,' he said to someone, softly. 'I love America.'

'That's fine,' I heard an American voice reply. 'Don't worry about it.'

Tony returned to the phone.

'America,' said Tony, 'is a fucking amoral disgrace.'

9. *Living A Diamond Life In A Rocky World*

In the months that followed Thom Robb's controversial keynote address at the Ku Klux Klan congress, in which he instructed his members not to use the N-word in public, word spread throughout the neo-Nazi movement that Thom had kissed a black baby for the benefit of the media. It was rumoured also that Thom planned to publish a Ku Klux Klan cookery book that included recipes for all his favourite dishes.

Throughout the United States, in compounds scattered around the wildernesses of the Appalachian hills and the Ozark mountains, and in underground Klaverns across the country, racists were scandalized. Nobody seemed entirely certain where the baby-kissing had occurred, or whose baby it was, but the widespread belief was that Thom had simply gone too far in his quest to be accepted by the mainstream.

I must admit I found myself siding a little with the outraged racists. A Ku Klux Klan leader kissing a black baby could have been a landmark in racial harmony, but

213

the gesture seemed hollow. Furthermore, I did not think that Thom was genuinely interested in cookery.

I wanted to learn more about Thom's standing within America's racist movement. I drove to Butler, Indiana, to visit Jeff Berry – Jeff 'Moron' Berry as he was referred to in Thom's keynote speech – the Imperial Wizard of the American Knights of the Ku Klux Klan, one of Thom's chief rivals, a man famed for saying 'nigger' freely on television.

This was a journey that many reporters before me had undertaken (much to Thom Robb's bafflement and annoyance). There have been so many exterior shots of Jeff Berry's bullet-riddled house (he has so far survived sixteen drive-by shootings) that he has cunningly erected a huge neon-lit sign in the garden that reads WHITE PRIDE WORLDWIDE alongside a toll-free contact number. You certainly can't miss it. (An advance deal is often made between the Klan and the TV networks in which Jeff Berry agrees to the interview on the condition that this exterior shot is included, lasting five seconds minimum, with the toll-free number clearly visible and un-pixelated.)

Jeff Berry has three guard dogs that jumped out in attempted frenzied attack whenever they saw me, only to be yanked back by their restraining chains. The yanking seemed to make them angrier. The dogs didn't get comfortable around me at any point during the time I spent at Jeff's house. Jeff has long, straggly, hillbilly hair and a wonderful, baritone speaking voice.

Jeff also has a young live-in armed bodyguard called Dakota. Dakota was polite to me and a little shy. He looks like a teenage skateboarder who watches MTV and endorses multi-culturalism. He searched me for weapons and he made us all coffee.

We sat in Jeff's office. His walls are covered with the sorts of posters and drawings that Thom criticized in his keynote speech at the Klan Congress. There's a drawing of a Klansman holding a noose. It says: 'Fetch the Rope'. There's also a 'Nigger Target', for gun practice.

'*Rumours?*' said Jeff. 'They ain't *rumours*. Thom Robb is chickenshit. He's a sissy. He kisses black babies. He had it all once, but now he's politically correct. Did you know Thom Robb's going round telling people not to say nigger?'

'*And* he's banned robe usage,' I said, bitchily.

'Well, that's just sickening,' said Jeff. 'Why is our organization the most powerful Klan group in America right now? Because we're doing the opposite of what Thom Robb says. I appeal to the working man. I don't think I'm God almighty like Thom Robb does. A man who tells people not to say nigger, he's a dictator. That's what the Klan's about, freedom of speech. If Thom Robb don't change his ways, and the way he runs his Klan, all he'll have left are his memories and that building he's got.'

The building Jeff referred to is the unusual white building in Thom's grounds. Now I learnt that the building was infamous amongst America's white supremacists for being showy. Some of Thom's competitors in the neo-Nazi movement have dubbed it his Bavarian Hunting Lodge.

Jeff Berry took me outside to show me his bullet holes.

He said, 'You know my house has been shot up sixteen

times? But I'm still here. If I want to say nigger, I'll say damn nigger and I'll say dirty baboon.'

'I'm going to visit a Ku Klux Klan historian called Richard Bondira this afternoon,' I said to Jeff. 'He lives about two hundred miles away from here, just south of Indianapolis. Do you know him?'

Jeff nodded.

'What kind of man is he?' I asked.

'He ain't no man,' said Jeff. 'He's a sub-human.'

I told Jeff that I ought to leave if I was going to make my appointment with Richard Bondira. Jeff replied, a little sulkily, 'How long did you spend with Thom Robb?'

'A few weeks, on and off, so far,' I said.

'So you spend *weeks* with Thom Robb and, like, an *hour* with me?'

There was a slightly awkward silence.

'I'm sorry,' I said.

I had found Richard Bondira on the internet, selling Klan merchandise such as posters and statuettes and advertising himself as the keeper of a Klan museum. He lives in Rockville, Indiana, in a ramshackle house at the end of a long suburban street. His windows are all blacked out with sheets. This is to stop the light coming in and fading his original Klan posters and pamphlets, but the overall impression is rather eerie: a ramshackle house with blacked-out windows and swastikas and Ku Klux Klan memorabilia stacked up in every corner.

But Richard turned out to be well dressed and welcoming and highly knowledgeable about Klan matters.

'I've just been to see Jeff Berry,' I said to Richard, by way of small talk, shortly after I arrived.

'That man, in my opinion,' replied Richard, 'is pus-infected maggot slime.'

Richard told me that he was an impartial observer when it came to Klan affairs. He wanted it on the record that he was a man of many interests that were unconnected to the Ku Klux Klan.

'I am a published poet,' said Richard. 'My poems have been published in racial harmony magazines. I am an artist as well as a taxidermist. All these paintings, and the stuffed birds and fish you'll see all over the house, are my own work. I am a sculptor too. Those cement lions over there, next to the painting of the Klansman on the horse, were my own work. I am a motorcycle mechanic also. Here are my certificates. So although I have been studying the Ku Klux Klan for eighteen years, I am a rather diversified individual, as you can see from my accomplishments, and all my certificates on the wall.'

Richard took me over to his bookcase.

'However,' he said, 'I am also an authority on the Ku Klux Klan. All these books about the Klan, from there to there, have featured contributions by me.'

'What do you know about Thom Robb?' I asked Richard.

'He's a word merchant, a dream seller,' said Richard. 'He's your old-style medicine man. He's a propagandist.'

'How's he doing, in terms of his image makeover?' I asked.

'He's a washed-up has-been,' said Richard. 'He just wants to make money. I call him Thom on the Robb. You send him your twenty dollars for a T-shirt and it arrives in the mail, like, *eight months* later. You know that song "Band On The Run"? Well, I've written some new words that apply to Thom Robb. It goes, "Thom on the Robb. Thom on the Robb". And I'll tell you this. He's lost a lot of support since he started kissing black babies.'

'Did Thom *really* kiss a black baby?' I asked Richard.

'Yes, sir,' said Richard.

'I can't imagine Thom kissing a black baby,' I said.

'Oh, really?' said Richard. He chuckled to himself. 'I can.'

There was a silence.

'Thom says he wants to become the voice,' I said.

'He's *always* wanted to be the voice,' said Richard. 'He wants to be the new Adolf Hitler. Jeff Berry wants to be the new Adolf Hitler. They've all got their eye on the number-one position and they are all pathological liars. Thom Robb is falling apart. A lot of your Klan groups today are people who split off from Thom Robb. And all these little fractured fragments continue to break down into their sub-atomic parts. Every group has in-fighting and rivalry. They split. More factions form, like individual little fingers that are never drawn together into a fist.'

Richard clenched his fingers together to form a fist.

'And Jeff Berry is ignorant low-life. In my opinion, he's rude, crude and lewd; he does *not* have a high IQ. Nobody is going to pay attention to an uneducated ditch digger, not even his own mother, but the minute you throw on a bedspread and a pillow case and proclaim yourself an Imperial Wizard of the Ku Klux Klan, you have instant stardom. Now everybody is listening to you. Maybe Jeff

Berry will do like Jim Jones and poison his congregation. You never know with these guys.'

Richard said, 'I want to show you something. Let's go downstairs.'

What Richard wanted me to see was a video exposé of Thom Robb.

'Who produced it?' I asked.

'One of Thom Robb's people who split off in disgust when he kissed a black baby,' said Richard. 'His name's Dennis Mahon.'

Richard pressed play. Dennis Mahon's video exposé consisted of two men, Dennis Mahon and someone identified only as Mike, sitting on an orange sofa in somebody's front room. The camera-work was anxious and jumpy, and Richard's tape looked to be around tenth generation, which gave the video even more of a jittery and restless feel.

Dennis Mahon was in his late thirties, and dressed in Klan uniform, a blood-drop patch sewn into his shirt. He was good-looking with tightly cropped hair and a handsome boxer's face. Mike was middle-aged and well dressed. He looked like a well-to-do lawyer. Like Dennis Mahon, Mike was once a friend and supporter of Thom Robb's.

Dennis and Mike's conversation lasted an hour. Every so often a kitten jumped, purring, onto the sofa, and Dennis suspended the discussion so he could grab it and fling it yelping across the room.

Dennis explained that both men were sad having to expose Thom Robb but that they needed to wake people up to his activities.

'You know,' said Mike, 'I once heard him interviewed and they asked him what was the problem with a race-mixing couple, and he said, "Well, if that's what they want to do there's no problem . . ." '

'He actually *said* that?' interrupted Dennis.

'Yes,' said Mike. 'He said, "As long as they don't force it on me . . ." '

'A Grand Wizard of the Klan saying this?' said Dennis, clearly startled. 'Oh, man!'

Back in real life, Richard Bondira sat curled up on his sofa, nodding supportively.

'Did you know,' said Mike, 'that in 1982 Thom Robb's trailer burnt down? He lived in a trailer with his family and it burnt down and he wrote in his newspaper, "Oh, it's such a terrible thing that happened. Our trailer burnt down," and he insinuated that the Reds or the Jews did it, or ZOG did it . . .'

Richard Bondira said, 'ZOG is the Zionist Occupied Government.'

'Thanks,' I said.

'. . . and please send money for him to find a place to live,' said Mike.

'I sent him several hundred dollars,' said Dennis, 'and he never did get another trailer.'

'So his trailer burnt down,' continued Mike, 'and he moved his family into a goat shed on their property, a goat shed about twenty-five foot square with no heat and he had his family in there for two years living like cavemen and God bless his wife Muriel how she put up with that guy I'll never know.'

'Can you tell me who really did burn down his trailer?' said Dennis.

'Nobody burnt it down,' said Mike. 'It was an electrical fire. His daughter's bedroom had a socket that was smoking.'

'That's dangerous,' said Dennis. 'A smoking socket is dangerous.'

'It was an electrical fire that burnt the trailer down,' said Mike, 'not the Jews.'

'Well, that's just carelessness,' said Dennis.

Richard Bondira picked up the remote control and pressed pause.

'Actually,' said Richard, 'it wasn't a goat shed. It was a tool shed. But everything else is true.'

He pressed play again.

'What really gets me,' said Dennis, 'is that he's going around saying awful things, like putting down Klan violence. *And* he's saying that we don't hate anybody.'

'Do I not hate mine enemy with a perfect hatred?' said Mike. 'That's theological.'

Dennis looked straight into the camera.

'I believe he has a deal with ZOG,' said Dennis.

'So do I,' said Mike.

Abruptly, the video exposé ended. Then Richard and I said our goodbyes. He saw me out. He stood on his porch, which was decorated with cement lions, hand-crafted by him, caught mid-roar. We both squinted in the winter sunlight.

Richard waved me off all the way until I reached the corner. Then I saw him look around. A young boy rode up the leafy street on a bicycle, swerving in and out of the leaves that gathered around the picket fences that belonged to his neighbours.

Richard shivered in the cold. He went back inside again and closed his door. I turned the corner.

The following week I did something that Randy Weaver had done. I visited Aryan Nations up in Idaho, a seventy-mile drive from the Weaver cabin. Swastika flags and American flags and the Union Jack flew on the main road. I drove in to see a skinhead mowing the lawn. I waved at him. He instantly stood to attention and gave me the Sieg Heil.

I parked up, jumped out of the car, and immediately found myself in an environment I can only compare to the scene in *Poltergeist* where everything in the room is spinning around. I was surrounded by a dozen skinheads, getting right up into my face, yelling questions at me.

'Who *are* you? What do you *want*?'

One of them took a photograph of me.

From the corner of my eye, I noticed someone scrutinize the profile of my nose and murmur something to his companion.

My perception of Aryan Nations was very different to Rachel Weaver's. I saw no treasure hunts, just rage and psychosis and I wished somebody could wipe this place off the face of the otherwise beautiful and idyllic Idaho. But perhaps this was unfair of me. I had invited myself to their compound. They hadn't come looking for me.

I explained I had been with Randy Weaver, and I wanted to meet Pastor Richard Butler, Aryan Nations' founder. Now in his mid-eighties, Butler was the grandfather of

American racism. There have been few racist murderers these past years who hadn't passed through Aryan Nations' doors.

And now I passed through their doors, stepping over an Israeli flag that they used as a doormat, and into their church, where Butler was sitting below a portrait of Adolf Hitler. During our short conversation, I was flanked by half a dozen skinheads and a man called Staff Leader Reichert Von Barron, who struck me as the least unpleasant of the neo-Nazis there. At least he smiled at me.

'Randy Weaver came out here to be away from the multicultural trash that's infected our nation,' explained Pastor Butler. 'Very sad his son and wife were murdered. The philosophy of the New World Order is to murder children.'

'Who is in charge of the New World Order?' I asked him.

'The anti-Christ Jew,' he said. 'The same one that murdered Abel.'

'All Jews or just some Jews?' I asked him.

'*All* Jews,' he said. 'It's a blood order. DNA has proved it.'

'But not all international bankers and multinationalists are Jews,' I said.

'If you are against the white race, you are anti-Christ. And if you are anti-Christ, you are a Jew,' he said. 'Simple as that.'

A big, bearded man holding a baby begged Pastor Butler's indulgence at this point. He said he would like to add something. Pastor Butler allowed it.

'Some of the people who control the banking system *say* they are not Jewish,' he said. 'But they *are* racially Jews.'

'So even if they are, say, Christian, they are actually Jewish?' I asked.

'Exactly,' he said. 'Look into their genealogy. You'll find a Jew in there somewhere, adulterating the blood. Then there's *no* going back.'

I was anxious to leave Aryan Nations. I felt that coming here was a stupid mistake. I said my goodbyes and I headed out towards my car, chaperoned by Staff Leader Reichert Von Barron. But my path was blocked by two skinheads.

'What's your genealogy?' asked one.

There was a silence.

'My *genealogy*?' I said.

'Yes.'

'I have no idea,' I snapped. 'I'm Church of England.'

The skinheads continued to stare at me. They didn't move. I could see they didn't believe me.

'Church of England, huh?' interrupted Staff Leader Reichert Von Barron. 'They're the ones that make you pay! Ha ha! Passing round the old collection bucket!'

He smiled at me. The two skinheads drifted away. I do not know why Reichert stepped in to alleviate the situation. But I was very glad that he did.

Reichert and I made small talk until we reached my car. I asked him what the skinheads were doing that night. He said that a bunch of them were planning to make a pilgrimage down to the Weaver cabin, and just sit there for a while and take it all in.

I got into my car and turned on the engine. I wasn't the

only person leaving. A young woman pulled out in front of me. She needed to do some chores in town. She headed off down the drive, and then she stopped, as if she had forgotten something. She reversed back, and wound down her window.

'Sieg Heil!' she yelled.

'Sieg Heil!' yelled the skinheads milling around in the car park.

Her Sieg Heil felt to me like fortification – like a multivitamin – something with which to steel herself, to carry with her into the evil lands that lay beyond Aryan Nations.

She drove off. I followed.

Some months passed. Then one day Thom Robb called to say that he was taking the Knights of the Ku Klux Klan on the road, for a rally in Michigan. This was an opportunity for Thom to show the people of Michigan that his Klan was different, that he ran a positive and cheerful Klan that didn't concern itself with slurs.

'Come along for the ride!' yelled Thom. 'We'll have *fun*!'

After my uneasy journey into the world of racism that lay beyond Thom's amiable Klan compound, it was nice to be back, sitting inside his no longer startling white building. Thom was happy to have me back too. He greeted me like an old friend who had been on a hazardous journey. We laughed and joked.

I suspect that Thom likes Jews when he doesn't realize we are Jewish. He seems to appreciate Jewish traits. Not, of course, the traits he consciously associates with Judaism – that we are direct descendants of Satan, that our Zionist Occupied Government secretly controls the world, et cetera – but the *other* traits, our urbanity and quick wit. Possessing these particular traits in spades, I was careful to tone them down when I first met Thom. But I soon stopped doing this because nobody seemed to mind.

We set off at dawn. There were four of us in the van. Flavis, Thom's deputy, was sleeping. He was once a hard-liner, a member of the notorious Aryan Brotherhood down in Mississippi. But now he was New Klan. He was big and unshaven with a bushy moustache and a pony-tail. Thom's grown-up daughter Rachel was asleep too.

Thom looked around and he saw that Flavis and Rachel were sleeping.

Quietly, and apropos of nothing, he said to me, 'Do you think I'm weird?'

There was a silence.

'I'm sorry?' I said. I looked over at Thom, assuming he was kidding around, but he wasn't.

'Do you think I'm weird?' said Thom. There was an intimacy, an awkwardness, in his voice. 'As a person,' said Thom. 'You know.'

I ummed and ahhed. Was Thom weird? He *is* the leader of the Knights of the Ku Klux Klan. But as a *person*. Thom wanted to know whether I considered him weird as a person. I felt that Thom, as a *person*, was in a transitional phase between weird and not weird.

Thom said, 'The thing is, I spend all my time with, you know, Klansmen. So how do *I* know if I'm weird? We're *all* weird.'

'There's no benchmark,' I agreed, 'if one spends all one's time with Klansmen.'

'That's the thing,' said Thom. 'That's exactly the thing. There's no benchmark.'

'There's no comparison point,' I said. 'I can see how that may frustrate you.'

'Exactly,' said Thom. 'So what do you think?'

'You have to be liked,' I explained to Thom. 'The thing is, most people don't *like* the Klan. They think that you are frightening.'

'That's exactly the thing,' said Thom. 'That's why we put on a show in our rallies. You know, David Letterman said "America wants cheap tricks". So we don't go out there and scream and holler at the protesters. We put on a show. You'll see that. We've got music, uniforms and flags, so there's certainly some entertainment in that.'

'People want to be entertained,' I said. 'You've got to be entertaining.'

'Exactly,' said Thom, thoughtfully. 'It's like those Hollywood movies that portray the Klan as ignorant tobacco-chewing rednecks. When you're watching a movie like that, your mind joins in with the storyline, and their message slips in through the back door.'

Thom showed me the book he'd brought with him for the journey, Tony Scott's *Living a Diamond Life in a Rocky World*. He read to me from the jacket:

Tony Scott takes you through an interpersonal look at the Diamond Life. How to get it and how to live it. You'll be challenged to look at your accomplishments and failures and dreams like you never have before. Multiple victories are yours.

Rachel was awake now, and reading *Laws of Leadership*.

Flavis was awake and reading *Tactics of Very Successful People*.

At 7 p.m., we arrived in Paw Paw, Michigan. We checked into a cheap motel in a horrible strip-mall. As soon as I arrived in my room, I put down my bags and started surfing the forty channels on offer. I stopped on Channel 22 to hear a CBS announcement: 'Coming up next. The new face of Ku Klux Klan hatred in America.'

I lay down on my bed. I wondered whether I should call Thom to tell him that there was a possibility that he was about to be featured on national television. But I considered that if the news report was going to feature him, he'd have known about it.

The ads ended and *48 Hours* began – *48 Hours* is a prime-time coast-to-coast news programme.

There was a woodland in moonlight. The music was foreboding, a single, menacing, throbbing note. The music warned me that something evil was in this forest, and it was about to come out and get me. A hooded figure appeared. There was a red glow to him, a glow emanating from a nearby burning cross.

'Meet Jeff Berry,' announced the commentary. 'He's the man some call the new face of hate in America.'

It's Jeff! I thought, in the way you think when you see someone you know on TV.

Then Jeff was standing on the steps of a courthouse. He was surrounded by his followers, who wore a variety of multicoloured robes. One man held up a noose, from which was hanging a lynched black baby doll wearing a nappy.

Jeff yelled, 'The Klan is getting bigger, aren't you glad you're not a nigger?'

And then, 'I have a daughter that's twenty-one and a son that's twenty-three, and you know what? *They hate niggers too!*'

As I lay on my bed, I wondered whether Thom and Flavis and Rachel were also watching this news report.

The next morning, as we drove from the motel into town, it turned out that all four of us, in our individual rooms, had turned on the television set the moment we'd checked in, and discovered the report while surfing the forty available channels. The mood in the hire van was understandably subdued. Flavis seemed haunted by Jeff Berry's good fortune.

'I did notice that he uses the N-word rather a lot,' I said.

'Nigger, nigger, nigger,' murmured Flavis. 'That's all they want. They don't want somebody up there telling white people to love their children. They just want somebody up there hollering nigger, nigger, nigger. He's speaking from a *script.*' Flavis gazed mournfully out of the window. He said, 'If it wasn't for Jerry Springer he'd be a nothing and a nobody and nobody would know him.'

'Flavis has called the *Jerry Springer Show* on countless occasions to suggest they have the real Klan on,' said Thom, 'but they don't want to know. They never call back. They just want the idiots up there.'

'The idiots,' said Flavis, 'who say nigger, nigger, nigger.'

Thom had a meeting in town with Christine Cox, a journalist on the local paper. Chris was Asian. The

American media routinely send non-whites to talk to white supremacists, to see if they will be abused or refused an interview. (No wonder the Klan thought that the media had been overrun by a multi-racial conspiracy orchestrated by the Jewish moguls.)

We wandered through the newspaper's corridors. Typists stopped typing mid-sentence and stared at the Ku Klux Klan. There were whispers.

'So,' said Chris, when we were seated in a private conference room, 'shall I call you guys the Klan? Would that offend you?'

'That won't offend us,' said Thom. 'Call me Thom.'

'So, I hear that you guys were on TV last night,' said Chris, brightly.

Flavis flinched. He stood up. He paced the room.

'No,' said Thom, patiently. 'That wasn't us.'

'Ah,' said Chris. 'OK.'

Flavis explained the differences between Thom and Jeff Berry, who was a clown and a moron and not even a real Klansman. Thom interrupted to tell Chris that he didn't hate anyone. He was, instead, filled with love and one day he hoped to represent white Christian heterosexuals in Washington, DC.

For an hour or so, Chris listened to Thom's vision of an upbeat Klan, a Klan that didn't hate anyone. Finally, she said, 'OK. So let's say that the Klan did get in control of government, and this became a homeland for white Christian, straight people. Do the rest of us get to stay or do we have to leave?'

'That's a hypothetical question,' said Thom.

'But that's what you're aiming for, right?' said Chris. She

pointed at Rachel. 'She's President.' She pointed at Flavis. 'He's Speaker of the House. You've got a White House full of Klansmen—'

'We'd take a vote,' interrupted Thom. 'OK? We'd take a vote. Thank you for your time.'

Chris held her hand out so Thom could shake it.

'Hey!' said Thom. 'Wow!'

He gave Chris a big, friendly handshake, and then they collected their papers and left the office.

Outside in the car park, and unaware that I was standing right behind them, Flavis and Thom discussed their feelings about Chris Cox. And I heard a strange Thom, a different Thom, say to Flavis, 'I thought she was a pretty good reporter. But she's a . . . she's a High Yellow, I think. I think she's a High Yellow.'

Flavis said, 'I think she's Asian. She's Asian and . . . uh . . .'

Thom turned around. He saw me standing there. I smiled awkwardly.

'She's Asian,' said Flavis, 'and . . .'

Thom touched Flavis lightly on his arm.

'She's Asian . . .' said Flavis, still unaware of my presence.

'We don't have to talk about that now,' said Thom.

Flavis saw me. He looked down. He adjusted his tie.

Then the three of us just stood there for a moment not saying anything.

'OK!' said Thom, brightly, clapping his hands together. 'Let's boogie!'

*

Saturday. The day of the rally. Thom's half-dozen flag-holders greeted us at a farmhouse in the countryside outside St Joseph, Michigan. They took turns in the bathroom, fixing their hair with hairspray provided by Rachel. Fully suited and lacquered, Thom called the flag-holders outside for a last-minute briefing.

'If the protesters throw anything,' he said, 'you simply move to the side. Like this. But don't give the appearance that it emotionally tore you apart, like you're going to whine about it now. If the protesters holler, "Your flies are open", just ignore them. OK? Don't look down.'

There were nods.

'I don't want to see you flip the finger at anyone. No smoking and no chewing tobacco. OK? And no chewing gum because it may look like you're chewing tobacco.'

Thom introduced me. He said, 'So I don't want to hear anybody say anything that will embarrass us in front of our friend from England.'

'Our *future supporter* from England,' added Flavis, slapping me heartily on the back.

'Be good,' said Thom. 'I don't want to hear any bad words slip out.'

'And try not to sway,' said Rachel.

We set off into town. The police were lined up on horse-back down Main Street, dozens of them. Thom wound down the window and gave them friendly waves. They nodded and their faces were masked by visors.

'The police are really great, really supportive,' said Thom, turning back to me. And again, to the police, 'Have a *good* day!'

And we parked up behind the courthouse. We passed through the metal detectors. We turned the corner through a doorway cut out of a tall steel fence, which was slammed shut behind us. And then we were in the car park.

The podium stood to our left. In front of us was a vast nothingness, a tremendous field of tarmac stretching out all the way down to another high steel fence, behind which stood two dozen people, little distant specks of colour – the audience.

This enormous space was what Thom had assented to in his negotiations with the town officials. He had agreed, albeit with reluctance, to this void that lay before us. He had hoped to hold the rally on the steps of the court house, just as Jeff Berry had on TV. Courthouse steps have a gravitas. One can picture weighty and legitimate declarations delivered on courthouse steps, imparted to the expectant crowds below.

But the town officials had said no to the steps. They insisted Thom spoke instead in the car park next to the courthouse. They also demanded a three-hundred-foot gap between the podium and the audience, for security purposes. Now – vast and empty of cars and bordered with high wire fences that separated the Klan from the audience – the car park suddenly resembled a cage for dangerous animals at a very humane zoo.

Most of the audience was black. They poked their fingers through the fence. They held their babies up to get a better view of the Ku Klux Klan.

'Why do you think it's such a low turnout?' I asked Thom.

'It *isn't* a low turnout,' said Thom. 'Look at those people over there, and those people way over there, and those people way over by the street corner over there.'

'So you're going to be speaking to the people beyond those people standing at the fence?' I said.

'Actually,' said Thom, 'I'm speaking to those people over *there*.'

Thom pointed at the press enclosure, fenced off to the right. It bustled. There were camera crews, TV news reporters, journalists with notepads. The press outnumbered the audience. They even outnumbered the huge police presence.

'So our object here,' said Thom, 'is to have some good soundbites and not make any mistakes, and not say anything foolish, so when they do report on us they're limited to *positive* statements.'

We walked back to the podium, now dressed with flags held by motionless Klansmen, much like a mini Nuremberg rally. Flavis hooked up the PA and he pressed play.

'Amazing Grace' thundered across the emptiness. This was the musical entertainment Thom spoke of in the van.

'You're going to have difficulties with body language,' I said to Thom.

'Yes I am,' concurred Thom.

'There doesn't seem any point in even trying out body language today,' I said.

'This is what I hate, you see?' said Thom. 'These town officials don't understand the nuances of what goes into public speaking.'

He took to the stage.

'Good afternoon my white brothers and sisters,' he said, and his words boomed through the public address system, across the cavernous car park, across the acres of tarmac, to the audience that stood such a terribly long way off, behind the faraway fence.

'Fuck YOU!' replied the protesters, their faint echoes reaching back to us at the podium.

Thom stood to attention and he smiled broadly, as if to say that this juvenile behaviour was hurting nobody's feelings. It was, however, impossible for the audience to note Thom's facial expression from such a long way away.

When the heckles finally subsided, Thom cleared his throat and he addressed the car park.

'That was delightful,' he said.

'*You're* delightful,' came the distant response.

'I heard a rumour just the other day,' said Thom, 'I heard that the local churches were having prayers that it would rain today. I heard they were having this *intense prayer* that it would rain all day and *rain us out*! Ladies and gentlemen, *God didn't hear their prayers today*!'

There was a moment's startled silence and then an incensed 'Fuck YOU!'

'My white brothers and sisters,' said Thom. 'We're not coming here today asking you to hate anyone.'

'Fuck *you*!' responded audience members.

'We don't want you to hate black people,' said Thom.

'I hate *you,* motherfucker!' yelled a black person.

'We don't want you to hate, because hatred doesn't accomplish anything,' said Thom.

'I hate *you*!' yelled the black person again.

'What we want you to do is feel love, feel an *intense* love for your children,' said Thom.

He said, 'You see those people standing there yelling that

nice little love word – well I guess they've got a limited vocabulary – they don't hate *me*, personally.'

'Yes we do!' yelled a protester. 'We hate you personally!'

'They don't hate *us*,' said Thom. 'They don't even *know* us. They don't hate our flags. They hate what we *stand* for. They hate white Christian America. *That* is what they hate.'

'Fuck you!' came a far off response. 'I hate your flags!'

Thom attempted to outline his message of love for white children. Much of the audience drifted away. The press area thinned out. In the absence of an actual audience, Thom began to address people who happened to be in the vicinity.

'You sitting on the street corner over there, you across the street, you up on the high-rise, you sitting round in your cars. You've been betrayed. I was born in Michigan . . .'

'You were born in *hell*!'

'I was born in Michigan, and I know your politicians, and they have *betrayed* you. My white brothers and sisters, I am not asking you to hate anyone. You've only heard words of loving. We've been speaking a message of love today. My white Christian America, we are going to close now . . .'

'Hooray,' replied a few tired voices, their echoes bouncing off the distant tower blocks that surrounded the car park. Thom sighed, and the amplifiers picked up his sigh and carried it back to the audience.

'That was awful weak,' said Thom.

Then his voice sharpened.

'We're going to try that again. Take deep breaths. Come on. Take deep breaths . . .'

I looked up. This was something new. Something had changed in Thom. There was an edge now. I couldn't understand it. There had been so few protesters, and they were such a terribly long way off. But they seemed to have got to him. The atmosphere was different now, and the flag-holders broke from their disciplined postures and looked over their shoulders at Thom because something was going to happen.

'Reach out way down deep,' yelled Thom into the microphone, 'way down deep, you know, way down deep, take a *deep* breath, try and muster up all the hatred you can in your little AIDS-infested lungs . . .'

I gasped. But positivity was beyond Thom now. It was as if he couldn't stop himself from sliding, sliding into caricature, sliding into becoming all the things everybody else wanted him to be – the press, the protesters, the supporters, the things that would get him onto TV, the things that had been *defined*.

'Come on! Deep breath! Count of three. Say your favourite little love word. Come on. You can do it. One . . . Two . . . Three . . .'

And Thom held the microphone out towards the audience. And, after Thom said 'three', there was silence, of course. Nobody rose to the challenge.

'Boy,' laughed Thom, through the microphone. 'They can't even talk, they're too dumbfounded. Duh! Duh! Duh! Doy! Doy! Doy-uhh! So anyway, my white brothers and sisters, there's *hope for America* . . .!'

We were back to the upbeat.

'Love your heritage, love your culture, love those things that came to you through *thousands* of years, bought down to you *at this very hour*. And my white, Christian brothers and sisters in the audience, what are you going to *do* with it? America will either be white and Christian, or America will be what *they* want . . .'

Thom waved his arm to indicate the remaining few protesters.

'. . . A multi-racial, anti-white, anti-moral America,' yelled Thom. 'Pray on it. Meditate on it. Look to the most *high* in heaven. Who *guided* our people. From the *very* beginning. And *brought* them to this land. And blessed them and nourished them and built them into a great nation that only in the last thirty or forty years has been turned into a cesspool by *faggot slime—*'

Thom stopped abruptly. The flag-holders relaxed and laughed. Thom's shoulders tensed, then they slumped a little. There was a sad silence, while the words *faggot slime* echoed through the car park.

Faggot slime.

Faggot slime.

Faggot slime.

'And that's the part they'll put on TV,' sighed Thom. The rally was over. Thom stepped away from the microphone. The silence lasted right up until Flavis turned on the tape recorder and played 'Amazing Grace' once again. Thom walked slowly to the back of the podium and climbed down.

10. *Dr Paisley, I Presume*

It was lunchtime in the countryside near Yaounde, Cameroon, West Africa. A dozen people were crammed into a small wooden hut in the grounds of a local fundamentalist church. Nobody said anything. Everyone waited.

The guest of honour examined the lunch that had been laid on for him – plantains, chicken wings, bread, pineapples, the centrepiece a dish of coleslaw, decorated with the words, written in carrot shavings, 'WELCOME D.I.P.'.

Dr Ian Paisley surveyed the shaved carrot abbreviation of his name, and we could see he was content.

Ian Paisley was dressed all in white. A large, floppy safari hat covered half of his face. He is not a tall man, but he seemed enormous. His colossal bone structure and lung capacity were to some extent responsible, but there was something more. He exuded an abstract, transcendental enormity. Standing among the locals who surrounded him in a courteous, expectant silence, he looked like a lithograph of a great missionary from another century.

*

'*O Father! We can see the great pan-nationalist conspiracy, with the Pope at its head, sending his secret messages to the IRA . . .*'

It was delightful, after all the code words, to spend time with a man for whom code words are anathema, the last of the great unreconstructed conspiracy theorists.

'*. . . the European Union is a beast ridden by the harlot Catholic Church, conspiring to create a Europe controlled by the Vatican . . .*'

For Dr Paisley, the occupants of the secret room were not Bilderbergers, nor Jews, but Machiavellian papists. But what he believes they are doing in there is essentially the same as what the others believe – a mystical cabal is conspiring to establish a European superstate and, ultimately, a nefarious world government.

This was January 1998, some months before the signing of the Good Friday Agreement at Stormont Castle. Ian Paisley had exiled himself from the Northern Ireland peace talks. He couldn't have been further away from the negotiating table, here in this hut in the Cameroonian outback. He was not prepared to sit back and watch Ulster fall to the ecumenists and the papist conspiracy and become 'rife with nuns'. So he had come to Cameroon to do God's old-fashioned work, plain and simple. He had come to preach to the sinners.

'Come on,' he announced in the hut. 'Let's have some *lunch*.'

He sat down and surveyed the still-silent crowd.

'What are you all waiting for? The Israelites shall sit at

the main table with me, but the sinner must sit on his own at the little table over there by the window.'

The sinner in question was, and there was no ambiguity about this, me.

My bad relationship with Ian Paisley could be traced back to the very first conversation I'd had with him, on the plane coming over from Heathrow some twelve hours earlier. I sat in 21F. He was in 21A. I smiled across the aisle a few times, but he just sat there, quietly reading his Bible. I could see that he had made notes in the margins. He later told me that he could recite the Old Testament in English *and* in fluent Hebrew. I, myself, had been raised to learn Hebrew, and nowadays all I can remember is the opening line of the *Shema*, the prayer Jewish children diligantly memorize with the aim of reciting it at the beginning and the end of every day and, in the long term, as our final words before dying. Any grown-up Jew who knows nothing but the *Shema* is, one can safely conclude, lapsed.

Feeling the urge to break the ice and form a relationship (I had been told back in Belfast that he had only very reluctantly allowed me to join the party) I cleared my throat and leant across the aisle.

'I imagine that the Cameroonian singing style must be very different to the Northern Ireland one,' I said.

'In *what way?*' he boomed. There was deep suspicion and gravity in his voice. I paused, sensing that I was entering some sort of minefield. In that moment I realized that people who were in proximity to Dr Paisley were required to adhere to a protocol that I had no knowledge nor understanding of.

'Well,' I continued, 'take the vocal harmonies. I assume that the Cameroonian approach to vocal harmonies must be very different from the hymn singing in Ulster . . .'

I trailed off. Perplexed, I could see that Ian Paisley was now furious with me. He went glassy-eyed and the lower part of his face trembled. He exhaled noisily and shook his head from side to side, like a wild horse, as though to expel the unpleasantness he had been unfortunate enough to hear. This was followed by a steely silence that continued for many hours – the entire flight, in fact. It continued all the way through the descent and the landing, through disembarkation and customs and passport control, through baggage, through the lobby of Yaounde airport, and into the courtesy bus, where it finally, and mercifully, ended.

'We Ulstermen are outgoing people,' he announced suddenly, as the bus bounced through the potholed suburbs of Yaounde. 'We're friendly people. We're hospitable people. We're *good singers*. These are characteristics which are sadly lacking in *some Englishmen*.'

Now, in the hut, Dr Paisley addressed the crowd.

'I'm under police surveillance. Everywhere I go, I have policemen sitting with me. Now I have a journalist. And he wants to *record* me, to use my words against me in future days.'

'Of course,' I said, 'David Livingstone had a journalist along with him too.'

'Well,' replied Dr Paisley, 'he had a journalist who *caught up on him*. Mr Dr-Livingstone-I-Presume. And Stanley, as a journalist, took all the glory. As if Livingstone was *lost*!'

I felt that the best course of action, at that point, was to deride journalism. So I mentioned that Stanley lived to regret uttering those famous words, because the music-hall comedians of the time mocked him for it. This information seemed to please Dr Paisley a lot.

'Well, don't you be saying it to me, or all the comedians will laugh at you too. And, anyway, *I'm* not lost in Africa. I'm *saved*. It's *you* that's lost. You're the lost soul. The lost sheep of the house of Israel. Am I right?'

'That's right,' murmured the Revd David McIlveen, Ian Paisley's travelling companion. 'The lost sinner in Africa.'

'That's right,' said Ian Paisley.

Recklessly, I took this as a new opportunity to ingratiate myself.

'As I am an Israelite myself,' I said, 'I will join you at the main table.'

I sat down. David McIlveen and Dr Paisley exchanged a glance.

'Are you a Jew?' said David.

'Yes I am,' I said.

'Are you practising?' said Ian Paisley.

'Well . . .' I began.

I then gave an impassioned speech about the importance of Judaism in my life. Although I am not practising, I said, and although to my shame I haven't visited the synagogue for many years, I still feel guided by my Jewishness. We discussed how the Jews and the Free Presbyterians share a commitment to the Old Testament. And I ended, with a flourish, by quoting the opening line of the *Shema*.

'*Shema Israel*,' I said, '*Adonai Elohaynu, adonai echad.*'

'Ah,' said Dr Paisley, ' 'tis a beautiful verse!'

'Thank you,' I said.

I added then that, by the way, my wife is a Presbyterian.

'Does she sing the Psalms?' asked Dr Paisley.

'No,' I admitted.

There was a silence.

'Oh,' he said.

Still, he seemed pleased that there was a Presbyterian in my life.

In stressing the sincerity of my Old Testament beliefs, while adding that I had married out of the faith to one of Dr Paisley's own, I felt I had had my cake and eaten it with aplomb. I had managed to portray myself as a good Jew and, by proxy, a good Protestant too. And, in admitting my shameful failure to keep up with the teachings, I had given myself an opt-out in case Dr Paisley tested me on the fundaments of my faith. It had gone terrifically, and I felt that I had forged some kind of Old Testament bond between the two of us.

The final member of the Paisley party sat to one side during all of this, eating coleslaw. A local man, Joseph Ename, he was there to translate the sermons, line for line, from next to Dr Paisley in the pulpit. Joseph had told me earlier that it was a golden opportunity for him to watch Dr Paisley preach and to examine his technique close up.

'It's all in the hands,' said Joseph. 'Watch his hands.'

'The way he raises his hands?' I asked.

'The rhythm of his hands,' said Joseph, 'and the rhythm of his voice. And the words too. He is a fantastic preacher.'

'Did you see the coleslaw?' said David McIlveen to Ian Paisley. 'It spelt out "Welcome Dr Ian Paisley". But Joseph spoiled it. He took a spoonful.'

'Did *Joseph spoil it*?' roared Dr Paisley. '*Thanks for spoiling it.*'

David McIlveen smiled softly to himself.

'Well,' said Dr Paisley, 'what can you expect from a friend but bad treatment?'

There was a distinct edge to this teasing. The coleslaw had said, 'Welcome D.I.P.', and so etiquette dictated that the first spoonful should be taken by Dr Paisley. Joseph looked contrite. He knew he had done wrong. He said nothing.

'Come on, my Jewish friend,' said Dr Paisley, standing up and heading to his jeep. 'Don't dilly dally.'

The visit to Cameroon was to last for eight days, during which time the four of us – Dr Paisley, David, Joseph and I – would travel across country in two hired Toyota jeeps, while Dr Paisley preached the gospel thrice daily to the unsaved locals.

We had walkie-talkies to ensure that nobody got lost on the long journeys down dirt roads between preaching engagements. Ian Paisley's jeep led the way. I followed. An hour into the journey, my walkie-talkie crackled into life.

'How are you doing back there, my Jewish friend?' roared Dr Paisley.

'Fine,' I said. 'Over.'

'I hope you're not going to try and overtake us!' he said. 'David McIlveen says you can try, but you won't succeed! Over.'

'Is that a challenge?' I said.

'That is a challenge from a gentile to a Jew,' said Dr Paisley. 'Did you hear me? Did you hear what I said?'

I was finding it difficult to respond in kind to Ian Paisley's teasing. My customary *esprit de corps* had eluded me since I joined the Paisley party. I think I realized instinctively that it was OK to receive his banter with cheerfulness, but unwise to return it with banter of my own – had I thought of any, which I had not. But I did my best to join in the spirit of the conversation by adopting, at least, a bantering tone of voice.

'I shall rise to the challenge,' I said.

'There's a good degree of racism in us all,' hollered Dr Paisley, over the walkie-talkie. 'Did you hear that?'

'Yes I did,' I said.

'Did you hear it? Did you hear what I said? Racism – in – us – all! Over and out!'

A few hours' driving followed. It had been impossible for me to attempt to pass the Paisley jeep along these tiny, rural dirt roads. But the truth was, I had forgotten all about his gentile–Jew overtaking challenge. Then, suddenly, the walkie-talkie crackled into life once more.

'Germany calling!' hollered Dr Paisley. 'Germany calling! Germany calling! Germany calling! I see you are still behind!'

There was a pause.

'I – um – got a bit of a crackle there,' I said. 'Could you repeat that, please?'

'You got no crackle at all,' he yelled, abruptly. 'You got

the message *loud and clear*. Do not tell lies. Over and *definitely* out.'

I was plunged, then, into a long radio silence.

I became paranoid. What had happened back there? Had Dr Paisley realized that 'Germany calling' was, under the circumstances, a tactless thing to say? Was he embarrassed? When I asked him to repeat it, did he take it as an opportunity to bat the guilt back to me? In visualizing his displeasure, I found myself all the more eager to please him, and I wondered whether that was what made Dr Paisley such a good leader. During the miles that followed, I even fabricated spurious reasons to call him on the walkie-talkie, just to see if he really was angry.

'Do we turn left?' I asked. 'Have you enough water?'

But my questions were met with an icy silence.

Finally, just as we reached the church, Dr Paisley crackled onto the walkie-talkie again.

'Are you all right?' he boomed.

'Yes,' I replied, hesitantly. 'And you?'

'Excellent,' he said.

And then he said, 'What we've got is . . . um . . . we've got some light . . . "Jew" . . . down on the road for you, so be careful not to skid if you overtake us! Ha ha! Over and out!'

Our destination was a small stone and wood church at the end of a long dirt track. We parked up. David McIlveen approached me. There was a smile on his face.

'Hello, Jon,' he said. 'How are you?'

'How are you?' I said.

'Very well,' he said. 'Did you have a good journey?'

'Yes,' I said. 'Did you?'

'Well,' said David, softly, 'we had a little bit of a laugh and a joke with you, didn't we?'

'Yes you did,' I said.

Ian Paisley wandered over.

'How are you?' he bellowed.

'Fine, thank you,' I said.

'Good!' said Dr Paisley. 'Good! How's your wife?'

'She's fine,' I said.

'Good,' said Dr Paisley.

There was a silence.

'So your wife's well?' he said. 'Very good.'

He clapped his hands together.

'Right!' he said. 'Time to work up a good pulpit sweat. As George Whitfield said, the cure for all ills is a good pulpit sweat.'

It was dusk. Fifty or so villagers were gathered on the grass outside the church. Dr Paisley knelt down. He retrieved from his pocket a torch he'd bought from Dixons at Heathrow airport. He rested it on the ground and propped it up with a small stone.

This was how it all began for him, as a young preacher evangelizing outdoors at night in Barry Island, South Wales, during the war, roaring the words so as to drown out the hullabaloo of the nearby fun fair and, I like to imagine, the fighter planes circling up above.

Now, Dr Paisley scrutinized the crowd for a moment, and he began.

'As the light goes down and as the night comes, can I ask you this? When the light of your life goes down and the night of death comes, *can you face death because you have Jesus Christ right beside you . . .?*'

There are people who like to expose powerful and famous preachers as frauds – as crooks and hypocrites. When this happens, such as in the case of Jimmy Swaggart or Jim Bakker, their sermons are brought back from the news archives to haunt them, as hard proof of their cunning and sanctimony: an adulterer evangelizing against adultery, a swindler condemning the coveting of thy neighbour's live-stock, and so on.

Many people have tried to find hypocrisy in Ian Paisley's private life, something with which to humiliate and disgrace him. Yes, Loyalist gunmen have proclaimed that attending one of his entrancing sermons was the turning point, the moment they saw the light and knew that violence was the way forward. Some say that Ian Paisley has done more – driven a car, as it were. Or even literally driven a car. Back in the sixties. To drop someone off somewhere, to meet other people. But that sort of thing is not so unusual in Northern Ireland, where men sit around the table at Stormont Castle, politicians like Martin McGuinness, whose previous posts were as IRA commanders.

The only kind of exposé that could really destroy the Reverend Ian Paisley would be revelations about drinking, or adultery, or pilfering from the funds, and there is nothing like that to be found. He is what he preaches.

'The world is a shore. Eternity is a great sea. The only way to face the sea is to have *that right posture before God . . .*'

Ian Paisley's voice swelled to something beyond a shout, a whole new sound the likes of which I had never heard before.

'A posture of *submission. Kneeling down* to God's perfect and blessed will.'

Joseph stood at his side, translating for the crowd, imitating his every movement. When Dr Paisley raised his hands in the air, clenching his palm for punctuation, so did Joseph. At the beginning of our trip to Cameroon, Joseph had limited himself to simply translating the words. But time passed and he began echoing the hand movements, then the tone of voice, the arch of the shoulders, as if the ultimate goal was for the two men to become as one in the pulpit. They stared out into the darkness, oblivious to the insects that were crashing into their faces, attracted by the torchlight. They didn't brush them away.

'CHRIST STANDS AT YOUR HEART'S DOOR WITH A *NAIL-PIERCED HAND*. HE'S KNOCKING TO GET IN. *LET HIM IN TONIGHT*.'

The torch cast a huge shadow onto the church wall and, as Dr Paisley raised his hand into the air, the spectre of each finger loomed enormously over us. It was quite mesmerizing.

When it was time to head back to the hotel, I jumped into the Paisley jeep. Joseph drove mine. Our journey took us through the gloom of Yaounde's red-light district. Local prostitutes screwed up their eyes against the full beam of the headlights, and disappeared into the shadows. Drunk pedestrians swerved in and out of the traffic. There were many posters advertising Guinness.

(A fortnight after we returned home, an oil tanker crashed in Yaounde. The crash itself claimed no lives, but then people gathered to scoop up whatever oil they could. Somebody lit a cigarette, and 120 people were killed.)

'This is a wild place at night,' muttered Dr Paisley.

'It's fearful,' said David McIlveen. 'That's Africa for you, I'm afraid.'

'Firewater!' said Dr Paisley. 'That's the curse of civilization.' He sighed. ' "Guinness is good for you"? It should be "Guinness is *very bad* for you".'

'The street lighting is very poor,' said David. 'That's one of the terrible hazards of driving here. You could hit a black person on the side of the road very quickly.'

'It must be dangerous,' I said.

'Oh, David's well used to driving in these conditions,' said Dr Paisley. 'This is nothing compared to Kenya.'

'Oh yes,' agreed David. 'Kenya's worse. So's Douala.'

'Oh yes,' said Dr Paisley. 'Douala is terrible. Kenya's a rough place.'

'And Jerusalem,' said David, 'is even worse.'

'Oh, Jerusalem's much worse,' muttered Dr Paisley. 'Terrible. Too many Arabs! Ha ha!'

Dr Paisley yawned for a long time. He had been on the road since just after dawn, and now it was midnight. I think he would have fallen asleep if it wasn't for the potholes in the road, shaking the jeep violently from side to side. The jeep fell silent. Nobody said anything – except for when we drove past a decapitated body lying on the side of the road outside a brewery.

'Look at that,' said Dr Paisley. 'Terrible.'

'Terrible,' said David McIlveen.

And we drove on to the hotel.

The next morning, Ian Paisley had ordered a 10 a.m. start, but by 10.30 a.m. there was no sign of Joseph. We waited on the sofas in the foyer of the Yaounde Hilton. It was strange to see Ian Paisley locked into this period of relaxation. He stood up and wandered around the foyer, busying himself.

'There's always something to do,' he muttered, wandering off.

I was left alone with David McIlveen.

'So . . .' I said. I paused. In small talk lay minefields. 'Who designed the hymn books for the trip?'

'That was Dr Paisley himself,' he replied.

'Really?' I said. I was impressed. 'For all his burdens and responsibilities, his constituency duties in Westminster and Strasbourg, his vigorous opposition to the peace talks, and so on, he still found time personally to design the hymn books?'

'Yes,' said David.

'Right down to choosing the typeface?'

'That's right,' said David.

'Is he not someone who likes to delegate responsibility?' I asked.

'Well,' David said, 'the day may come when Dr Paisley isn't with us, and others will have to carry on where he has left off. Therefore, it is good that we can benefit from his wisdom, his understanding and his expertise in these matters.'

'Do you ever say to him, "I'll do that?" '

'Oh no.' David seemed astounded by the question. 'Oh no. I have never said *that* to him. I make myself available for him. I'm happy for him to make the decisions. That is very much a measure of the man.'

Dr Paisley bounded over in time to hear these last words. 'A person who doesn't like to work, a person who gets deputies to do things he doesn't need to do, he's not a man at all. He thinks he's the *Pope*. And I don't think I'm the Pope!'

He laughed, and I remembered the occasion in October 1988 when the Pope visited the European Parliament. As he began his address, Ian Paisley rose to his feet, and held up a sign upon which was written POPE JOHN PAUL II ANTICHRIST in bold red letters.

'*I denounce you and all your creeds!*' he roared.

He was surrounded by a dozen deputies who tore the banner from his hands. Other members of the European Parliament booed and hurled objects at him, some of which hit him on the head. He was dragged from the building and hospitalized for his injuries.

Twenty more minutes passed in the foyer of the Yaounde Hilton.

Ian Paisley looked at his watch.

'Where do you think Joseph is?' I asked.

'You always have to give these people half an hour,' he replied. 'They're always late. That's African time.'

'That's right,' said David, softly. 'African time.'

'I may be wrong,' I said, 'but—'

'You definitely *are* wrong,' said Ian Paisley. 'Let there be no doubt about that.'

He turned to David McIlveen.

'He's definitely wrong!' he said.

'That's right,' agreed David.

'Don't get into ground that you have never run through,' said Ian Paisley, turning back to me. 'Keep out of long grass. I never go into ground that I haven't investigated first. But we'll hear your question anyway.'

'All I was going to say,' I said, 'is, uh, I've noticed Joseph carefully studying your preaching techniques. When you raise your hand, he raises his hand. I think he's very fond of you. And I was wondering if you'd noticed that too.'

'Well,' he replied, 'I would never say to a youngster, make that man your model. Because you'll just become a poor imitation.'

'On our last visit here,' said David, 'Dr Paisley put his trousers into his socks to keep the ants away, so the interpreter did exactly the same thing!'

'And one day,' said Dr Paisley, 'one of my trouser legs fell out by mistake, and he pulled his trouser leg out too! Ha ha!'

Ten minutes passed. There was still no sign of Joseph. Dr Paisley scrutinized his watch and disappeared again, leaving the two of us alone.

'Are you Ian Paisley's best friend?' I asked David.

'Oh no,' he said. He blushed. 'Oh no. Dr Paisley has many, many very great friends.'

David paused. 'I would say that I have been very convenient to Dr Paisley over the years.'

'Convenient?' I said.

'Well,' said David, 'one of my very pleasant duties over the years used to be transporting Dr Paisley's children to school. When they were going to school. But now they are all grown up.'

David smiled. It was a warm smile.

'What makes him angry?'

David's smile vanished.

'I have no idea,' he said. 'You cannot be in his company and not share the joy and the happiness that he exudes.' He turned his back to me and said, 'Stick to the agenda.'

The agenda was that my line of questioning would be limited to enquiries about the tenets of Dr Paisley's faith and Protestant fundamentalism in Cameroon. If I mentioned the peace process, even the words 'Northern Ireland', I would no longer be welcome in the entourage.

We sat in an uncomfortable silence, our backs turned away from each other, awaiting Joseph's arrival.

And he did arrive, at 11.20 a.m., flustered and contrite.

'The traffic was terrible,' he said to David. 'I'm so sorry. I couldn't get a taxi.'

David locked eyes with Joseph.

'You slept in,' said David.

'And we had such a late night . . .' Joseph looked down. When he looked up again, he saw that David was continuing to stare at him.

'Did you sleep well?' said David.

From across the hotel foyer came the booming laughter of Ian Paisley. He bounded over, grinning and pointing theatrically at his watch. When he reached us all, he turned to David.

'Well?' he roared. 'What happened to Joseph?'

'He overslept.'

'Did he now?' laughed Ian Paisley. 'Well. We've got to fly.'

'It is a great privilege to be here this afternoon . . .'

Dr Paisley leant forward on the pulpit. He surveyed the crowd. Joseph did the same. Ian Paisley straightened his shoulders. Joseph straightened his shoulders.

'I *was* to be here this morning . . .'

Joseph translated.

'. . . but *Joseph slept in*!'

There was a long silence. Joseph turned plaintively to Dr Paisley. But there was no escaping this elaborate punishment.

'Confess your sins!'

And with unease, Joseph did.

The congregation laughed, quietly at first, but the laughter grew. Soon, the whole congregation was laughing at Joseph. Ian Paisley hushed the crowd with his hands.

'I'm the oldest man in the party,' he said, 'and, try as they may, they all fail to keep up with the old man . . .'

Lunchtime. David McIlveen picked up a bowl full of soapy water. He held it out while Dr Paisley washed his hands.

'I thought you were offering to wash my feet there, David,' he laughed.

'I am one among you who serveth,' laughed David.

'And I am one among you who has one that serveth,' laughed Dr Paisley.

The pastor produced a large metal pot full of fruit and hard-boiled eggs. He rested it at Ian Paisley's feet.

'Thank you, thank you, thank you,' he said. 'But I am

not permitted to bring any fruit into the United Kingdom. So, please, give it to the children. And David McIlveen would have liked to have taken the hard eggs because he's a hard-boiled egg himself! But he has to say goodbye to his associates. Ha ha!'

The English speakers all laughed. Joseph translated. Everybody else laughed. The pastor responded. Joseph nodded and translated.

'According to the programme,' he said, 'they say you were supposed to be here at 1 p.m. So they thought you'd eat the lunch, and then take a rest, and then eat the fruit.'

'Ah!' roared Dr Paisley. 'Well, let me explain. *This man* was *supposed* to be at the hotel at *10 a.m.* Now, we moved it from 8 a.m. to 10 a.m., *thinking* he would be on time. He turned up *after 11 a.m.*!'

He looked at Joseph. '*Confess your sins!*' he roared.

'It is a great privilege to be here this evening . . .'
    (Translation)
    'I *was* to be here this afternoon . . .'
    (Translation)
    '. . . but *Joseph slept in*!'

'It is a great privilege to be here on this beautiful night . . .'
    And so on.

'*Are* you a hard-boiled egg?' I asked David McIlveen. It was 11 p.m. The day's preaching engagements were over, and we were checking into our motel.

'I don't know what that means,' he smiled.

'I think it means a hard man.'

He paused for a beat.

'Is that right?'

'I think so.'

'We would really prefer concentrating on the religious aspect of the missionary work while we're here.'

'OK,' I said.

'So maybe I *am* a hard-boiled egg,' he said.

'I understand,' I said.

The Ranch motel in Ebulowa is a sprawl of pre-fabricated chalets, each one decorated with a red light bulb and a soft-core painting of a naked woman lounging on a bed. The first thing Ian Paisley did, after putting down his bags, was to remove the painting from his wall and place it, with gentle rectitude, inside the wardrobe.

The roar of the insects was almost as loud within the rooms as it was outside. I hoped this was a result of the wafer-thin walls rather than the possibility that I might be sharing my bedroom with a swarm of mosquitoes and little grubs. I was later informed that both scenarios were true. The last time the Paisley party slept at the Ranch a worm burrowed into David's ankle and laid eggs. Back home, David cut open the swelling on his ankle and lots of little worms crawled out.

I stood rigid in the middle of my bedroom, holding my suitcase, afraid even to put it down on this infested floor, this ever-moving carpet. Ian Paisley wandered past my open door and looked in.

'It's not so bad,' he said.

He gave me a friendly smile. I smiled back.

'This is really quite a horrible motel,' I said to David in the foyer. We had been invited for dinner at a local pastor's house.

'This is Africa,' he said. 'This is Cameroon. You have to be a hard-boiled egg to experience the hard life. And I understand that a hard-boiled egg is *soft* on the outside and *hard* on the inside. So, maybe I *am* a hard-boiled egg.'

'I'm sorry about that . . .' I said.

But it was too late. David informed me that he and Dr Paisley had discussed my hard-boiled egg comment in detail and I was to be suspended from the entourage for twenty-four hours, pending a decision on the long-term situation which would be made in the fullness of time.

I watched the Paisley jeep drive off into the darkness. It was a melancholy night. I sat in the bar, replaying the day's events in my head. The waiter brought over the menu, and I ordered the chef's special: porcupine.

'I've never eaten porcupine,' I said as it arrived.

'Oh, it's very, very tasty,' he said.

'Mmm,' I said. 'It *is* tasty. Are they local?'

'Very local,' he said.

'I'm glad the chef took the spikes out!' I joked.

'Spikes?' he said, mystified.

'Oh, nothing,' I said.

'Good morning,' said Dr Paisley, sternly.

'Good morning,' I said.

'Did you have a good evening?'

'I just had supper and went to bed.'

'Was the food good?'

'Very good. I had the special. Porcupine, can you believe it?'

David McIlveen's eyes widened. 'Did you say porcupine?'

'I ate a rat?'

'I'm afraid you did,' grinned David.

'A *rat*?'

Ian Paisley doubled up with laughter.

'Did it still have the fur and the teeth?' he hollered.

'Are you *certain* that porcupine is the local word for rat?'

'Did you see any spikes?' chuckled David.

'They said it was local,' I said. 'I ate a *local* rat.'

'Be glad of that,' said Dr Paisley.

In the end, something good came out of the events of the evening. Ian Paisley and David decided that rat-eating was a just punishment for my impudence, a chastisement of appropriate proportions. I was back in the entourage.

On our last day in Africa, Dr Paisley stopped off to inspect his mission house in the countryside near Yaounde. There used to be full-time Paisleyite missionaries in Cameroon, but their wives kept getting sick. The mission house was said by the locals to be a diseased house, and nobody went near the place nowadays.

But behind the locked doors the house was preserved and ready, with a dining table, a sideboard and some wicker chairs. There was an Ulster flag nailed onto the wall, alongside a bunch of faded postcard-sized photo-graphs of missionaries past.

Dr Paisley wandered outside, and we sat on the porch. David McIlveen bought us out some Marks & Spencer's biscuits.

There was time to kill before we needed to be at the airport. Dr Paisley said it was nice to have had some time away from his bodyguards. Being under police surveillance twenty-four hours a day could get trying, he said. He silently surveyed the scene, anthills and ferns. Perhaps now the trip was over he was thinking about the future, about the peace talks at Stormont, wondering what might happen.

'There are various ways to martyr a man,' he said to me. 'You can lie about him. And I have been *lied* about. You can ostracize him, and fundamentalists have been ostracized. You can defame him. You can seek to destroy him. You can, first of all, kill his character. And my character has been assassinated across the world by the media, simply because . . .' He smiled. 'They're not against me *personally*. I recognize that. They're against my preaching, because I won't give in. As one person said to me, "If it wasn't for your religious views, you'd have taken Northern Ireland *by storm*." But I am not sacrificing my religious views for anybody. I am a captive to the Bible. I am a prisoner to the Bible . . .'

I myself would occupy a small place in Dr Paisley's future. For months to come, whenever a journalist would ask an inappropriate question at a press conference, Dr Paisley would reply, 'Who do you think you are? The *Jew*?'

*

We caught our plane home. Although I was sitting only a few seats away from Dr Paisley, we didn't talk to each other during the journey. Finally, we arrived at Charles de Gaulle airport in Paris. Dr Paisley was going straight to the European Parliament in Strasbourg. David McIlveen was going home to Belfast. I was staying in Paris. I had arranged to meet Alexander Walker, the London *Evening Standard*'s film critic. Like Dr Paisley, Alexander Walker is an Ulster Presbyterian with resolute views about moral probity. Alexander was in Paris on a visit to see Adrian Lyne's potentially controversial remake of the movie *Lolita*, which was opening that day. He intended to write about the film before anyone else did, to discover whether it was worthy of his high-profile denunciation. I wanted to write about Alexander's responses to the movie.

On the transit bus from the plane to the terminal, David McIlveen asked me why I was staying in Paris. I suspected that if I came right out and said I was about to see a film about underage sex, it might cause an unpleasant scene. So I chose my words carefully.

'I'm meeting a film critic,' I said. 'A very moral man, and an Ulster Presbyterian just like yourselves.'

'Oh,' said David. 'Why?'

'Well,' I said, 'we're going to see a film which may cause a furore when it opens in Britain.'

David's attention perked up.

'Why?' he asked.

'Well,' I said, carefully, 'this film critic, who is forthright in his deeply held moral convictions, has travelled from London to see if the film deserves his condemnation.'

'What's the film?' said David.

'*Lolita*,' I said.

'What's wrong with it?' said David.

'Underage sex,' I murmured.

Suddenly, Dr Paisley perked up.

'What's all this?' he roared.

David turned to him.

'Just another example of filthy immorality,' he muttered.

Dr Paisley scrutinized me.

'Oh,' he said, darkly.

And, before I had a chance to explain the situation in any more detail, David McIlveen and Dr Paisley were out of the transit bus, into the arrivals lounge, and I lost them in the crowd.

11. *The Way Things Are Done*

In my attempts to find out whether the world really was being secretly ruled from inside the Caesar Park golfing resort that June weekend, I contacted dozens of Bilderberg members. And, of course, nobody returned my calls. Nobody even wrote back to decline my request and thank me for my letter, and these are people whose people always write back and decline requests – Peter Mandelson's office, for instance – which is why I began to envisage these silences as startled ones.

I did manage to speak to David Rockefeller's press secretary, who told me that Mr Rockefeller was thoroughly fed up with being called a twelve-foot lizard, a secret ruler of the world, a keeper of black helicopters that spy on anti-Bilderberg dissenters, and so on.

The Rockefeller office seemed to have an encyclopedic knowledge of the conspiracy theories. They troubled Mr Rockefeller (his press man said). They made him wonder why some people are so scared and suspicious of him in particular and global think-tanks such as Bilderberg in general. Mr Rockefeller's conclusion was that this was a battle between rational and irrational thought. Rational people favoured globalization. Irrational people preferred nationalism.

I asked him why he thought no Bilderberg member had returned my calls or answered my letters.

'Well,' he shrugged, 'I suppose it's because they might want to be invited back.'

I persevered. I wanted the information. I felt I deserved to have the information, and I simply couldn't believe that, in this day and age, there was some information that I couldn't get my hands on. It was driving me crazy.

I learnt that being followed around by a man in dark glasses was tame in comparison to the indignities suffered by some of the few prying journalists who had travelled this road before me. In June 1998 a Scottish reporter tracked Bilderberg to the Turnberry Hotel in Ayrshire, and when he started asking questions he was promptly hand-cuffed by Strathclyde police and thrown into jail.

Bilderberg members continued to ignore my enquiries through the end of 1999 and into 2000. It was around the same time that my former Islamic fundamentalist friend Omar Bakri decided to take against me in a big way.

It began innocently enough. I wrote an article about him in the *Guardian* newspaper, and a few days later he phoned to say that as a result of it he had been asked to appear on a TV discussion programme entitled *Fanatical Debate*.

'*Fanatical Debate*!' sighed Omar. 'What a name! See how you've typecast me, Jon.'

We laughed about it.

The next day Omar called back. Something had changed.

'I am very angry with you,' he said.

'Why?' I asked.

'You said you'd portray Omar the husband, and you lied.'

'How could I portray Omar the husband if you never introduced me to your wife once during the entire year we were together?' I said.

'Anyway,' said Omar, 'I am not angry. I am happy.'

'Why?' I asked.

'Because it was a funny article,' said Omar. 'It made me laugh.'

Three hours later, I received a telephone call from Helen Jacobus, a journalist on the *Jewish Chronicle*.

'I've just been speaking to Omar Bakri,' she said. 'He's very angry. He says that you have personally destroyed relations between all Muslims and all Jews in the UK. He says that if there is a violent aftermath, you will have nobody to blame but yourself. He says that the Zionist-controlled British media has demonized him, and it is all your fault. Would you care to comment?'

'But,' I said, 'I haven't.'

'Is that it?' said Helen. 'Is that your comment?'

'I haven't,' I said. 'I just haven't.'

'My God, Jon,' said Helen. 'This is *all* we need.'

'What else did Omar say?' I asked her.

'He said that you will burn in hell,' she said.

*

This was the worst possible news. Here I was, still smarting at the heavy-handed treatment afforded to me by the Bilderberg security guards in Portugal, and Omar was going around telling people that I was *part* of the international media-controlled Jewish conspiracy. I seemed to be in a unique, and not pleasant, position in the grand conspiratorial scheme of things.

I debated whether to phone Omar and remind him that journalism is very much a team effort. There are researchers, publishers and so on. I realized then, with shame, that I do not cope well under pressure.

I telephoned Omar.

'Omar,' I said, 'did you tell the *Jewish Chronicle* that I have destroyed relations between all Muslims and all Jews?'

'Yes,' he said, merrily.

'Don't you think it's getting out of hand?' I said.

'Oh, Jon,' said Omar. 'I know how to work the media! Ha ha! Don't you think it is all very funny? I'm going to cause as much trouble as possible, ha ha!'

'But what if some of your followers take your words seriously and – you know – kill me?' I said.

'Oh, Jon,' he muttered. 'Don't be silly. We are all very mature. All Muslims are very mature.'

'So we're friends?' I said.

'Of course,' said Omar.

'Maybe I can come over?' I suggested.

'Oh no,' said Omar. 'I can never trust you again. You lied. I am very angry. You have caused much unhappiness amongst the Muslims.'

'But you said you were very happy.'

'Oh yes,' said Omar. 'I am very happy.'

'Omar,' I said, 'are you happy or angry?'

'Happy,' said Omar.

There was a silence.

'There's something else,' I said.

'What?' he said.

'Helen Jacobus said that you said that I would burn in hell.'

'Ha ha ha!' said Omar. 'I was *joking*! I say that to my *children*! If you don't do your homework you will go to the hellfire! Ha ha! I can't believe that you believed me!'

'So I won't go to hell?'

'You will go to paradise,' said Omar. 'And if you go around telling people that I said you will burn in hell then I will give you sixty lashes.'

'Will you?' I said.

'Jon!' said Omar. 'I'm joking again! Ha ha!'

'Ha ha,' I said.

'Sixty lashes for you!' said Omar.

In 1999, three nail bombs exploded in London – in Brixton and Brick Lane and at a gay bar in Soho. The bomber, David Copeland, believed that Tony Blair's government was being secretly controlled by a clique of powerful Jews who call themselves the Bilderberg Group and meet once a year in a five-star hotel at an undisclosed location. He also believed that this Judaic-Satanic elite attends a secret summer camp every year called Bohemian Grove where they sacrifice children on an altar to their owl god.

The Serbian leader Slobodan Milosević publicly blamed the Bilderberg Group for starting the war against him in the former Yugoslavia. His accusation was barely reported. I suppose that the journalists at the press conference had never heard of the Bilderberg Group and simply didn't know what to write.

The Iraqi government announced in November 2000 that the vote-rigging scandal that convulsed the American elections in Florida was all part of the great Bilderberg Jewish conspiracy to get their man, Al Gore, into power. Other conspiracy theorists contended that this could not be true because George W. Bush was himself a regular attendee at Bohemian Grove and must, therefore, also be part of the conspiracy.

I thought about Timothy McVeigh visiting the remains of Randy Weaver's cabin and rummaging through the family's scattered belongings, like an archaeologist, or a pilgrim, shortly before blowing up the federal building in Oklahoma City – a building he considered to be the local headquarters of the global elite. I realized just how central these conspiracy theories were to the practice of terrorism in the Western world.

In October 2000, in Gaza, a twelve-year-old boy called Mohammed al-Direh went out looking for used cars on a Saturday morning with his father. They blundered into a street battle with Israeli soldiers. The boy hid behind his father's back for safety. He was killed. It was a clean and deliberate shot. The Israelis appeared to the world like old-fashioned monsters.

A series of posters appeared overnight in London and Birmingham calling, in vast letters, for the murder of the Jews.

THE FINAL HOUR WILL NOT COME UNTIL
THE MUSLIMS KILL THE JEWS . . .

At the bottom of the poster was a telephone number. I recognized it straight away. It was Omar's mobile phone number.

That night, a Jewish student was brutally stabbed while reading the Talmud. Britain's Jews were becoming scared. I was becoming scared. I felt that things were getting out of control. I was one of the only Jews in Britain on speaking terms with Omar, so I telephoned him.

'Hello, Jon,' he said. 'How are you? It is lovely to hear you.'

'Omar,' I said. 'Why have you done this? Why are you bringing all of this to Britain? I think that you have done a terrible thing.'

'Oh, Jon,' said Omar, sadly. 'You know me. I had nothing to do with the posters.'

'But your phone number was printed at the bottom,' I said.

'Some terrible person must have found my number,' said Omar.

'But why would they do that?' I asked.

'To frame me,' said Omar. 'To get me into trouble. I had nothing to do with the posters. I promise you that. We are not at war with the Jewish community but with the terrorist state of Israel. The posters were nothing to do with me.'

'Oh, Omar,' I said.

'What?' said Omar.

'Nothing,' I said.

What else was there to say?

*

I continued dutifully to write to Bilderbergers, although I held out no hope of a breakthrough.

And then, one Tuesday morning, the phone rang. It was the instantly recognizable voice of a Bilderberg founder member, for thirty years one of their inner circle, their steering committee, a Bilderberg agenda setter, a head-hunter – a secret ruler of the world himself, should you choose to believe the assorted militants I had spent the last five years with.

It was Denis Healey.

'How can I help you?' he said.

'Well,' I said, 'would you tell me what happens inside Bilderberg meetings?'

'OK,' he said, cheerfully.

There was a silence.

'Why?' I said. 'Nobody else will.'

'Because you asked me,' he said. Then he added, 'I'm an old fart. Come on over.'

Once Lord Healey had agreed to talk to me – and I had circulated this information far and wide – other Bilderberg members became amenable too (albeit on the condition of anonymity).

These interviews enabled me to, at least, piece together the backstage mechanics of this most secret society.

So this is how it works. A tiny, shoestring central office in Holland decides each year which country will host the next meeting. Each country has two steering committee members. (The British ones have included Lord Carrington, Denis Healey, Andrew Knight, the one-time editor of *The Economist* magazine, and Martin Taylor, the ex-CEO of Barclays Bank).

They say that each country dreads their turn coming around for they have to raise enough money to book an entire five-star hotel for four days (plus meals and transport and vast security – every packet of peas is opened and scrutinized, and so on). They call up Bilderberg-friendly global corporations, such as Xerox or Heinz or Fiat or SmithKline Beecham or Barclays or Nokia, who donate the hundreds of thousands of pounds needed. They do not accept unsolicited donations from non-Bilderberg corporations. Nobody can buy their way into a Bilderberg meeting, although many corporations have tried.

Then they decide who to invite – who seems to be a 'Bilderberg person'.

The notion of a Bilderberg person hasn't changed since the earliest days, back in 1954, when the group was created by Denis Healey, Joseph Retinger, David Rockefeller and Prince Bernhard of the Netherlands (a former SS officer while he was a student – ironic that a former Nazi, albeit a low-ranking and half-hearted one, would give birth to an organization that so many would consider to be evidence of a Jewish conspiracy).

'First off,' said a steering committee member to me, 'the invited guests must sing for their supper. They can't just sit there like church mice. They are there to *speak*. I remember when I invited Margaret Thatcher back in '75. She wasn't worldly. She'd probably never even been to America. Well, she sat there for the first two days and didn't say a thing. People started grumbling. A senator came up to me on the Friday night, Senator Mathias of Maryland. He said, "This lady you invited, she hasn't said a *word*. You really ought to say something to her." So I had a quiet word with her at dinner. She was embarrassed. Well, she obviously thought about it overnight because the next day she suddenly stood up and launched into a three-minute Thatcher special. I can't remember the topic, but you can imagine. The room was stunned. Here's something for your conspiracy theorists. As a result of that speech, David Rockefeller and Henry Kissinger and the other Americans fell in love with her. They brought her over to America, took her around in limousines, and introduced her to everyone.

'I remember when Clinton came in '91,' he added. 'Vernon Jordan invited him along. He used it as a one-stop shop. He went around glad-handing everyone. Nobody thought they were meeting the next President.' (Of course, Jim Tucker would contend that they *all* knew they were meeting the next President – for they huddled together that weekend and decided he would *be* the next President.)

At times I become nostalgic for when I knew nothing. There are so few mysteries left, and here I am, I presume, relegating Bilderberg to the dingy world of the known.

The invited guests are not allowed to bring their wives, girlfriends or – on rarer occasions – their husbands or boyfriends. Their security officers cannot attend the conference and must have dinner in a separate hall. The guests are expressly asked not to give interviews to journalists. Rooms, refreshments, wine and cocktails before dinner are paid for by Bilderberg. Telephone, room service and laundry bills are paid for by the participants.

There are two morning sessions and two afternoon sessions, except for on the Saturday when the sessions take place only in the evening so the Bilderbergers can play golf.

The seating plan is in alphabetical order. It is reversed each year. One year Umberto Agnelli, the chairman of Fiat, will sit at the front. The next year Norbert Zimmermann, chairman of Berndorf, the Austrian cutlery and metalware manufacturer, will take his place.

Whilst furiously denying that they secretly ruled the world, my Bilderberg interviewees did admit to me that international affairs *had*, from time to time, been influenced by these sessions.

I asked for examples, and I was given one:

'During the Falklands War, the British government's request for international sanctions against Argentina fell on stony ground. But at a Bilderberg meeting in, I think, Denmark, David Owen stood up and gave the most fiery speech in favour of imposing them. Well, the speech changed a lot of minds. I'm sure that various foreign ministers went back to their respective countries and told their leaders about what David Owen had said. And you know what, sanctions were imposed.'

The man who told me this story added, 'I hope that gives you a flavour of what really does go on in Bilderberg meetings.'

This is how Denis Healey described a Bilderberg person to me:

'To say we were striving for a one world government is exaggerated but not wholly unfair. Those of us in Bilderberg felt we couldn't go on for ever fighting one another

274

for nothing and killing people and rendering millions homeless. So we felt that a single community throughout the world would be a good thing.'

He said, 'Bilderberg is a way of bringing together politicians, industrialists, financiers and journalists. Politics should involve people who aren't politicians. We make a point of getting along younger politicians who are obviously rising, to bring them together with financiers and industrialists who offer them wise words. It increases the chance of having a sensible global policy.'

'Does going help your career?' I asked Denis Healey.

'Oh *yes*,' he said. Then he added, 'Your new understanding of the world will certainly help your career.'

'Which sounds like a conspiracy,' I said.

'Crap!' said Denis Healey. 'Idiocy! Crap! I've never heard such crap! That *isn't* a conspiracy! That is the *world*. It is the way things are done. And quite rightly so.'

He added, 'But I will tell you this. If extremists and leaders of militant groups believe that Bilderberg is out to do them down, then they're right. We *are*. We are against Islamic fundamentalism, for instance, because it's against democracy.'

'Isn't Bilderberg's secrecy against democracy too?' I asked.

'We aren't secret,' he snapped. 'We're private. Nobody is going to speak freely if they're going to be quoted by ambitious and prurient journalists like you who think it'll help your career to attack something that you have no knowledge of.'

I noticed a collection of photo albums piled up on his mantelpiece. Denis Healey has always been a keen amateur photographer, so I asked him if he'd ever taken any pictures inside Bilderberg.

'Oh yes,' he said. 'Lots and lots of photographs.'

I eyed the albums. Actually seeing the pictures, seeing the set-up, the faces, the mood – that would be something.

'Could I have a look at them?' I asked him.

Lord Healey looked down at his lap. He thought about my request. He looked up again.

'No,' he said. 'Fuck off.'

12. *The Clearing In The Forest*

The fog rolled in over the giant redwoods of northern California and settled for the night outside my motel room in the logging town of Occidental, giving the place a menacing air which became less menacing when the fog lifted the next morning and I saw that the motel's restaurant specialized in low-cholesterol egg alternatives and breakfast smoothies.

I spent the day sitting in my car and watching limousines pick elderly men up from Lear jets at the nearby Santa Rosa airport. I followed them along Bohemian Highway to a lane that read 'NO THROUGH ROAD'. There, the limousines disappeared up the hill.

This was the lane that led to Bohemian Grove, the clearing in the forest where, it had long been said, the rulers of the world, President Bush, for instance, and Bilderbergers Kissinger and Rockefeller, dress in robes and hoods and burn effigies at the foot of a giant owl. As far as Randy Weaver and Alex Jones and David Icke and Thom Robb and all the others were concerned, the very heart of Luciferian globalist evil lay at the top of this hill.

I wanted to attempt the impossible. I wanted to somehow get in, mingle, and witness the owl-burning myself. After all I had heard about the global elite these past five years – the claims and the counter-claims – I believed this to be the only tangible way I could finally learn the truth. What *were* they doing in there?

I had no clear idea how to accomplish this. My original plan had been to enter the forest alone, perhaps climb up some hills, and basically just scout around until I found it. Recognizing that this was an ill-conceived strategy, I telephoned some of the anti-New World Order radicals I had met during my travels to ask their advice.

David Icke warned me against it. He said the reptilian bloodlines transform themselves back into giant lizards at Bohemian Grove. Furthermore, he said, Henry Kissinger, Jimmy Carter, Walter Cronkite and the male members of the British royal family routinely sexually abuse their harem of kidnapped sex slaves – brainwashed through the MKULTRA trauma-based mind-control programme – at the Grove. I asked David how he knew this, and he explained that one of the sex slaves, a woman called Cathy O'Brien, escaped and wrote a chilling memoir about her experiences called the *TranceFormation of America*.

'If you read Cathy O'Brien's book,' said David, 'you'd know not to go anywhere near the place. People disappear in those forests.'

I called Alex Jones, the radio and TV talk-show host I had met while visiting Texas with Randy Weaver. He instantly invited himself along.

'That place is sick,' he yelled. 'You've got presidents and governors and prime ministers and corporate chieftains running around naked. They have orgies. They worship their devil owl. I'll smuggle a camera in and get right up in their faces.'

'I think stealth might be a better approach if we want to witness the owl-burning ceremony,' I said.

'You're right,' said Alex, thinking aloud. 'Let's liken it to Indiana Jones. Getting in their faces will be like going for the little emeralds along the way to the big ruby in the head of the idol, which would be to actually witness the owl-burning itself.'

'Exactly,' I said.

I was glad Alex was joining me. He struck me as someone who would behave fearlessly in the face of danger. He also had five million listeners. He was a high-profile person. He had personally organized the re-building of David Koresh's Branch Davidian church at Mount Carmel in Waco. He had a can-do attitude. I could not imagine that, with Alex around, they would dare to do anything should we be caught.

I had arranged to rendezvous with Alex, his girlfriend Violet and his producer Mike at the Occidental Motel on Wednesday evening, but they didn't show up. Instead they telephoned me from somewhere along the road at 10 p.m.

'It's all fogged out,' yelled Alex, 'so thick you can't see. Weaving roads. Deer jumping in front of us. I'll tell you, the hairs on the back of my neck are standing up.'

Alex called again at 11 p.m. to report on their progress.

'There's fog everywhere,' he yelled, 'and there's all these strange people, old men and old women just standing on the side of the road watching us. I know the Bohemian Grovers have their snitches all over this forest. We're going to take a more circuitous route down side roads. I'll call you back.'

At midnight, I received a final call from Alex's increasingly crackly mobile phone.

'A jeep has come off the side road and has started following us. We're going to turn around. Oh my God, it's turning around too! It's following us back down the road. Write this down. A red jeep. Newer model. Write down the licence plate. Hang on a minute.'

Alex handed the phone to his producer, Mike.

'If something happens to us make a big stink about it!' yelled Mike. 'Promise me that.'

'I promise,' I yelled.

I did not hear from them again that night. The motel receptionist informed me at breakfast that their beds had not been slept in.

I spent the morning leaving concerned messages on Alex's mobile phone. Then I shrugged and thought, well, life goes on, and I paid a visit to Mary Moore, a local anti-Bohemian Grove activist who lived a mile from my motel. Mary was once a beauty queen, the winner of the 1953 San Luis Obisbo County Fiesta, but she became radical in the 1960s and moved to Occidental. Mary protested the Grove every summer for three decades, holding up placards, yelling at the warmongers cruising past in their limousines, but now she is sixty-five and retired. Her cabin was decorated as a monument to her participation in left-wing causes. There were posters and bumper stickers pinned everywhere reading 'NUCLEAR WAR? NO THANKS' and 'WHO KILLED KAREN SILKWOOD?' and 'SPLIT WOOD NOT ATOMS' and 'VOTE JESSE JACKSON'.

'Is it dangerous to try and get into Bohemian Grove?' I asked her.

'Yes, if you get caught,' she said. 'They do not want publicity. But I will tell you this. Getting in is easier than most people think.'

She paused, and added, with a cryptic smile, 'Easy when you know how to do it, that is.'

I asked her if she'd help me, but she said she had been burned in the past. In 1991 she had gone to great lengths to help a journalist from *People* magazine smuggle himself in – she had co-opted her deep throats and her people who knew people – but he was spotted inside by two executives from Time Warner, *People*'s publishers. They called security and had him removed. His article never appeared.

'I don't know who your On High is,' said Mary. 'I don't want to get burned again.'

We talked for an hour. She gave me a detailed map of the Grove that had been published by the Bohemians themselves. The Grove's 2,700 acres do not appear on any normal map of the region. She warned me of the nearby Russian River's treacherous currents and the surrounding sheer rocky canyons. She said that penetration via the encircling terrain was not a good idea.

She showed me the lists of Bohemian attendees she had managed to surreptitiously acquire over the years. They read much like a Bilderberg roll-call, with Kissinger and Rockefeller, alongside Presidents Bush and Reagan and Ford and Nixon. There were movies stars like Clint Eastwood and Danny Glover, the ex-Tory cabinet minister

Chris Patten, Alan Greenspan of the Federal Reserve and Caspar Weinberger and George Shultz.

'What do you know about the owl-burning ceremony?' I asked her.

'They call it the "Cremation of Care",' she said. 'Is it deeply occult as many people think? Some say they're killing children up there and sacrificing them on the altar. Maybe they are. But I doubt it. I think we'd have heard about it by now, at least locally.'

Mary rifled through her filing cabinet and she found a copy of an old 'Cremation of Care' programme from the 1980s. One of Mary's deep throats had smuggled it out to her. The front cover depicted a cartoon of a giant red owl with a snarling grin clutching a small man in its claws, about to throw him into a giant fire.

'Goodness,' I said.

'Make of that what you will,' said Mary.

Mary said there was much evidence of prostitutes from San Francisco being flown in en masse to the nearby village of Monte Rio to service the all-male encampment for the two-week duration, reports of a great deal of alfresco urination against the redwood trees – even though the campsite was equipped with a great many toilets – and world leaders wandering around in drag, with giant fake breasts.

I tried to remain objective, but it all seemed uncommonly strange and unexpected and hard to rationalize.

'The truth is,' said Mary, 'I couldn't care less about what they do in their private lives. I don't care what their sexual habits are. Men are men. That's not news to me. I care about the *networking*. This is where the ruling class bonding happens. This is the ultimate back room.'

Mary told me about the 'lakeside talks', the unofficial power-meetings that occur in an open-air amphitheatre in the grounds of the Grove. One of these lakeside talks, said Mary, had conceived the Manhattan Project, which gave birth to the first US atomic bomb. In 1978, she added, the chief of the US Airforce gave a lakeside talk in which he directly pleaded for, and later received, congressional approval for the B2 Stealth bomber. Mary said that the future of the world is discussed at the Grove by men like Henry Kissinger who have the power to change the course of history, men who actively thrive on secrecy, hence the mystique that has grown up around any secret society Kissinger belongs to, especially if that very same secret society undertakes berobed ceremonies involving owl effigies.

'It's strange to see the left and the right coming together on this issue,' I said.

'Well,' she shrugged, 'we all hate Henry Kissinger.'

'My colleague Alex Jones hopes to smuggle in a hidden camera and film the owl-burning ceremony,' I said.

Mary brightened.

'Well, if you guys can do that,' she said, '*that* I'd like to see. That has *never* been done. Hang on a minute.'

Mary went into the other room to make some calls. She returned some minutes later to tell me the good news. A friend of hers called Rick – a local lawyer who had twice successfully infiltrated the Grove – was prepared to meet with Alex and myself.

'He says he'll even come in with you,' said Mary. 'He

looks the part. He could be one of them. You'll be OK with Rick.'

Alex and Violet and Mike finally showed up at the motel mid-afternoon. They explained that their circuitous route down mountainous side roads had proved unsuccessful, so they had retraced the road back to town and checked into a hotel.

I laid out Mary's map of the Grove on Alex's bed. They gathered around to study it.

'OK,' said Alex. 'Here's the lake. Here's the shrine of their devil owl.'

'Where does it say that?' I asked.

'Right there,' said Alex, pointing to a spot marked Shrine. 'Here's Bohemian Highway. I guess our hotel must be right over there. Hey. Where did you *get* this secret map?'

'Deep throat,' I said.

'Now wait a minute,' said Alex. 'This map is unheard of. This map isn't widely available.' He narrowed his eyes and scrutinized me. 'Where *did* you get it?'

I could tell that dark thoughts had entered Alex's mind.

'I am *not* one of them,' I tutted. 'I am *not* luring you into a trap. Can we have some trust here, please?'

'Yeah, yeah,' said Alex. 'I'm sorry.'

The treacherous currents and the sheer rocky canyons did not seem intimidating to Alex and Mike. They had made their plans. They intended to rent a boat, sail it down the Russian River, moor it, climb a mountain, shimmy down the other side, and get in that way.

'Hiking in two thousand seven hundred acres is not

hard,' said Alex. 'We need to catch these people at their Luciferian worship.'

The cleaning lady wandered past the open bedroom door holding a vacuum cleaner. Alex slammed the door shut. He pulled the curtains together.

'I saw her before,' whispered Alex, 'just standing there staring at me. Really. Standing there and just staring. She had her hand to her ear like this.'

Alex cupped his ear.

'All the literature I've read on the net says the Bohemians have got their snitches all over this town,' he explained.

'The actual clearing seems to be only about five hundred acres,' said Mike, still studying the map. 'The rest is undergrowth.'

'God only knows what's really going on in the other two thousand two hundred acres,' said Alex. 'I would guess that's where they perform their more nasty or beastly activities. But that is only speculation. We've got two hidden cameras. We've got a tie camera and one that looks like a pager.'

'Do you think that Alex's temperament is such that he'll be able to maintain the stealth needed to undertake the operation?' I asked Violet.

'Alex is not only a great activist and a great broadcaster but also a great actor,' she said.

'Thank you, honey,' said Alex. They kissed each other on the lips.

'Do you worry for Alex?' I asked.

'I do,' said Violet. 'Alex gets so impassioned. I'm afraid

sometimes he might be a little *too* fearless. And it's creepy at night up here in the woods.'

There was a silence.

'I just wish we were armed,' said Violet, wistfully.

'Well,' muttered Mike, 'guns would be no good out here without silver bullets.'

'I've arranged for us to meet a local lawyer called Rick,' I said, 'who has twice infiltrated the Grove.'

'I'll meet your guy,' said Alex.

'I think his advice might be valuable,' I said. 'I think you should just listen and not say anything.'

'Why not say anything?' asked Alex.

'He comes from a different political persuasion to you,' I said. 'I don't want your words to disturb him.'

'A socialist, huh?' said Alex. 'Well, if he wants to consolidate power and enslave the world's population and kill eighty per cent of us like the UN are publicly stating then he ought to be *all for* Bohemian Grove.'

'I don't think Rick wants to sacrifice eighty per cent of the world's population,' I said.

'Well, you said he was from a different political persuasion to me,' said Alex.

'Still,' I said, 'the important thing is for you to not say anything.'

At 6 p.m. Rick and Alex and myself sat by the pool at the Occidental Motel. Rick was sixty but he looked ten years younger. He wore a plaid shirt and khaki trousers. Alex laid out Mary's map, which he and Mike had annotated with little red arrows, plotting their proposed route along the torrents of Russian River, up a mountain, and down the other side. Alex's arrows ended at the spot on the map marked Shrine.

'Going in that way,' said Rick, 'will get you killed. We are talking about a sheer rocky canyon.'

Alex produced a notepad and wrote down, 'Sheer rocky canyon – Killed.'

'So what's the secret?' I asked. 'How *do* we get in?'

'The secret?' said Rick. 'Just walk right in up the drive. That's what I did. There'll be one or two security guys sitting on the side of the road looking bored. You're just going to nod to them as you walk in. Just nod and say hi. And that's it.'

'That's it?' said Alex.

'What you don't do,' said Rick, 'is stand out. You don't dress young. Even the young ones in there don't dress young. Dress casual. Khakis. Cotton pants.'

'Preppy?' I asked.

'Preppy, yes,' said Rick. 'It's a preppy crowd. Wear a baseball cap.'

'Flip flops?' asked Alex. 'Sandals?'

'Sandals would be fine,' said Rick. 'Flip flops might not be such a good idea.'

Alex wrote down 'sandals'.

'What time do they have the owl-burning ceremony?' asked Alex.

'The "Cremation of Care",' corrected Rick, 'is at dusk tomorrow night.'

'Have you witnessed the ceremony?' asked Alex.

'Yes,' said Rick. 'It's pretty elaborate. They do it down at the lagoon. The crowd is on one side of the lagoon on a grassy slope and the ceremony is on the other side. So the crowd are quite a way away from it. Some people bring cushions or little lawn chairs. There's a chorus. There's a symphony orchestra. A good symphony orchestra, right there by the lagoon.'

'Wow,' said Alex. 'What type of music?'

'Boston pops type music,' said Rick.

'Sounds pretty eclectic,' said Alex.

I smiled at Alex. He smiled back. He was saying the right things.

'What is the owl made out of?' asked Alex.

'I have no idea,' said Rick. 'I know there's a druid type of ceremonial altar in front of it.'

'A druid type of ceremonial altar?' repeated Alex, writing down 'druid type of ceremonial altar'.

'It has that look,' said Rick. 'Very old. Very pagan. I'm sure it's meant to be harmless pranky type fun.'

Alex raised his eyes.

'This is not harmless pranky type fun,' he snapped. 'You have all these super powerful men in druid outfits, as you witnessed, Rick, burning an effigy in front of an owl. It just so happens that other primitive cultures have had that same owl, they just throw children inside the burning innards. That's historically based.'

Rick looked perplexed.

'And if you ask them what it's all about,' Alex continued, 'they'll just say, *Oh! I don't know what you're talking about. Get away from me little man or I'll set my dogs on you. You snivelling twit. I'll have you removed immediately. How dare you! Wretched fool!*'

I shot Alex an annoyed look.

'You're probably right,' Alex shrugged, calming down. 'It could be just big kid grown-up fraternity behaviour.'

'The important thing,' said Rick, 'is to look like you know where you're going. Smile. Just walk right in. Hell, I'll walk in with you. And dress preppy.'

Alex wrote down 'preppy dress'.

The next morning we drove into town to buy preppy clothes at Eddie Bauer. I nearly gasped when Alex and Mike stepped out of their dressing rooms. The visual transformation was astonishing. They no longer looked like highly strung Texan right wingers. Now they were the very picture of Ivy League graduates, the east coast elite, in sports shirts and khaki trousers, cashmere sweaters draped with carefree abandon over their shoulders.

'You look very handsome,' said Violet.

'Thank you, baby,' said Alex. They embraced and passionately kissed right there in Eddie Bauer, and Mike and myself and the shop assistants shuffled uncomfortably.

Back at the motel, Alex and Mike practised being preppy by wandering up and down the corridor in a preppy fashion, their hands in their pockets, a slightly effeminate lilt to their gait.

'The point is,' said Alex, 'we belong here. We're just normal.'

I didn't join in with the rehearsals. I felt I already knew how to behave preppily.

Rick had advised that Alex should assume a profession familiar to him – a talk-show host from Austin, for instance – but after much deliberation he and Mike decided to pretend to be high-flyers from Silicon Valley.

Alex was to be the CEO of a microprocessing firm, and Mike the technical brains with a doctorate in molecular science.

'What are our names?' asked Mike.

'I'm David Hancock and you're Professor Mike Richards,' said Alex. 'We're just going to talk. We're just going to walk normally as we would. Calmly. La la la. We're fat cats.'

Alex and Mike began rehearsing preppy conversations.

'But seriously,' said Alex, adopting a recondite tone of voice, the two men rambling delicately along the corridor, 'as fast as microprocessors are beginning to move . . . it's getting down to a molecular level . . . the question is, at what level will the actual basics of science stop us from making these systems smaller? It's the entire nanotechnology revolution that I find most dynamic . . .'

I could see that Mike's hands were shaking, making his polo shirt quiver.

'I agree,' he murmured, unsurely.

They looked over to me for approval.

'I'm not sure about "I agree," ' I said.

'I don't think we should practise talking,' snapped Mike. 'What comes up comes up. It's got to be natural when we do it.'

'No,' said Alex. 'We're going to go over it and over it until we get it right.'

'OK,' said Mike.

They resumed wandering along the corridor.

'But I really want to know your opinion of nanotechnology,' said Alex. 'You've been studying it so closely. You've already got these transistors down to the size of molecules. What I want to know is when will the science, just the basic laws, stop our progress in the miniaturization process. Doctor?'

Mike smiled wisely but he said nothing.

'What do you think?' said Alex to me.

'Are you sure you don't look *too* preppy?' I said.

'I need a prop to stop my hands from shaking,' said Mike.

'Mineral water,' said Alex. 'They drink mineral water.'

We abandoned rehearsals to purchase mineral water from the local General Store. In the few moments it took us to cross the road, two limousines and an open-top BMW cruised past us towards the Grove.

Rick's logic was that no security guard would risk his livelihood by insulting potential VIPs with impertinent questions about their right to be there, but Alex was still unsure.

'You think we can trust Rick?' he asked. 'People have recommended him to you? I'm not going to end up tied to a pentagram with Henry Kissinger's fat belly hanging over me while he's necking with a big dagger, am I?'

I could see Alex's point. Rick's tips seemed so contrary to everything we had heard about Bohemian Grove. How could we just walk in? That seemed incorrect.

'Have you worked out something to say as a last resort in case you get caught?' I asked.

'Yes I have,' said Alex.

'What is it?' I asked.

'I'll say, "*DON'T COME ANY CLOSER!*" ' screamed Alex.

'I'm sorry?' I said.

'I'll say, "BACK OFF! *JUST BACK THE HELL OFF!* DON'T TAKE ANOTHER STEP!*'*"

'Oh my God,' I said. 'That's a threat.'

'It won't come to that,' said Alex.

' "Don't come any closer" is not preppy talk,' I said.

'Definitely not,' said Alex. He smiled slightly and looked me squarely in the eye.

There was a silence.

'Are you dangerous?' I asked Alex.

'Are *these people* dangerous?' he replied. '*They* certainly are. I'm completely non-violent. Dangerous? I'm definitely dangerous to corrupt bureaucrats and their financial bosses that like to control the people on the planet.'

'But not in a violent way,' I said.

'Not in a violent way,' he said.

'Alex is one of the best guys you'll ever meet,' said Mike.

'This world government is dangerous,' said Alex. 'Henry Kissinger and George Bush are the dangerous ones. This degenerate in-bred New World Order crowd are the dangerous ones. I have no criminal record.'

'He's not dangerous,' said Mike. He turned to Alex. 'You need to clear that up,' he said.

'This is really a gross analogy,' said Alex, 'but I'll use it. I see most of these elitist individuals as a whole bunch of dog turds being laid all over this society. I don't run around stomping on them because I don't want to get it on my feet.'

Alex paused. His voice became sombre.

'I just say to the general public, "Let's clean these dog turds up. Let's tell these people they can't do this any more." '

Mike nodded in earnest agreement.

'They can't shit on us,' said Alex. 'That's really what I'm saying. You can't shit on us any more.'

There was a silence.

'I just want them to stop shitting on us,' said Alex.

'OK,' I said. 'Sorry.'

On Saturday afternoon at 4 p.m. – three hours before our allotted rendezvous with Rick – Alex had a private meeting with Mike and Violet in Mike's bedroom. Then he took me to one side to inform me formally of their change of plan. Yes, Alex was grateful for Rick's clothing advice and, yes, they were willing to walk up the driveway, just as Rick recommended. But, no offence, Alex said, they were not prepared to actually walk into the Grove with either Rick or myself. They had decided to go it alone.

Alex didn't admit it outright, but his reason was clear. He simply could not know for certain that Rick or I were not them: undercover Feds, or worse, part of some complex trap to capture an outsider and perhaps even offer him up as a sacrifice to the owl god. I considered launching a defence, but the truth was I had no tangible evidence to prove that I was not one of them. Furthermore, as crazy as it sounds, those suspicions had also crossed my mind about Rick, and I too was finding it difficult to shake them.

'When are you going to attempt your penetration?' I asked him.

'Right now,' said Alex.

'Well, at least let me come along to see you off,' I said.

*

The journey to the gates of Bohemian Grove was undertaken in an anxious silence. Violet pulled up in a lay-by near the entrance.

'If we're not here at 11 p.m., come back at 11.30,' said Alex.

'And every half-hour after that,' said Mike.

'What time do I get in touch with the police?' asked Violet.

'Six a.m.,' said Alex.

'If something does happen to us make a big stink about it,' said Mike. 'Promise us that.'

'I promise,' said Violet.

'Here we go,' said Alex.

Alex and Mike climbed out of the car. They strode away from us in a conspicuously preppy manner. They were looking good. I could tell by their hand gestures that they had already begun debating the miniaturization process of microprocessors, even though they were still a hundred yards from the driveway.

'It seems to be going well so far,' I said.

And it did seem to be going well, right up until the moment, some ten seconds later, that Alex and Mike, for no apparent reason, suddenly dived frantically into the undergrowth at the side of the road.

'Bloody hell,' I said.

For a second the two men became visible as they stood up in the bushes, brushed themselves down, turned around, gave Violet and me a surreptitious thumbs up, took a step forward, cascaded headfirst down into a gully, and were gone.

Violet gasped.

'Hmm,' I said.

'Where are the Texans?' asked Rick.

It was two hours later. Violet had gone back to the Occidental Motel. Rick and I were steeling ourselves for our impending penetration with cocktails at the Village Inn, a lovely riverside bar on the edge of the Grove.

'I last saw them diving into the bushes,' I said.

'Boy scouts,' tutted Rick. '*So* predictable. You know there's poison oak all over these forests.'

'Will they die?' I asked Rick.

'I don't know,' he said. 'Depends how many times they get stung. Anyway. Are you ready?'

'As I'll ever be,' I said.

I took a last big swig, we paid up, walked the hundred yards to the entrance, up past the sign that read 'NO THROUGH ROAD', and were immediately approached by a security guard.

'Hey there,' said Rick.

'You guys should have driven up here,' smiled the guard.

'Oh, we wanted to walk,' said Rick. 'You know. Enjoy the air.'

'Hey!' said the guard. 'No problem. Have a good time at Care.'

He gave us a little salute. We walked on.

'That was easy,' I whispered.

'Told you,' whispered Rick.

We walked the length of the car park – there were perhaps five hundred cars, Mercedes and BMWs and Range Rovers and Jeeps – and up to a second wooden

THEM: Adventures with Extremists

guardhouse, manned by a bored-looking security officer and some young valet parkers. Nobody seemed to notice us as we walked past.

And then we were in Bohemian Grove.

The bank of sixteen public telephones offered the first indication that this was no ordinary campground. The piano music drifting down from a nearby hill was another. There were clusters of canvas tents everywhere, some just off the road, others perched in the hills, as if built out of the trees. Each encampment was equipped with a bar, a grand piano, a huge stone fireplace, a stone barbecue and a wooden owl sculpture.

One had an open-air jacuzzi. A live band played rock and roll standards in another – 'Lucille' and 'Shout' and 'Go Johnny Go' – to a group of men, most elderly, some middle-aged, dancing and shouting and gulping down cocktails. I did not recognize any of them. But we kept our distance.

From time to time an open-top tram drove bumpily past us – decorated with a drawing of an owl – carrying khaki-wearing Bohemians from one end of the camp to the other. Again, I recognized nobody, although they all had an unmistakable aura of wealth and power. They all looked like they *were* someone.

Rick and I continued to explore. The camps were each marked with wooden signs: 'Cave Man' and 'Wolf' and 'Dragons' and 'Lost Angels' and 'Stowaway'. Red lanterns hung in the trees behind Dragons, like little devil eyes. The Grove's ambience seemed deliberately spooky, as if a designer had been instructed to utilize the shadows of the giant redwoods – the whole place was in shadow – to give it some kind of chic druid-Satanic milieu.

Everywhere we walked we discovered the remnants of a recently defunct party. Dozens of empty bottles of Moët et Chandon were scattered around a secluded lawn. The ice had not yet melted in the silver bowl that stood on a wooden table. Three strawberries remained. I ate them.

'Look at this,' said Rick. He was standing by a notice-board, full of snapshot photographs presumably taken at the previous night's entertainment. In these photographs, elderly preppy-looking gentlemen stood around, drinking and laughing. Some were dressed in full drag, with fish-net stockings and hideously applied make-up, humorously oversized fake breasts protruding from their nylon blouses. They struck burlesque erotic poses, their legs wide apart, fingering their buttocks, tongues out, etc. Others were dressed as Elvis impersonators, with fake chest wigs. Next to the photographs was a notice advertising the following Tuesday's concert, MC: George Bush.

There was a further notice, locked in a glass case. It was the guest list. I quickly scanned the names. Bohemians were wandering past me and I didn't want to appear too nosy. Under C was the name Cheney, Richard. It would be reported on CNN a week later that George Bush, Sr learnt of his son's decision to appoint Dick Cheney as his presidential running mate while he was camping on holiday in northern California.

And there was the list of guest speakers for the following week's lakeside talks: Henry Kissinger and John Major.

Black linen drapes hung from a bank of trees near the lagoon. We walked between them. I turned around to find myself face to face with a giant stone owl, nestling between two huge redwoods. It must have been fifty feet high and covered in moss.

'The shrine,' whispered Rick.

Bohemian Grove was, all in all, an unusual place. Besides the photographic remnants of the Drag/Elvis costume party, which I had found decidedly unpleasant in a palpably woman-hating way, and the cod-spooky *Rocky Horror Show* touches, this was a very beautiful spot. The ancient redwoods were vast and breathtaking. The tents looked luxurious and opulent, and I imagined myself sipping cocktails at twilight, discussing preppy issues with like-minded world leaders.

We wandered along the winding path. We found a private beach at the edge of a tranquil part of the Russian River, the sand perfectly manicured. There was a landing stage and a diving board. A handful of Bohemians were swimming naked in the waters below.

Rick and I gazed out at the trees and we discussed world events. How did we feel about the break-up of Microsoft? Rick was on balance in favour. I hadn't made up my mind. How about G8? Rick was on balance against. I hadn't made up my mind. I realized that my preppy demeanour was not a camouflage. I was genuinely interested in these matters. I didn't have a care in the world. I had made it to the inner enclave. Dusk was falling and the owl-burning was soon to begin, and with Rick as my cover I knew I would not be caught.

'Hey, look,' said Rick. 'There's your friend Alex.'

Sure enough, Alex and Mike were heading down the path towards us.

'Hi, you two!' I said.

'*Don't go that way!*' hissed Alex. '*There are cameras in the trees!*'

'*There are owls everywhere!*' hissed Mike, his eyes wide in terror.

'*Just keep walking!*' said Alex. '*Just keep walking!*'

And before I could say another word to them, they had gone.

'Hmm,' I said.

'They seem to be trapped in some sort of paranoid state,' said Rick, breezily.

'They certainly do,' I said.

'Ah,' said Rick. 'Can you see the osprey?'

'Oh yes,' I said. 'A lovely seabird.'

Nine p.m. There was no formal announcement. No bell was rung. But the Bohemians instinctively knew that the time had come for them down at the lagoon. The ceremony was about to begin. Rick and I found a prime spot, directly opposite the giant stone owl. We sat on the grass and we rested our backs against a tree. Soon the grassy bank was packed. A thousand men had drifted down, in groups of twenty or thirty, and were crowded together, sitting cross-legged on the grass. Many lit cigars. A few scrutinized me. I was probably the youngest person there.

I glanced behind me and spotted Alex and Mike. They spotted me. We looked away.

'First timer?' asked a big man wearing glasses.

'Yes,' I said.

'You're going to love the ceremony,' he said. '*Fools! Fools!* Ha ha!'

'Sorry?' I said.

'You'll see,' he laughed. 'Here. Have this.'

He handed me a colour programme. The cover read, 'Cremation of Care. July 15th 2000. 121st Performance. Bohemian Grove.' I thanked him and flicked through it. It was a cast list.

High Priest – Jay Jacobus.

Voice of the Owl – John MacAllister.

Funeral Cortege – The Gentlemen of Lost Angels Camp. And so on.

From across the lagoon, a single violin began to play. A hush descended. A figure appeared before the owl. He wore lederhosen. His lederhosen were covered in leaves. He resembled some kind of elfin Germanic Tarzan. He was, I learnt from my programme, Eden's Garden Soloist.

He stretched out his arms and began to sing, with operatic grandeur: '*Glorious! Glorious! Oh twigs! Oh boughs! Oh trees . . . !*'

For the next ten minutes or so, Eden's Garden Soloist eulogized nature's splendour, his voice ringing through loudspeakers concealed in the trees. Spotlights picked out individual redwoods. They glowed green.

Then we were plunged suddenly into darkness. The drums thundered. Boom! Boom! At each boom a robed man carrying a flaming torch appeared amid the trees. There were perhaps thirty of them. It was, without question, a berobed torchlight procession. Their hoods were red, their robes black. They resembled posh Klansmen, or the cast of a Broadway musical, should Broadway ever decide to do the Moloch Pagan Cult of Sacrifice story.

They lit a pyre at the foot of the owl.

'*Hail, Bohemians!*' said the High Priest, and it was clear he was the highest of all the priests because his robes were silver and gold and made of silk. The High Priest reprised Eden's Garden Soloist's eulogy of the great outdoors. '*The ripple of waters, the song of birds, such music as inspires the soul . . .*'

To summarize, he informed the crowd, these men of wealth and power, that Dull Care, arch-enemy of Beauty, must be slain, right here and right now!

'*Bring fire!*' he roared.

I wondered what Alex and Mike were making of this. I, personally, took Dull Care to mean the burdens and responsibilities of business, but I imagined that Alex was interpreting the scene differently. A naysayer could easily presume that Dull Care meant the world beyond the Grove, the average Joes, and that the High Priest was suggesting the world leaders in the crowd should not give a damn about ordinary people.

As I pondered this, a startling thundercrack rang out through the trees, followed by a scary, cackly voice. It was the voice of Dull Care.

'*Fools!*' he roared. '*Fools!* Ha ha *ha*! When will ye learn that me ye cannot slay?'

Dull Care suggested to the High Priest that he was invincible.

'When ye turn your feet to the market place,' he mocked cacklingly, 'am I not waiting for you as of old? *Fools!* To dream ye conquer Care.'

At this, and in a breathtaking display of pyrotechnic wizardry, the spirit of Dull Care spat fire onto the High

Priest. From the treetops, a gob of fire rained down upon the High Priest's hat. This infuriated the High Priest.

'Nay, thou mocking spirit,' he spluttered. 'We know thou waitest for us when this our sylvan holiday shall end. But this too we know: year after year, within this happy Grove, our fellowship has banned thee for a space. So shall we burn thee once again and in the flames that eat thine effigy, we'll read the sign. *Midsummer set us free!*'

And the crowd roared and cheered and yelled the last line back at the priest.

'*Midsummer set us free!*'

At this moment, Death appeared on a gondola on the lagoon, carrying a papier-mâché effigy towards the giant owl. Dry ice floated upon the lagoon's surface. It was a beautiful sight. The effigy was retrieved from the boat by (my programme informed me) the Brazier Bearers, held out to the owl's midriff, and then thrown – by the Mourning Revelry Dancers – into the fire.

'*Aaaargh*,' said Dull Care, his grotesque death rattle filling the forest.

'*Hooray!*' said the crowd.

Then fireworks erupted. Then everybody sang 'And When The Saints Go Marching In'. Then it was over. We clapped. The Grove descended once again into silence, broken only by the sound of many elderly men murmuring to their neighbours, 'Could you possibly help me up? Thank you so much.'

'Well, well, well,' I said.

'Pretty spectacular,' said Rick.

'I guess we should go,' I said.

We wandered back towards the exit. A ragtime band

was playing near a bonfire. All along the path, men unzipped their khakis and urinated up against the trees and straight onto the road. This did not strike me as mere convenience. There were public toilets everywhere. It was a statement. I needed the toilet myself, so I urinated too, my urine joining theirs, forming a little golden stream down the path and into the mud.

At 1 a.m., back at the Occidental Motel, Alex and Mike and Violet knocked on my bedroom door. We nodded to each other. Alex locked the door behind him. He pulled the curtains closed. Violet hooked the hidden camera up to the TV set. She fiddled around with the wires. We sat on the bed.

'OK,' said Violet. 'I think we've got it.'

She switched on the TV to reveal an indistinct blob of green to the right of the screen. We squinted our eyes.

'I don't understand what I'm seeing,' said Violet. 'The picture is very blurry and crooked, honey.'

'Nobody has ever lived to get this footage out before,' snapped Mike.

'I think it might be Eden's Garden Soloist,' I suggested.

'Who?' said Mike.

'The elf in the leaf-covered lederhosen,' I said.

'*Glorious! Glorious! Oh twigs! Oh boughs! Oh trees . . .!*' sang Eden's Garden Soloist.

'Look!' said Alex. 'Torches! Two torches! Now there's three torches! See them? More torches! It was some kind of sick torchlight procession.'

Sure enough, specks of light had appeared at a perplexing 90-degree angle in the corner of the TV screen.

'Damn,' said Alex. 'The camera must have toppled over.'

'That's so scary,' said Violet. 'I would have been terri-fied. How terrifying is that?'

'That's nothing,' said Alex. 'They start worshipping the owl any minute.'

'*Hail, Bohemians!*' began the High Priest. '*The ripple of waters, the song of birds, such music as inspires the soul . . .*'

'Were you scared?' Violet asked Mike.

'I'm not going to lie,' he replied. 'I was scared to death in there. The whole place was full of owl statues and gods. Just *owls everywhere.*'

'But surely that's like going to a Hilton and getting freaked out because they had H's everywhere,' I reasoned. 'The owls were a motif.'

Mike stared at me as if I was mad.

It was clear that the Texans' interpretation of the ceremony differed from my own. My lasting impression was of an all-pervading sense of immaturity: the Elvis impersonators, the cod-pagan spooky rituals, the heavy drinking. These people might have reached the apex of their professions but emotionally they seemed to be trapped in their college years. I wondered whether the Bohemians shroud them-selves in secrecy for reasons no more sinister than that they thought it was cool.

I remembered something that my Bilderberg deep throat had said to me on the telephone one Sunday evening shortly before I set off for the Grove. He said that far from being fed up with hearing wild conspiracy theories about themselves, many of the Bilderbergers actually thoroughly enjoy it.

He also said that, in all honesty, neither Bilderberg nor Bohemian Grove attract the calibre that they used to. The current members are getting older and older, and the prospective newcomers – the world leaders of tomorrow – don't seem all that interested in getting involved.

'Let's face it,' my deep throat had said to me, 'nobody rules the world any more. The *markets* rule the world. Maybe that's why your conspiracy theorists make up all those crazy things. Because the truth is so much more frightening. Nobody rules the world. Nobody controls anything.'

'Maybe,' I said, 'that's why you Bilderbergers love to hear the conspiracy theories. So you can pretend to yourselves that you *do* still rule the world.'

'Maybe so,' he said.

'*Fools!*' roared Dull Care on the video in my bedroom.

'Oh my God!' shrieked Violet, clutching Alex's arm. 'How is that *normal*? That is *so* Satanic!'

Mike washed his face at my sink. He said he wanted to get the hell out of northern California. He said that as long as only one copy of the videotape existed all our lives were in danger.

'We should make copies,' said Mike, 'give one to Jon, post another back home, and keep the third with us at all times.'

Alex and Mike and Violet plotted the future of their video. Once home, they would stream it on their website. Then they would release the complete version as a mail order VHS.

'Look,' said Alex, 'I'm not into the occult. I deal with concrete things. Waco. Ruby Ridge. I deal with hard-core things. But this was *much* worse than I expected. The cat-calls and the insane cackling. After it was over I was walking through the crowd and I was hearing little bits of conversation. Old men were going, "Yes! That's the *key*! We *must* burn him again! I *do* want to burn him again." These people were in a *fever*.'

'Even so,' I said, 'it isn't as if you overheard any of them secretly discussing global control or anything like that.'

There was a short silence.

'Yes I did,' said Alex.

'Did you?' I asked.

'Yes,' said Alex. 'I heard old men going around bragging about how they manipulate the world. I heard two guys going, "Yes, we're going to get him elected." '

'Did you hear someone say, "Yes, we're going to get him elected?" ' I asked.

'I swear to God,' said Alex. 'Mike was right there with me.'

'Is that word for word?' I said.

Mike nodded.

'Another guy said, "Our new missile system is really on top form. They're delivering the reactor next week," ' said Alex.

'You're making this up,' I said.

'No I'm not,' said Alex.

'These people are sick,' said Mike. 'This was sick for America.'

'You do seem freaked out,' I said.

'I am *very much* freaked out,' he said. 'I'm so tired of

these people telling us that David Koresh ran a cult. *That* was a cult. I have never seen the Branch Davidians worship an idol.'

This was a good point. I wrote the line down in my notepad.

'Write *this* down,' said Alex. 'The government is so good at calling people weirdos and . . . and . . . cult members . . . ' Alex paused, stumbling on his words. 'I'm so tired,' he said.

'The government,' prompted Violet, 'are saying the Branch Davidians are a cult but here's a bunch of old guys that run America in their black robes . . .'

'I'm exhausted,' said Alex.

'I'd be exhausted too if I'd been through what you've been through,' said Violet. She leant over to hug Alex. But he flinched away.

'The point I'm trying to make is this,' said Alex. 'These people point their fingers every day. If you're against the government you're an extremist. You're crazy. But this was a *pagan ceremony worshipping the earth and engaging in human sacrifice.*'

'Oh, come on,' I said. 'Mock human sacrifice. At worst.'

'I *know* the Branch Davidians,' continued Alex. 'They have their little five-hour Bible-study meetings every Saturday. They are really boring, to be frank . . .'

'That wasn't boring,' I admitted.

'That was occultic,' said Alex. 'You've got former and current Presidents, all these old men in the crowd chuckling their mirthful death rattles. "*Burn him! Burn him!*" '

'They're cheering for this guy to be killed,' yelled Mike. 'It's disgusting.'

'That's not normal,' said Violet.

'It just got weirder and weirder and weirder,' said Alex. 'You've got eighty-year-old men peeing on trees and going, "Here! Let's *pee*!" You've got the *Fortune 500* crowd, politicians, peeing on trees, out in public. I mean on concrete paved roads. Even though they've got toilets, like, *five feet* away. Whipping it out and peeing and peeing and peeing. It's running down the street. Now they're worshipping owls and burning humans in effigy. You've got death on a black boat bringing a papier-mâché person so they can burn him for some idol, some owl god, some demon.'

'Oh, come on,' I said. 'They were only saying that for two weeks they should forget their worldly cares. Be reasonable.'

'Look,' snapped Alex, 'we understand that they're not *literally killing a person*. OK? We *understand* that. But, Jon, let's get this straight. They were *burning a human* in effigy in deference to their great owl god. This was a *simulated human sacrifice* complete with the person begging and pleading for his life. This was bizarre Luciferian garbage.'

Mike stood up. He paced the room. He rapped the walls with his knuckles.

'They did *not* kill an effigy of a person,' I said. 'They burnt a symbol of their troubles so they can *enjoy their bloody summer holiday.*'

'THEY *WERE* KILLING AN EFFIGY OF A PERSON!' roared Alex.

'THEY BLOODY WERE NOT!' I yelled. 'YOU'RE DOING TO THEM' – I pointed furiously at the TV screen – '*EXACTLY* WHAT THEY DID TO RANDY WEAVER AND

DAVID KORESH! SURE! THEY'RE BEROBED! SURE! THEY RULE THE WORLD! SURE! THEY'VE GOT A GIANT STONE OWL AND THEY'RE BURNING A – UM – HUMAN-ISH EFFIGY IN FRONT OF IT! BUT YOU'RE PUTTING TWO AND TWO TOGETHER AND MAKING FIVE IN *EXACTLY* THE SAME WAY THAT THEY SAW THAT RANDY WEAVER WAS HIGHLY ARMED AND HE FREQUENTED ARYAN NATIONS AND THEY CONSEQUENTLY DECIDED THAT HE MUST BE A HIGHLY ARMED – UM – *WHITE SUPREMACIST*!'

I paused for breath and saw that Alex and Mike and Violet were staring at me with incredulity.

'Look, I'm sorry,' I said. 'It's just been an exhilarating night.'

'This will not fly with the American people,' said Mike. 'How do you think the American people will react when we tell them?'

'What *are* you going to tell them?' I asked.

'*That it's all true!*' yelled Mike. 'I looked the New World Order in the *face* out there! I saw a bunch of old rich white men, our leaders, out there sacrificing something to an owl god. I think they're sacrificing people in the *real world* too. Ruby Ridge. Waco. Oklahoma City.'

Mike splashed cold water onto his face.

'There *will* be an outcry about this,' he said. 'These are the *doctors* who make the vaccines that get pumped into our children. These are the people who make the *movies* our children watch. They're at the top, bringing all that stuff down on us. These are the people that bomb innocent countries and justify it by making them demons. It wasn't fun and games to me. I had a tear in my eye.'

Mike had a tear in his eye now. I gave up. I believed I was right, but who knows? Perhaps Alex and Mike's interpretation was equally correct. Alex patted Mike on the shoulder.

'Good job, Mike,' he said.

The next morning, as Mike had recommended, Alex copied all of his undercover Bohemian Grove footage for me. I watched the tape being transferred. I watched the ceremony again in my hotel room in Los Angeles on my way back home to London. I placed the tape underneath my clothes in my suitcase. I checked my suitcase in at the airport. I retrieved it at Gatwick. When I arrived home, I put the tape into my video recorder and pressed play. There was Alex and Mike diving into the undergrowth. There they were wandering through the grounds. There they were heading down to the lagoon at dusk. And then – and I offer no explanation for this, no theories – the tape blanked out. The ceremony had somehow been erased.

BOMBSHELL: ELITIST BOHEMIAM GROVE CULT
BLOWN WIDE OPEN!

In the weeks that followed, Alex did, indeed, stream his video on his website. It immediately became an underground blockbuster. Everywhere I looked, the internet was aflame with news of the daring raid.

FIRST EVER VIDEO FROM INSIDE THE NORTHERN
CALIFORNIAN GLOBALIST RETREAT OBTAINED!
LEADERS FROM POLITICS, BIG BUSINESS,
ACADEMIA AND THE ARTS CAPTURED ON TAPE

WORSHIPPING A 50-FOOT HORNED OWL AND
ENGAGING IN MOCK HUMAN SACRIFICE.

Radio Talk-Show Host and Documentary Filmmaker
Alex Jones infiltrated the cult on one of their highest
holy days to witness the infamous 'Cremation of
Care'. On July 15, 2000, Jones, carefully disguised
as a 'Grover', spent four hours inside the elite cult
compound. Armed with two hidden digital video
cameras, he observed and documented bizarre public
urination and the worship of a giant stone horned owl
deity.

Other news:

THE BUSH GANG: WANTED FOR INTERNATIONAL
MURDER, CHILD ABUSE, DRUG RUNNING, AND
GENOCIDE. YOU KNOW THE FATHER NOW MEET
THE SON.

NATO LEADERS CONTROLLED BY BILDERBERG.
BILDERBERG SUMMIT CLOSES IN PORTUGAL
UNDER MASSIVE SECURITY

... Reporter Jon Ronson was understandably dis-
turbed by the experience of being trailed by security
men in a green Lancia K throughout Wednesday.
According to Ronson, the British Embassy had told
him not to provoke any incidents and that his fate was
in his own hands ...

WHY WAS THE *SPOTLIGHT*'S JIM TUCKER AND
REPORTER JON RONSON CHASED BY BILDERBERG
SECURITY IN PORTUGAL?

Perhaps the whole reason was just so Tucker could write an outlandish article about it that nobody would believe because of the *Spotlight*'s racist tendencies. Perhaps they were chased *just so* nobody would believe them.

I got tired. I turned off my computer.

Afterword

And then thirteen years passed, and now I'm turning my computer back on to bring you up-to-date on how life unfolded for some of the people in this book.

Today is May 27th, 2014. Yesterday, Lebanese authorities arrested Omar Bakri for 'contributing to the logic of terrorism'. They had tracked him to his hiding place – a tiny apartment in a Beirut suburb. This was twelve weeks after one of Omar's people – a Crawley man called Abdul Waheed Majeed – rammed a truck filled with explosives into a Syrian prison. He'd once been Omar's chauffeur. He'd drive Omar from the railway station to the jihad training camp in the scout hut in the forestry centre. Another of Omar's one-time people, Michael Adebolajo, murdered the soldier Lee Rigby on the streets of southeast London a year ago. Omar's people have committed a lot of acts of terrorism these past years.

I've always felt pleased that I wrote *Them* before 9/11, and as a result got to portray Omar as – to an extent – likeably absurd. It's possible that if I'd met him post-9/11 I'd have felt compelled to depict him in a harder way. I feel the same way about the conspiracists in *Them*. I'm glad I found the lightness in them. The conspiracy movement blossomed and hardened after 9/11. The 'truthers' were a special sort of awful. They utilized social media to grimly troll those victims of terrorism who dared to disagree with their conspiratorial beliefs. People who had survived actually being blown up on trains were getting hounded by paranoid Miss Marples who'd been watching too many Alex Jones You Tube videos.

Of all the people in the book it's Alex Jones I'm most often asked about. I feel that I really star-spotted Alex. Nowadays he's the king of the conspiracy world. In 2010 *ABC News* called him 'arguably the Nation's premier purveyor of what could be called paranoia'. People kept asking me if he was honestly that crazy. They seemed let down when I replied that I didn't think he was crazy at all – just a great showman.

Jim Tucker stopped kicking the can and hunting the macaroon on April 26, 2013, at the age of seventy-eight. It was a fall that killed him. He lived to see huge crowds converge on Bilderberg perimeters – journalists and TV crews and conspiracy theorists and Occupy protestors. Bilderberg perimeters are very different now to when it was just Jim and me and a couple of men from the local English-speaking newspaper. I think this book has got something to do with it. I think it de-stigmatized the idea of writing about Bilderberg.

I look back on my car chase with Jim from Sintra to Estoril with great fondness, now that my fear has subsided. I have very happy memories of Rachel Weaver too, of course, and also David Icke and Alex Jones. I didn't realize just how fond my memories were until a few years ago, when I was queuing for the toilet at Heathrow Airport and I noticed David Icke queuing behind me. He spotted me and we hugged like two old warriors who had been through a great adventure together. It didn't matter to either of us that we'd been on opposite sides – the memory of the adventure was all that mattered. These were some of the happiest days of my life.

JON RONSON
May 27th, 2014